LEGENDARY LOCALS

OF

ROCKWALL

TEXAS

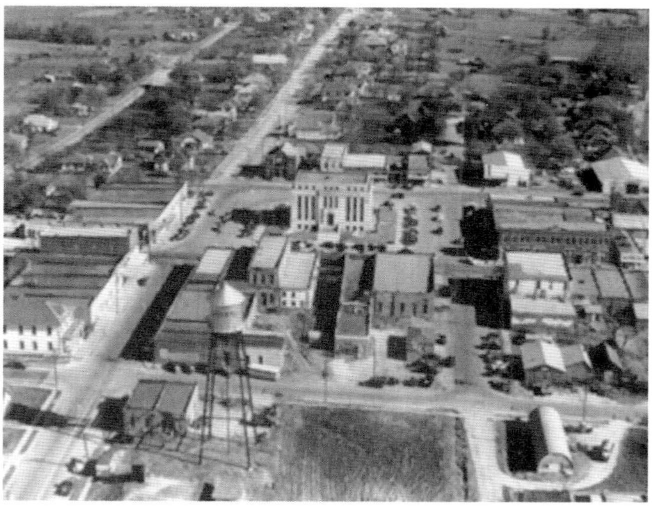

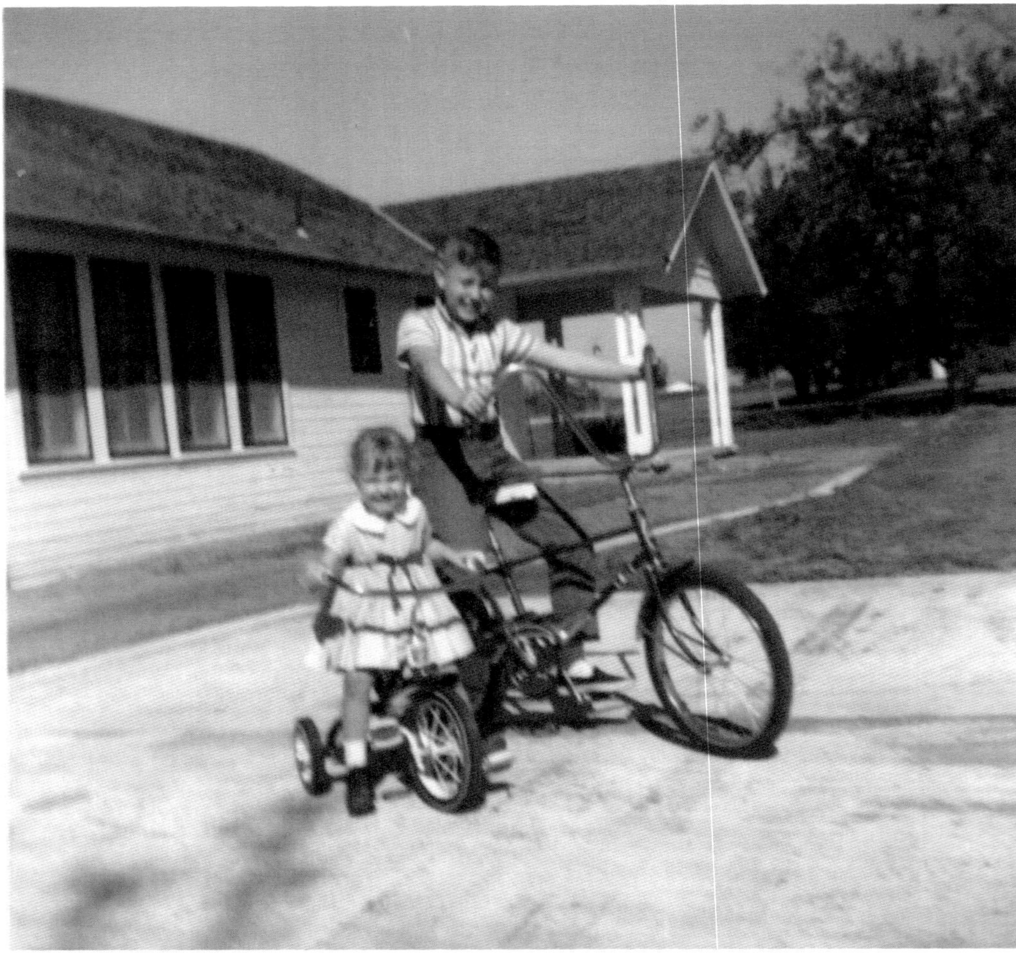

Rockwall County Heritage
Sheri Sue Stodghill and her brother Steven Hall Stodghill, children of Patsy (Hall) Stodghill and Donald R. Stodghill, are pictured above in 1970 at the home of their maternal grandparents, Emma (Lofland) Hall and William Curtis Hall, in Heath, Texas. Sheri and Steven can trace their Rockwall roots back six generations, through at least 14 different families: six generations—Lofland, Isabell, Garner, McLendon, and Burch; five generations—Hall, Seay, Myers, Russell, Nowlain, and Moorman; four generations—Stodghill, Dromgoole, and McFarland. (Photograph courtesy of the Stodghill family.)

Page 1: **Historic Downtown Courthouse**
Pictured is an aerial view of the courthouse in the center of historic downtown Rockwall, taken in the early 1940s, when there were still vast amounts of open farmland surrounding the courthouse square. A mere 20 years later, that land was occupied by a number of businesses, as well as Rockwall's city hall. (Photograph courtesy of the RCHF.)

LEGENDARY LOCALS

OF

ROCKWALL

TEXAS

SHERI STODGHILL FOWLER

LEGENDARY LOCALS

ISBN 978-1-4671-0189-9

Legendary Locals is an imprint of Arcadia Publishing
Charleston, South Carolina

Printed in the United States of America

Library of Congress Control Number:

For all general information, please contact Arcadia Publishing:
Telephone 843-853-2070
Fax 843-853-0044
E-mail sales@arcadiapublishing.com
For customer service and orders:
Toll-Free 1-888-313-2665

Visit us on the Internet at www.arcadiapublishing.com

Dedication
To my brother Steven, who is legendary far beyond the borders of Rockwall County and who has done absolutely everything in his ability to help me in all my endeavors. He is my personal superhero.

On the Front Cover: Clockwise from top left:
Dr. Sherman Sparks (right), civic leader, with wife Billie and builder Johnnie Parrigan (Courtesy Dr. Robert Sparks; see page 89), Congressman Ralph M. Hall (Courtesy Congressman Hall; see pages 32 and 33), Harvey Sanders, stadium namesake (Courtesy Rockwall Independent School District; see page 79), Maurine Cain, school namesake (Courtesy the Cain family; see pages 68 and 69), Dorris A. Jones (lower left corner), principal and school namesake (Courtesy Rockwall ISD; see page 65), Dr. Hal Manson, civic leader and newspaper owner (Courtesy Rockwall County Historical Foundation; see pages 20 and 21), Billie Marian Stevenson, school namesake and community volunteer (Courtesy the Stevenson family; see pages 76 and 77), and Dr. Jessie Castle LaMoreaux, the first formally trained female dentist in Texas (Courtesy Rockwall County Historical Foundation; see pages 82 and 83).

On the Back Cover: From left to right:
Jim Lofland, long-tenured deputy sheriff and tax assessor for Rockwall County (Author's collection; see page 34); the Reese Mansion, built by Judge James Reese in 1911 (Courtesy the Rockwall County Historical Foundation; see pages 28 and 29).

CONTENTS

ACKNOWLEDGMENTS

When Arcadia Publishing contacted me about doing a Legendary Locals edition for Rockwall, I was so excited to be able to highlight our wonderful community members. Since I had previously produced three other titles for Arcadia, I naively thought the process would be smooth and straightforward. However, I was diagnosed with cancer just weeks after signing the contract for the book, which produced an unforeseen and possibly insurmountable obstacle. The prognosis was not a simple one, and I sat down with my fiancé and my mother and said, "Can I still do this book? Can *we* do this book?" The answer was complicated. The fact is that I love history—particularly the history of the community my family has called home for seven generations. If working on this book would be a positive distraction that would keep me motivated and active doing something that I absolutely loved during an arduous cancer battle, then Arcadia had provided me with the gift of a lifetime. On the other hand, if my health deteriorated, then I worried about whether I would be able to fulfill my obligations. We unanimously decided that we should move forward with positive thoughts and a determination that we could absolutely accomplish the task. Everything started smoothly, but eventually I was sidetracked with 19 unexpected days in the hospital and a lengthy recovery. More than 26 chemo treatments and some devastating setbacks slowed me down considerably, but the book moved forward, thanks to a wonderful support team that assisted me in every way possible. My mother, Pat Stodghill; our dear family friends Sharon Shannon, Autumn Quinton, Diana Chapman, April Guest, and Shelley Garrett; and my fiancé, Stacy Parks, did whatever I asked, including gathering photographs, talking with families, and doing the legwork that I was unable to do myself. Carolyn Francisco and the Rockwall County Historical Foundation (RCHF) once again provided invaluable support and resources. The Rockwall Independent School District (RISD) provided photographs and information on school namesakes and other school-related topics. Dozens of families searched their photograph albums and family histories to provide information for the book. My cousin Sue Ann Yasger was of great assistance researching and helping with the completion of this project. I am eternally grateful to all those who helped me in so many ways. Finally, I would like to thank my editor, Erin Vosgien, who always had a kind, understanding, and uplifting word for me when I had to e-mail and say, "Sorry I'm delayed. I'm not feeling too well this week." The understanding and support of many contributed to the "legendary" completion of this volume.

INTRODUCTION

In any community, what qualifies a local resident to be classified as "legendary"?

There are obviously vast and varied reasons that a person is considered to be legendary. A long-tenured elected official, the founder of a local nonprofit, a sports hero, or a supporter of the arts might qualify. However, the fact is that no matter how many legendary locals are rightly included in a book such as this, there will be others whom some think have been unfairly overlooked. To cover all of Rockwall's legendary locals would take volumes, so as you read about the people who have helped to make Rockwall wonderful, know that this is meant to be a sampling—an overview of some of those who have made significant contributions to our community. Also, understand that, to some extent, it is a practical matter. A pioneer settler or a 1950s businessman might have been very well known and contributed greatly to our area, but if there isn't a way to track down a photograph or a family biography, then there isn't a way to include him or her in the narrative. This being said, what does make a legendary local?

All of the early pioneers who traveled by horseback and wagon to bring their families to the new, adventurous frontier of Texas were certainly legendary. Some names are lost, but men such as Benjamin Boydstun, Sterling Barnes, and Terry Utley Wade will forever be recorded in the pages of Rockwall's early history. Both Barnes and Boydstun settled communities, and Terry Utley Wade was responsible for the discovery of the famous rock wall. As the local communities began to take shape, civic responsibilities expanded and business opportunities grew. Men such as Dr. Hal Manson, Dan Anderson, Milton Stanhope Austin, and John Summerfield Griffith not only became the area's new business leaders, but they also took an active role in the politics of the day. In 1873, when Rockwall became the smallest county in Texas, Griffith and his business partner, C.L. Jones, rode to Austin by horseback to obtain the charter.

In 1886, the Missouri-Kansas-Texas Railroad would be charted directly through Royse City and Rockwall, forever changing the economy of the time. Although the line did not initially travel through Fate, astute local businessmen knew that the local shops would not survive unless they provided immediate services for the rail passengers. The town itself was moved, with many current businesses being located to Royse City and new establishments being built by the railroad in the relocated area of "New Fate." Access to the shipping rail made a huge difference for the locals. Rather than having to take wagons of cotton to Terrell or Dallas for shipping, Rockwall County residents could simply take their crops to the gin and then ship them directly from Rockwall. By this time, cotton was already the most prominent local crop, but after the arrival of the railroad it was a only a few years before cotton was the full-blown king.

As Rockwall grew into the 1900s, numerous community leaders and elected officials became prominent. Claude Isbell was a local boy who went on to serve as county judge, as representative to the Texas Senate, and as Rockwall's only secretary of state. A number of local men, including Ephraim Heath and James Reese, served in the Texas House of Representatives. Ralph Hall served first as a Texas state senator and then went on to serve 34 years as a member of the US House of Representatives from Texas's 4th District. Others became legendary because of their long-tenured local service. Lannie Stimpson served 53 years in elected office (the majority as county treasurer); Derwood Wimpee served 35 years in office, including terms as both county clerk and county judge; Jim Lofland served 29 years as deputy sheriff and tax assessor-collector; and Paulette Burks served as Rockwall county clerk for 20 years (working a total of 35 years in that office).

A countless number of businessmen and businesswomen also grew to prominence. Dr. Jessie Castle LaMoreaux was the first formally trained female dentist to practice in Texas. George Vaught, who started his harness business with very little to go on except talent, developed the Vaught brand into an international mail-order concern specializing in everything from common harnesses to ornate silver-embellished parade saddles. The local newspaper, the *Rockwall Success*, became a family business under the ownership of the Bounds family, who worked diligently to balance journalistic integrity with community pride, producing issues for decades that were eagerly devoured by readers. Local businessmen such as Dick Pickens brought jobs and industry to Rockwall. Others, such as the Payne family, Wayne Rogers, and Ted Cain, strived to provide quality goods and services to the community. Professionals such as veterinarian Joe Loftis, banker Larry Parks, and attorney Don Stodghill used their skills not only to assist their clients but also to serve a number of philanthropic and civic organizations. No list of respected Rockwall business leaders would be complete without the mention of Raymond and Elizabeth Cameron. The Camerons developed real estate and, more importantly, generously donated land for a number of projects, including Amanda Rochell Elementary School and the First United Methodist Church.

Throughout the years and leading up to today, a number of hometown heroes have taken on legendary status. Gloria Williams was the first person of African American heritage from Rockwall to earn a high school diploma, although her journey eventually took her on two buses twice a day so she could travel to Booker T. Washington High School in Dallas to complete her education. The 1963 Yellowjacket football team achieved legendary status with a dramatic, come-from-behind victory thanks to a last-minute extra point that secured the state championship. Artists, performers, and writers such as Pat Stodghill, Ruth Peck, Barbara Montgomery, and more recent additions, such as Jason Castro and Amber Carrington, highlight Rockwall's creative successes. There are also countless people who have furthered the causes of local nonprofits, including Robert Reeves and Margo Nielsen, whose success with the Helping Hands assistance center is a benchmark for a community reaching out to those in need. Throughout the years, Friday Study Club, Rotary Club, National Charity League, Rockwall Women's League, and so many other organizations have offered both social and civic outlets for Rockwall residents wanting to serve.

Of all the people Rockwall has chosen to honor, those whom many think are the most prominent and special are the educators chosen for the namesake school program. Almost all of Rockwall's schools are named after local educators. Imagine teaching first grade for 35 years! That is exactly what school-namesake teacher Amy Parks accomplished prior to her retirement. Doris Cullins served RISD for 42 years, moving out of the classroom after 20 years to serve as principal. She eventually opened three new campuses for Rockwall students. Other examples of namesake educators include Nebbie Williams, who served 43 years in education; Ouida Springer, who served 32 years; Dorothy Smith Pullen, who served 40 years; Virginia Reinhardt, who served 35 years; Celia Hays, who served 42 years; and Maurine Cain, who served 38 years in the classroom. RISD's most recent school namesakes include Sharon Shannon, who served 29 years at Rockwall High School; and Billie Marian Stevenson, who taught for 26 years. Administrators Howard Dobbs, Dorris A. Jones, Herman Utley, and Jimmy Williams taught in classrooms but also held distinguished administrative careers.

Finally, there are those who are legendary simply because they did the things necessary to build the community of Rockwall. The farmers who helped establish a flourishing economy may not be remembered because of an office they held or a popular business they owned, but they are remembered because they farmed thousands of acres of Rockwall's blackland soil, helped implement the best practices in farming, and formed the absolute basis of the Rockwall County economy for well over a century. As tribute, city and county leaders named roads after many of these families, including Bourn, Rochell, Clem, Springer, Cornelius, Smirl, Darr, Garrett, Zollner, and Cullins. Roads in Rockwall are still named for politicians and civic servants, but the namesake roads are a fitting and unique way to honor farmers who were, without doubt, legendary in their own right.

So, quite simply, what does make a local legendary? A love of community; a desire to contribute to the civic, economic, and social aspects of the area; and a deeply held belief that Rockwall is home. The people whose stories are included in this book did not quickly capitalize on periods of growth or prosperity. Instead, they invested in a community. Enjoy this sample as a celebration of those who worked, served, and loved in this unique place called Rockwall.

CHAPTER ONE

Settlers and Pioneer Personalities

In 1845, Texas was the newest state in the Union and was ripe for pioneer settlement. Thousands of families looking for new opportunities and financial security traveled from Arkansas, Illinois, Tennessee, and other states to the newly established Texas colonies. Rockwall's earliest settlers were among those travelers who crossed the prairie lands of Texas looking for rich soil and strong communities. At that time, the area that would one day be Rockwall County was known as Mercer's Colony. Peter's Colony—which would grow into Dallas—was a nearby and well-advertised pioneer settlement, but Mercer's Colony was less prominent and was primarily settled by those who were drawn to its blackland soil and the possibility of agricultural prosperity.

These early-day settlers were civic-minded and set about building a strong community of schools, churches, businesses, and civic organizations. Pioneers Benjamin Boydstun, Watson B. Bowles, and Elijah Elgin share the distinction of being considered the founders of the city of Rockwall, while Terry Utley Wade is known for suggesting the name Rockwall after the unusual rock formation originally found on his property. John O. Heath and Sterling Barnes were some of the area's earliest settlers and also hold the distinction of being some of the area's first businessmen.

The late 1800s were a time of prosperity and growth in the Rockwall area. In 1873, John Summerfield Griffith and C.L. Jones rode to Austin on horseback to obtain the original charter that provided for the formation of Rockwall County. The formation of the county provided new challenges, and dedicated residents such as Tom Shaw, Milton Stanhope Austin, and Dan Anderson stepped forward to fulfill the civic duties of a growing community.

While farming was the main occupation, businesspeople such as Dr. Hal Manson (who was a local physician and owned the community newspaper) and the Truitt family (who operated the first gin in the area) enjoyed the prosperity of the Rockwall community. The arrival of the Missouri-Kansas-Texas rail line in the mid-1880s marked a period of unprecedented growth in the area. Rockwall entered the 1900s as a flourishing farming community.

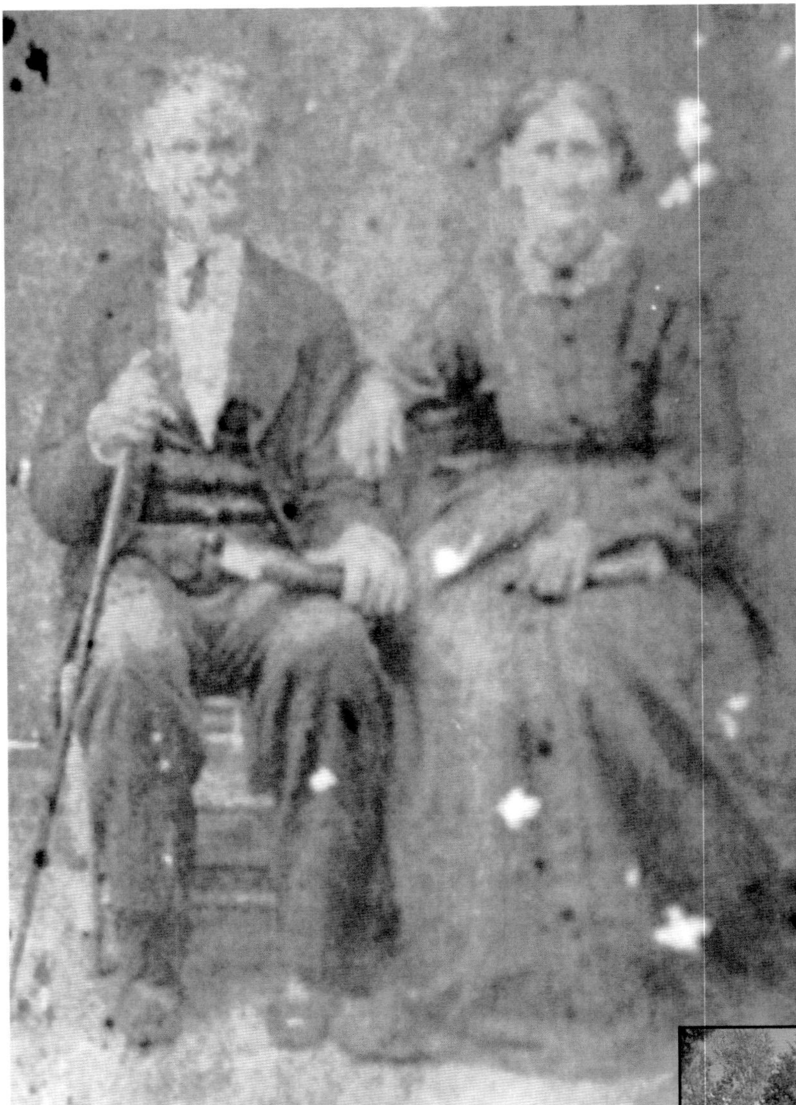

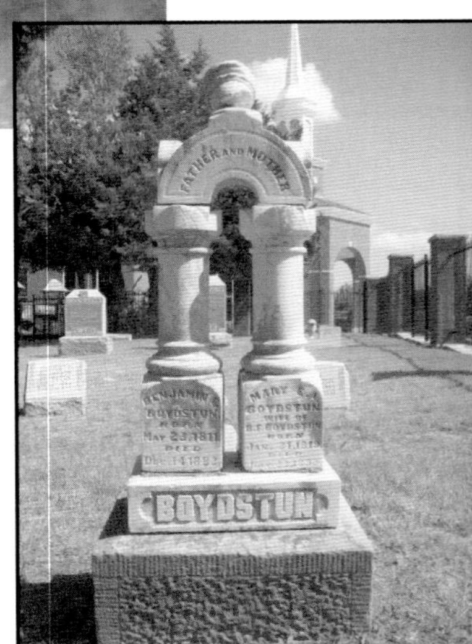

Benjamin Boydstun

In 1848, Benjamin Boydstun left his home state of Illinois and brought his family to Texas with the intention of settling in Peter's Colony, the site of present-day Dallas. When he reached the East Fork of the Trinity River, he encountered heavy rains. The swelling of the East Fork made a crossing impossible, so the Boydstuns waited for the flowing water to subside. Seeing the rich, blackland soil, Boydstun decided to obtain a grant for a 572-acre tract of land in Mercer's Colony—the land that would one day become the city of Rockwall. (Photograph courtesy of the RCHF.)

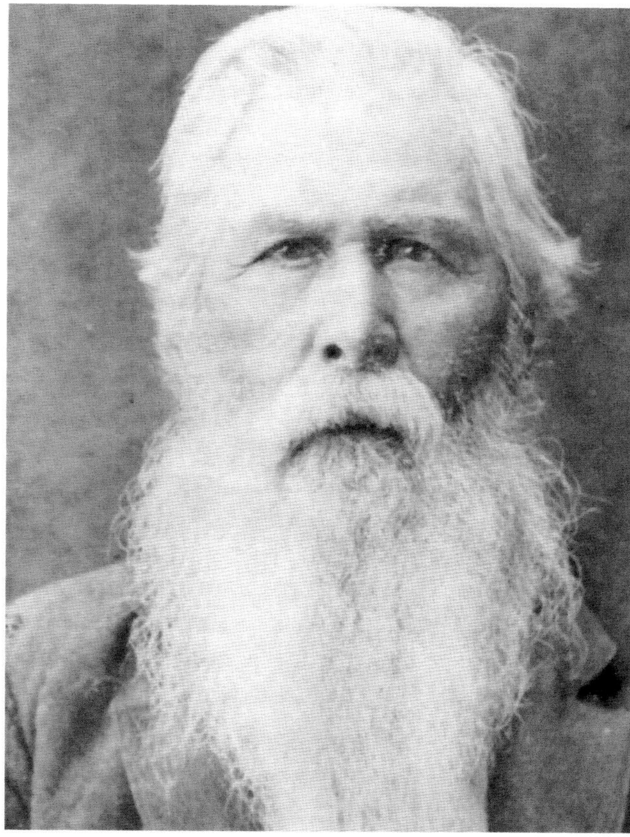

Terry Utley Wade

Born in 1830 in Kentucky, Terry Utley Wade became one of the original pioneer settlers in what would one day be Rockwall County when he established a farmstead in the area in 1852. In need of a well, Wade and two neighbors began digging in the dense blackland soil and soon struck a hard surface that resembled stacked rocks. The men noted their discovery of this unusual "rock wall" and continued to dig to the full depth of the well, utilizing the rock wall as one side of the finished structure. This was the first documented discovery of the rock wall. Two years later, in 1854, when local leaders were looking for a name for their new city, Wade suggested Rockwall. In 1873, when a new county was formed, the name Rockwall was again utilized as tribute to the unusual underground formation. (Above photograph, courtesy of the Wade family; below photograph, courtesy of the RCHF.)

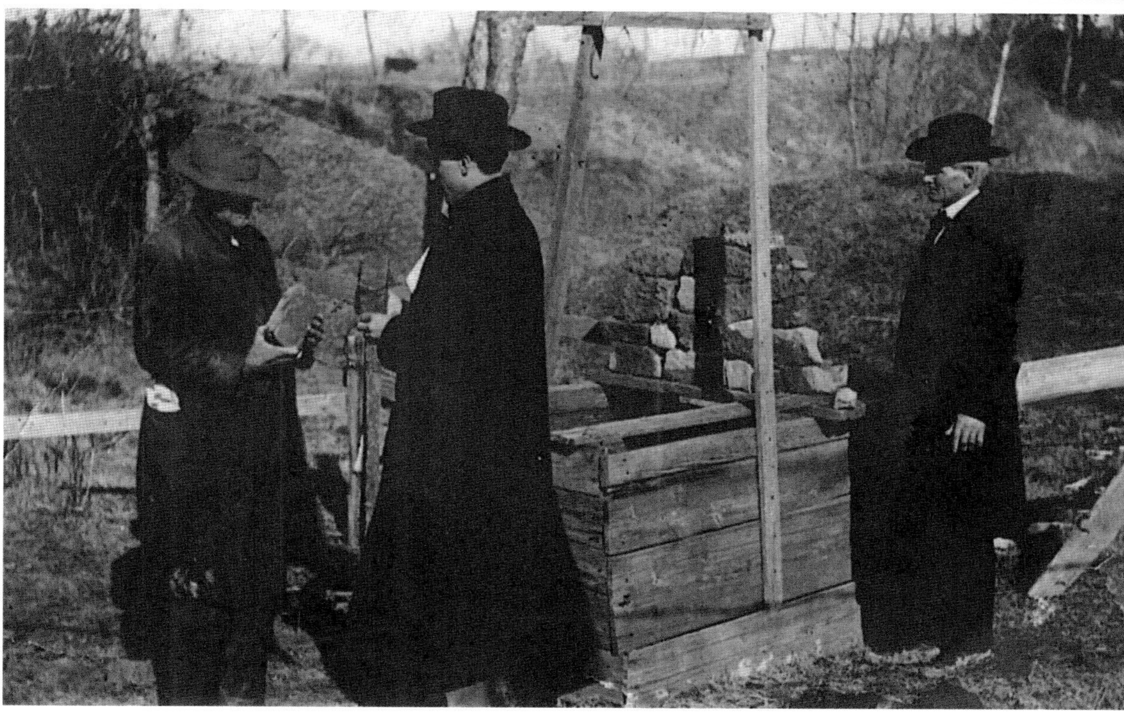

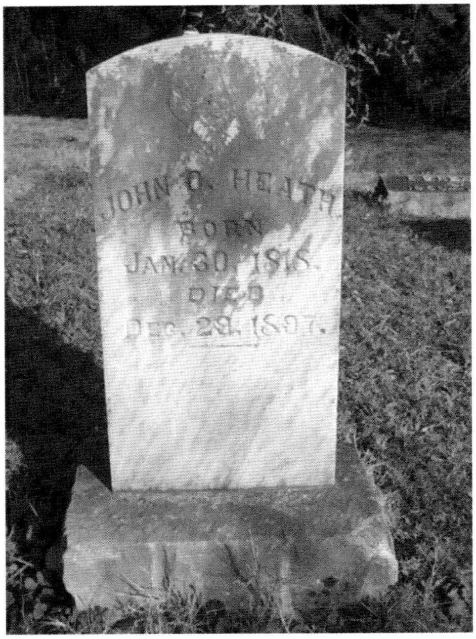

John O. Heath

John Heath was born in Kentucky in 1818 and came to Texas in the spring of 1846. He scouted the land to see if it would make a good homestead, returning to Kentucky in the fall to bring back his wife and child, and his wife's young brother, C.L. Jones. They settled near the present-day town of Heath, which was named after him. (Photograph courtesy of the RCHF.)

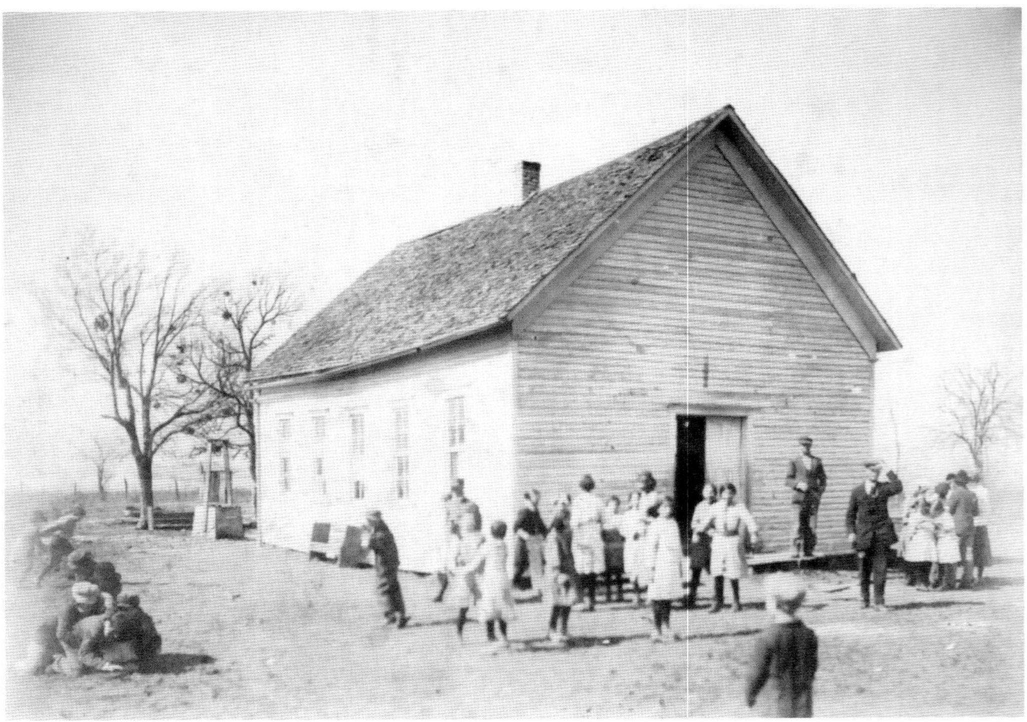

James Truitt

In 1849, James Truitt brought his family from Illinois to Texas. He settled about two miles north of what is now the city of Rockwall. The Truitt family established the first cotton gin in the area in 1866. Truitt was a lieutenant in the Confederate army and fought in the Texas army against Mexico. He and his wife, Celia Ann, gave one acre for a school that was called Locust Grove. (Photograph courtesy of the Truitt-Willess family.)

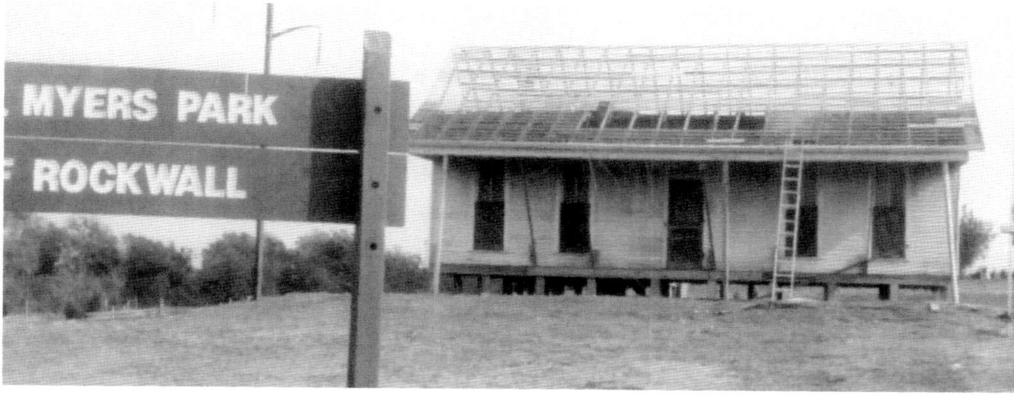

Watson B. Bowles

An original pioneer to the area, Watson Bowles moved to what is now Rockwall in 1847 and remained until his death in 1874. In 1852, he purchased 160 acres of land from Benjamin Boydstun. In 1854, he sold 40 acres of that land to Elijah Elgin, who platted Rockwall's original townsite. As a result, Benjamin Boydstun, Watson Bowles, and Elijah Elgin share the distinction of being the city founders. Bowles was very active in the affairs of the community and became partners with John O. Heath in the first full-sized corn-grinding mill in Rockwall. This significantly improved travel for farmers, as the next nearest full-service corn mill was near the Red River—a week's round trip. Bowles is also known for donating a portion of the land for the Rockwall cemetery with the understanding that no charges would ever be made for any grave lots. (Photograph courtesy of the RCHF.)

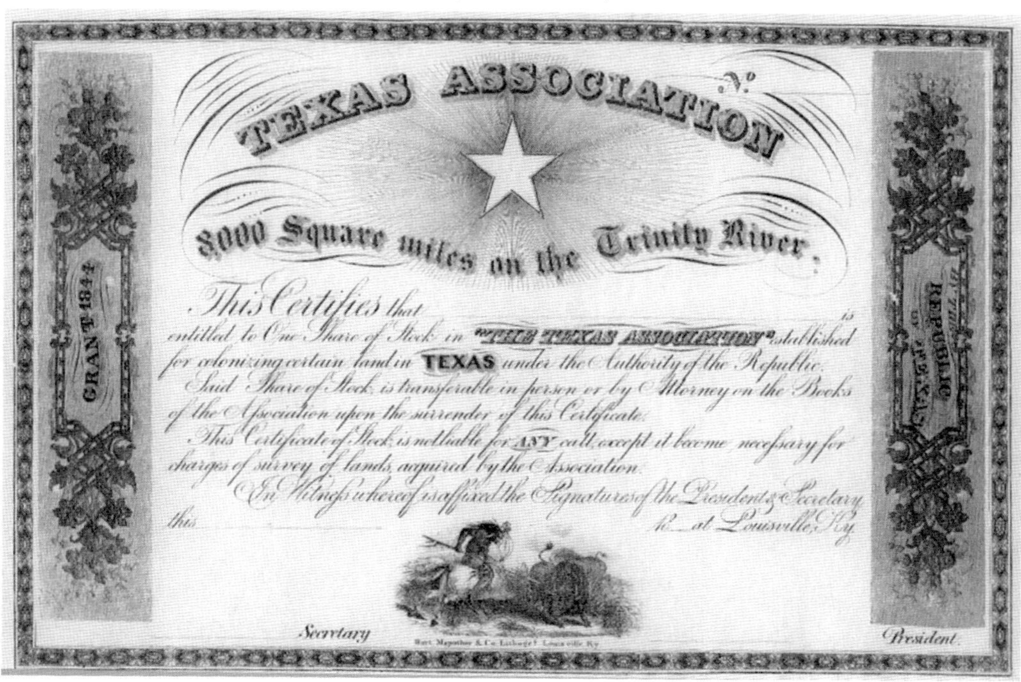

Elijah Elgin

In 1854, pioneer settler Elijah Elgin contracted to purchase 40 acres of land from Watson B. Bowles. The location was prime property on a hill that overlooked the East Fork of the Trinity River, and Elgin platted the original town site of Rockwall on this 40 acres. The plat included a public square and surrounding streets for businesses and homes. (Photograph courtesy of the RCHF.)

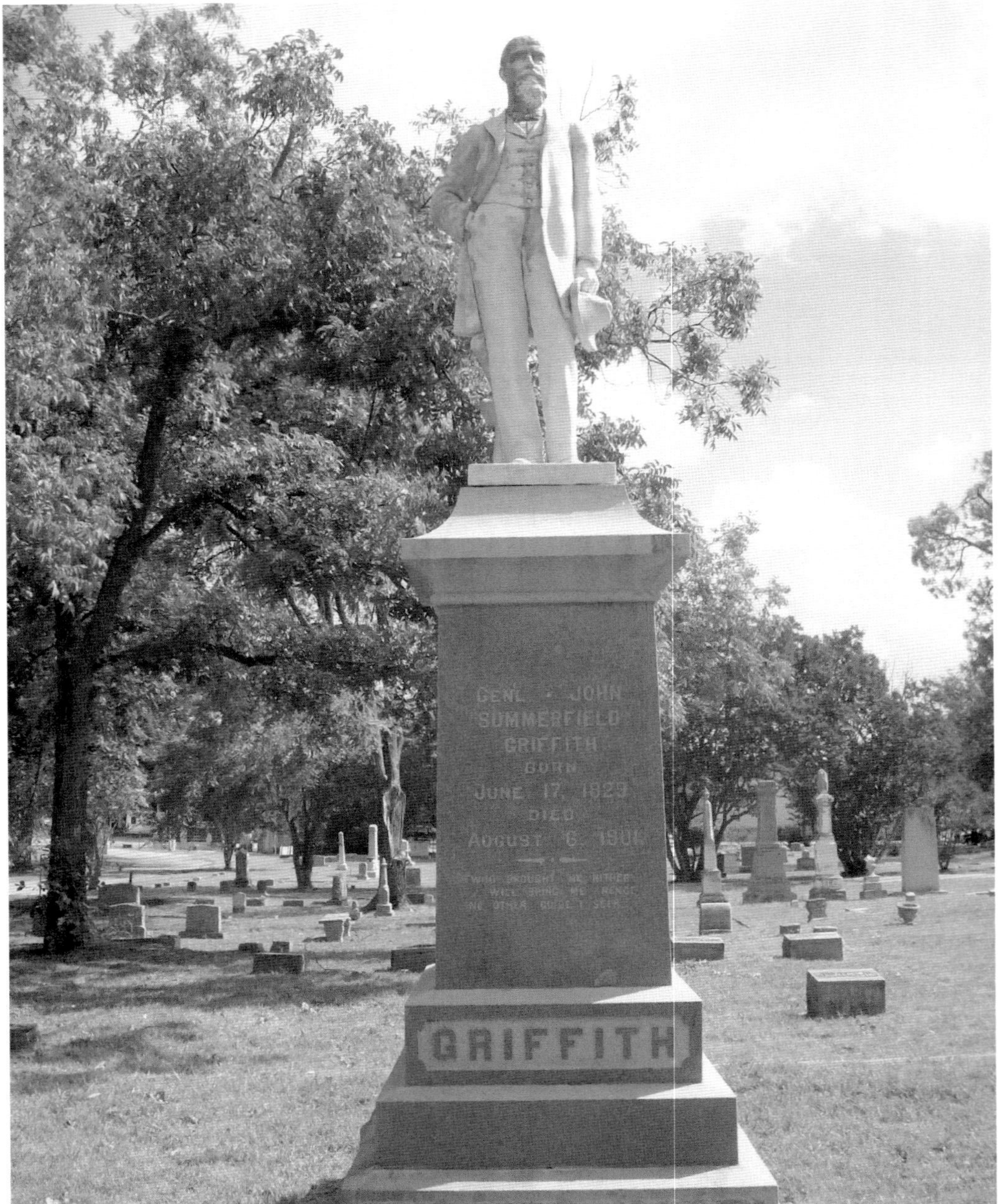

John Summerfield Griffith

In 1859, John Summerfield Griffith settled in Kaufman County, opening a store in Rockwall and establishing himself as a prominent cotton farmer and rancher. With the onset of the Civil War, he organized a group of volunteers from the Rockwall area that eventually became part of the Sixth Texas Calvary. Under Griffith's leadership, the group was instrumental in leading a raid on the Union arsenal at the Battle of Holly Springs, Mississippi. After his Civil War service, Griffith returned to Kaufman County and was elected to the Tenth and Fifteenth Texas Legislature. In 1873, he and fellow businessman C.L. Jones rode by horseback to Austin to gain the original charter for Rockwall County. (Both photographs courtesy of the Texas State Preservation Board.)

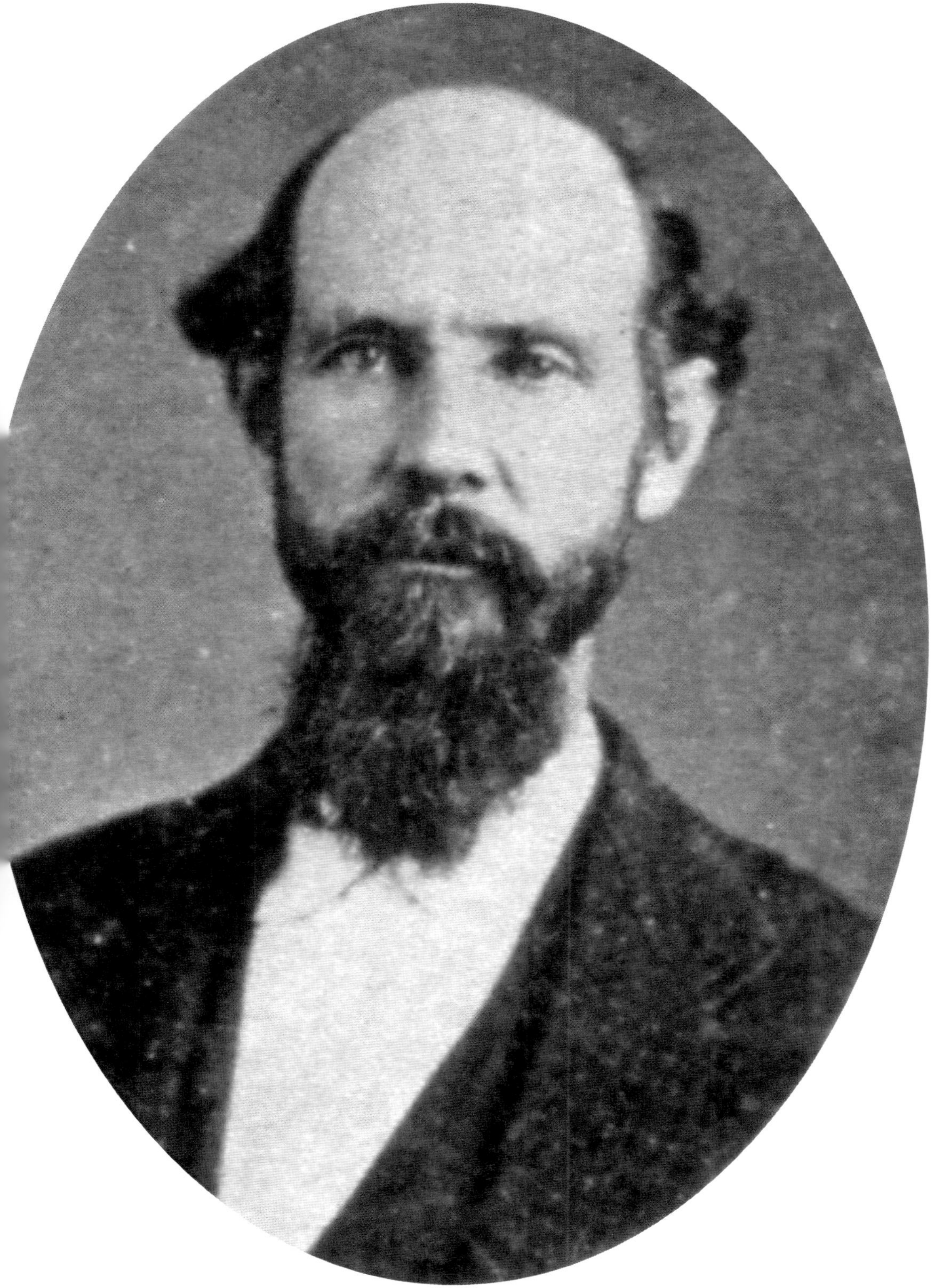

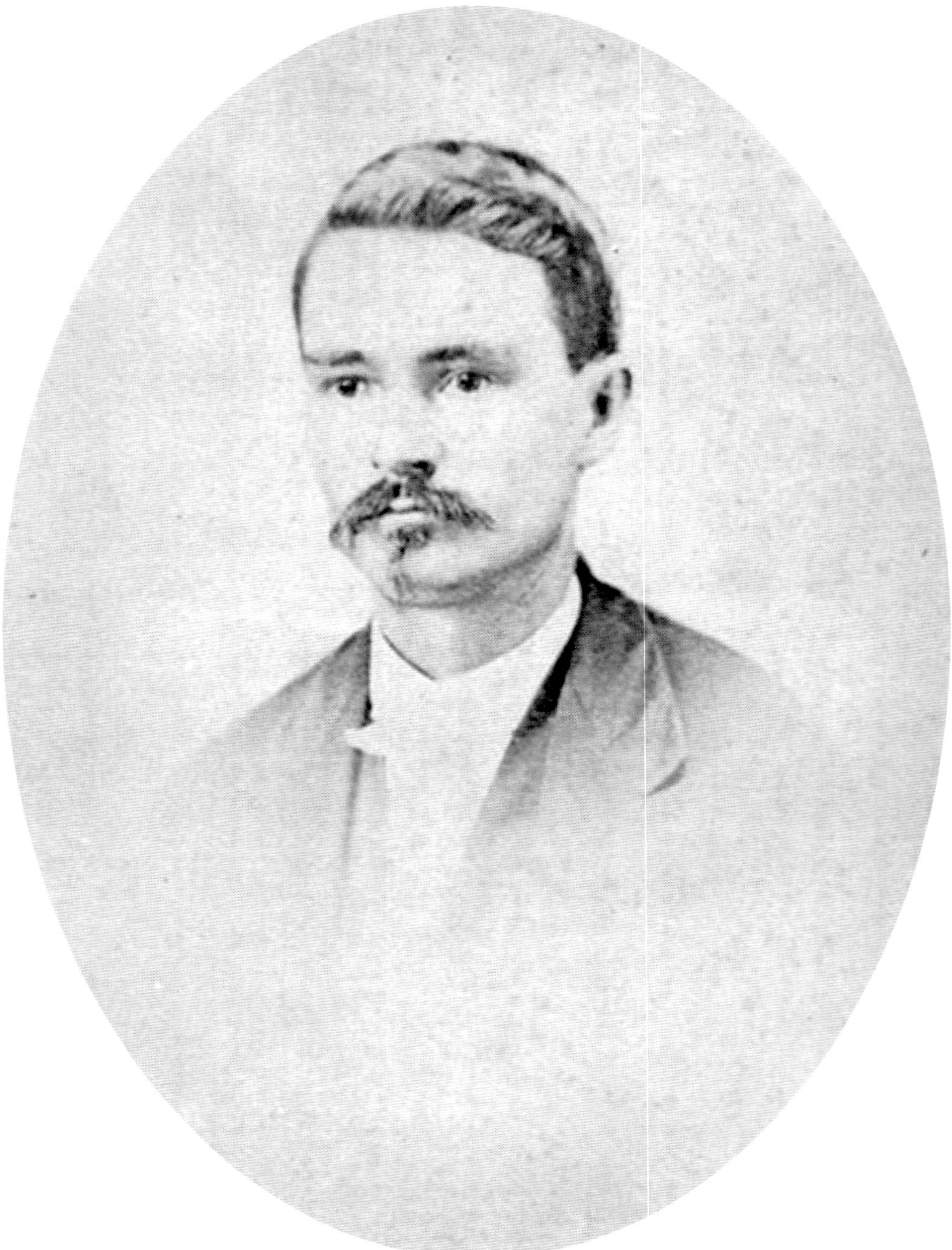

Tom Shaw

When Rockwall County was formed in 1873, Tom Shaw was appointed as its first sheriff. According to local lore, several years prior to his appointment, Shaw witnessed a robbery at a local general store. He shot at the thief as he was trying to escape on horseback. The bullet missed the intended target but hit the horse instead, which led to the robber's capture. This display of bravery led to Shaw's appointment as the first sheriff of Rockwall. (Photograph courtesy of the RCHF.)

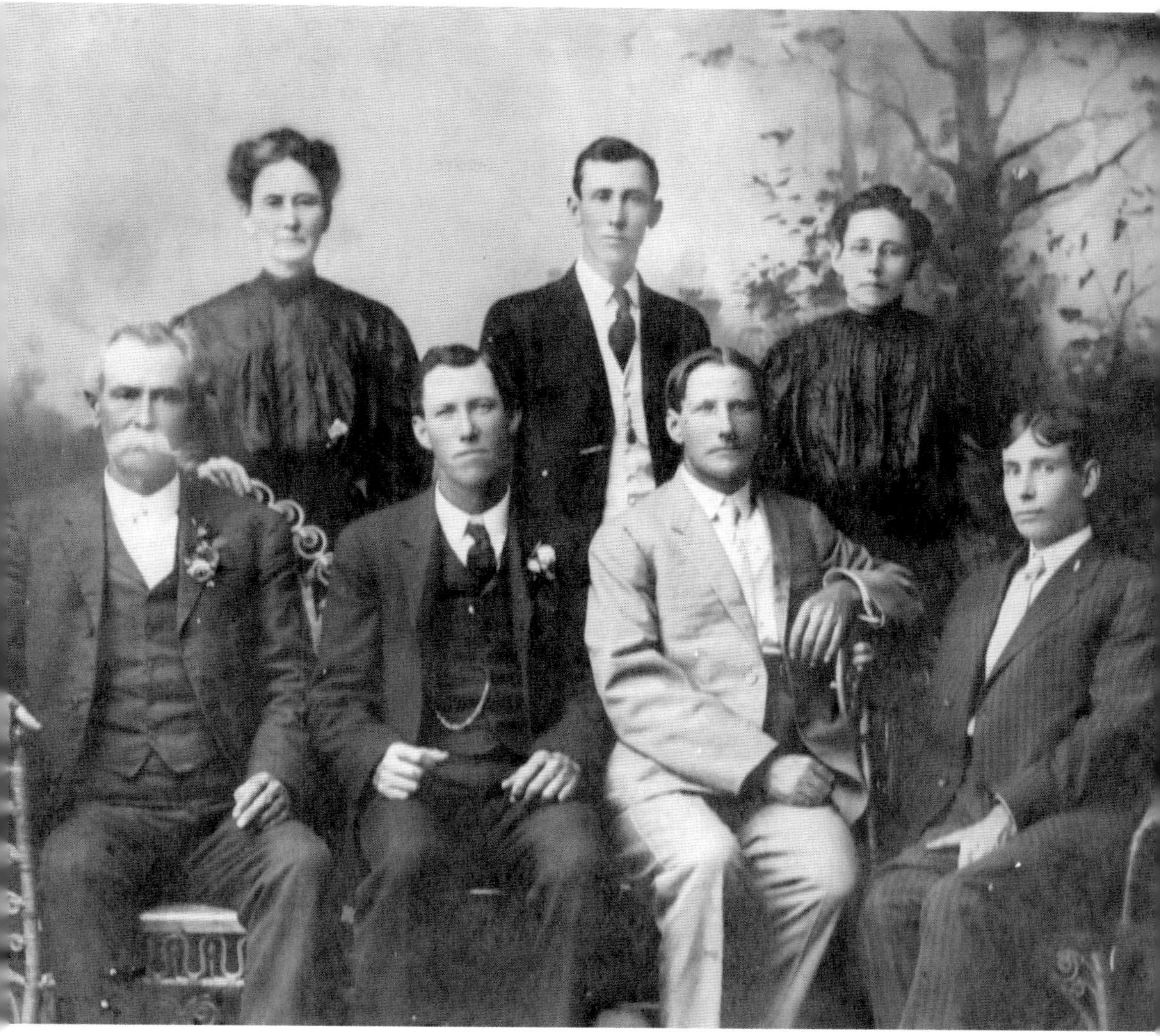

Dan Anderson

Daniel James Anderson married Julia Ann Raines in 1883, and they began their life on a ranch in the eastern part of Rockwall County. The ranch had first been acquired by Dan's father prior to the Civil War. The Andersons were accomplished ranchers and oversaw large herds of cattle and horses. Around 1896, the family moved into the town of Rockwall in order for the children to enjoy better educational opportunities, but they still maintained their ranching operations. Dan was elected sheriff and tax collector for the county in 1898 and again in 1902. He also served as president of the Guaranty State Bank. The Andersons were very active in church and civic activities throughout their lives. Dan is pictured bottom left at a family reunion. (Photograph courtesy of the Loftis family.)

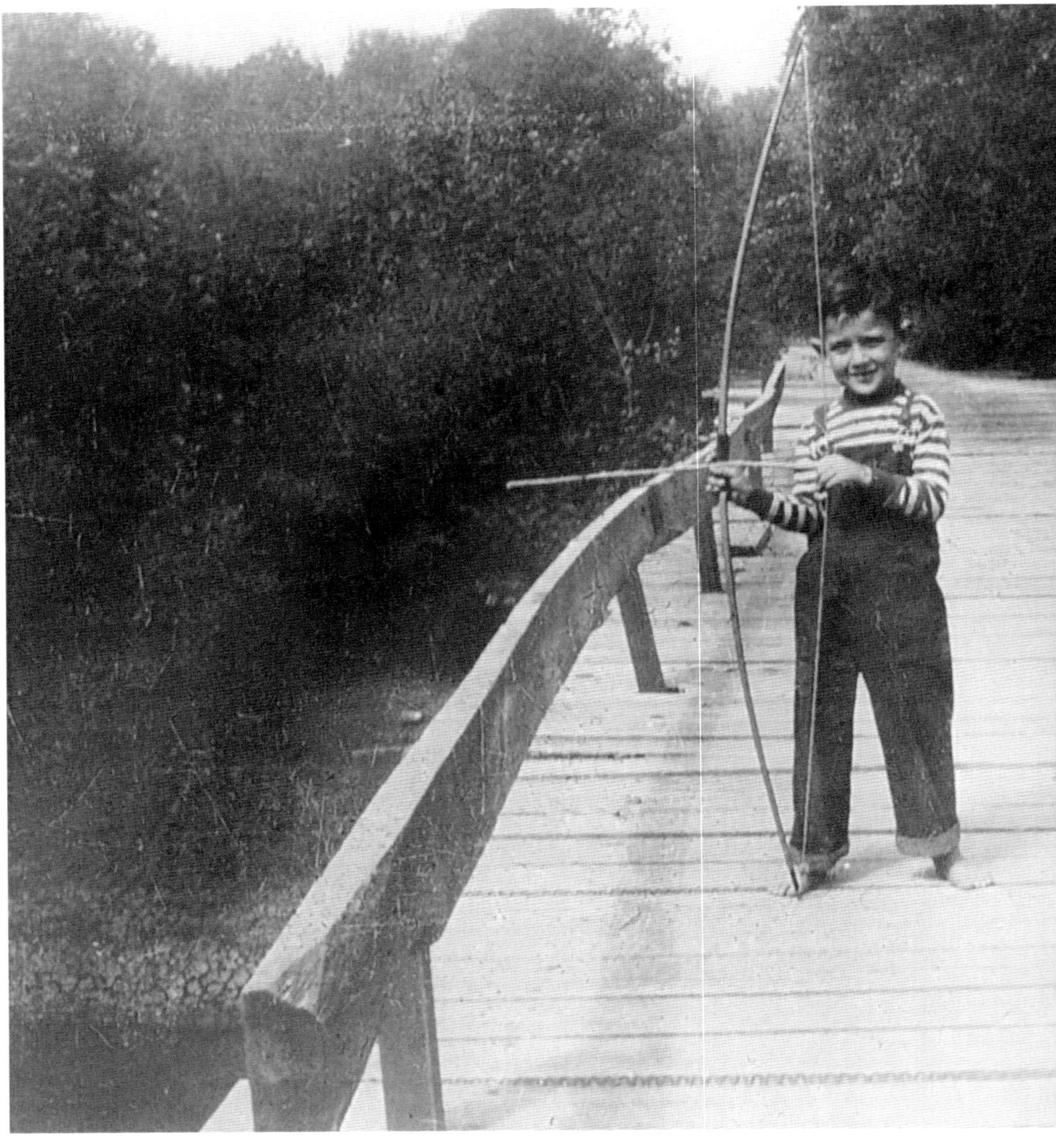

Sterling Rex Barnes

Born in Virginia in 1799, Sterling Barnes lived in Alabama and Mississippi prior to immigrating to Texas in 1846 with his wife and children. The family temporarily settled about two miles south of present-day Rockwall but eventually obtained a land grant for a homestead on the banks of the East Fork of the Trinity River. They built their home near the present-day city of Heath. At that time, a ferry was used to cross the river, but Barnes bought out the operation in 1854 and built a toll bridge known as Barnes Bridge. It crossed the East Fork of the Trinity near the Dallas County line. According to the 1877 minutes of the Rockwall County Commissioners' Court, the toll fees for that year were approved as 5¢ for a man on foot, 10¢ for a man and horse, 25¢ for a horse and buggy, 40¢ for a two-horse wagon, 5¢ for loose horses, 3¢ for cattle, and 2¢ for sheep, hogs, or goats. The Barnes family continued to operate the bridge until it was taken over by the county around 1880. Today, Barnes Bridge Road still marks the old crossing, which is now covered by the waters of Lake Ray Hubbard. Pictured is Ronnie Terry, seven years old, on the Barnes Bridge in 1949. (Both photographs courtesy of the Terry family.)

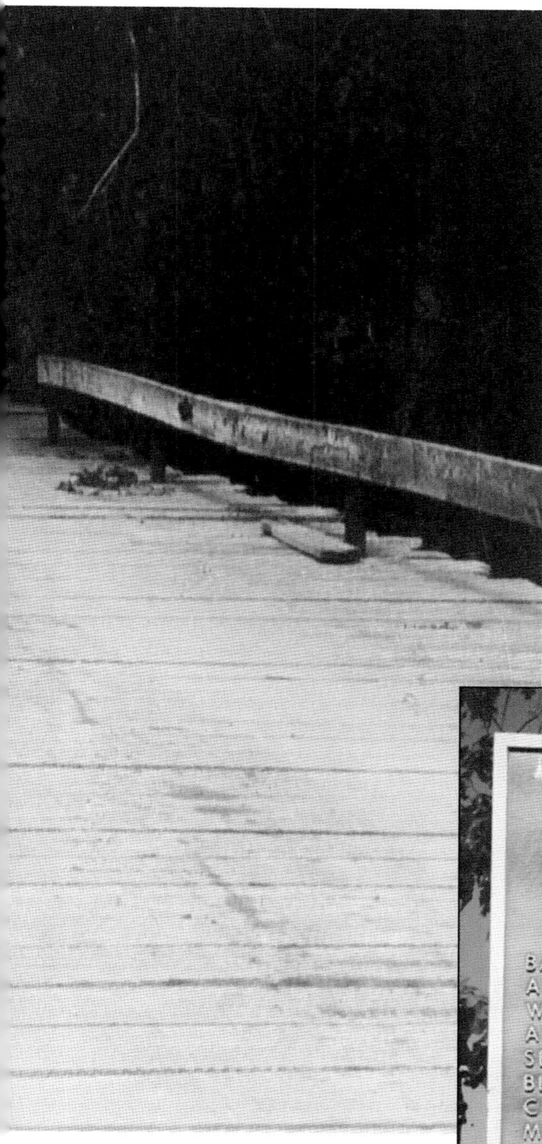

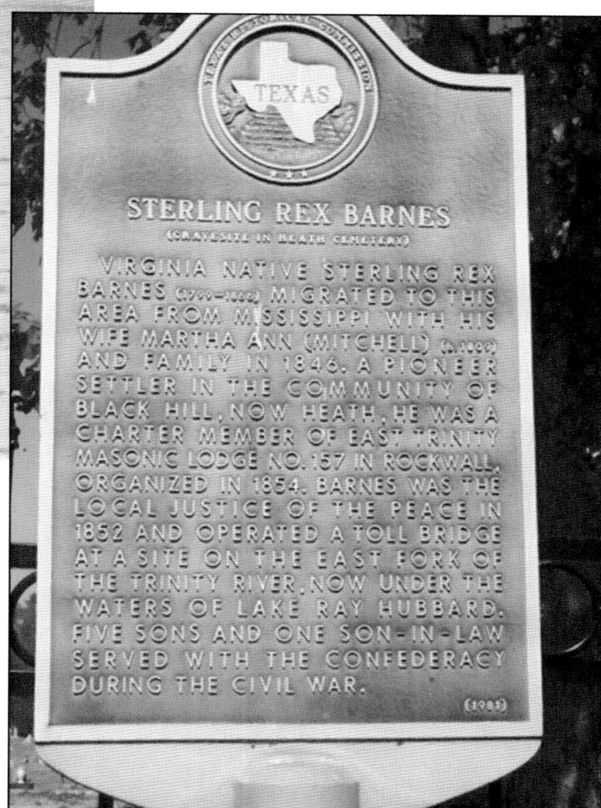
TEXAS
STERLING REX BARNES
(GRAVESITE IN HEATH CEMETERY)
VIRGINIA NATIVE STERLING REX BARNES MIGRATED TO THIS AREA FROM MISSISSIPPI WITH HIS WIFE MARTHA ANN (MITCHELL) AND FAMILY IN 1846. A PIONEER SETTLER IN THE COMMUNITY OF BLACK HILL, NOW HEATH, HE WAS A CHARTER MEMBER OF EAST TRINITY MASONIC LODGE NO. 157 IN ROCKWALL, ORGANIZED IN 1854. BARNES WAS THE LOCAL JUSTICE OF THE PEACE IN 1852 AND OPERATED A TOLL BRIDGE AT A SITE ON THE EAST FORK OF THE TRINITY RIVER, NOW UNDER THE WATERS OF LAKE RAY HUBBARD. FIVE SONS AND ONE SON-IN-LAW SERVED WITH THE CONFEDERACY DURING THE CIVIL WAR.

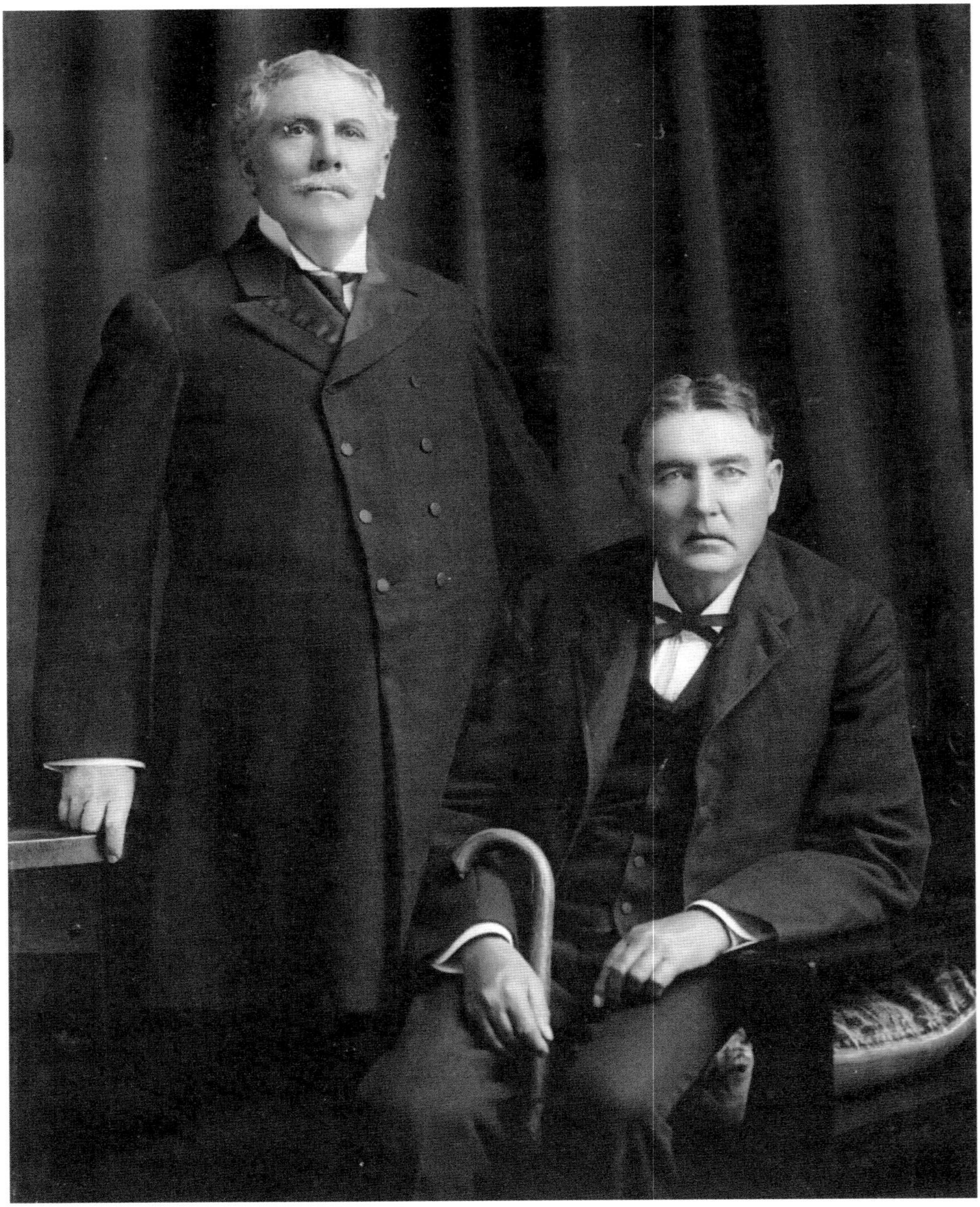

Dr. Henry (Hal) Walker Manson

Dr. Manson was born on February 12, 1843, in Tennessee, studied medicine at Cumberland University, and served the Confederacy during the Civil War. He moved to Rockwall County, along with his first wife, around 1870. Dr. Manson was a physician, a farmer, and the publisher of the *Rockwall Success* newspaper. He ran for state representative in 1897, winning the at-large seat for Dallas and Rockwall by approximately 8,000 votes. Following the death of his first wife, Dr. Manson married Myrta Bell Castle of Dallas. They settled in his home in Rockwall. One of his close friends was Cyrus Scofield (pictured at left), author of the famous *Scofield Reference Bible*. They served together during the Civil War and remained close until Dr. Manson's death in 1905. (Both photographs courtesy of the RCHF.)

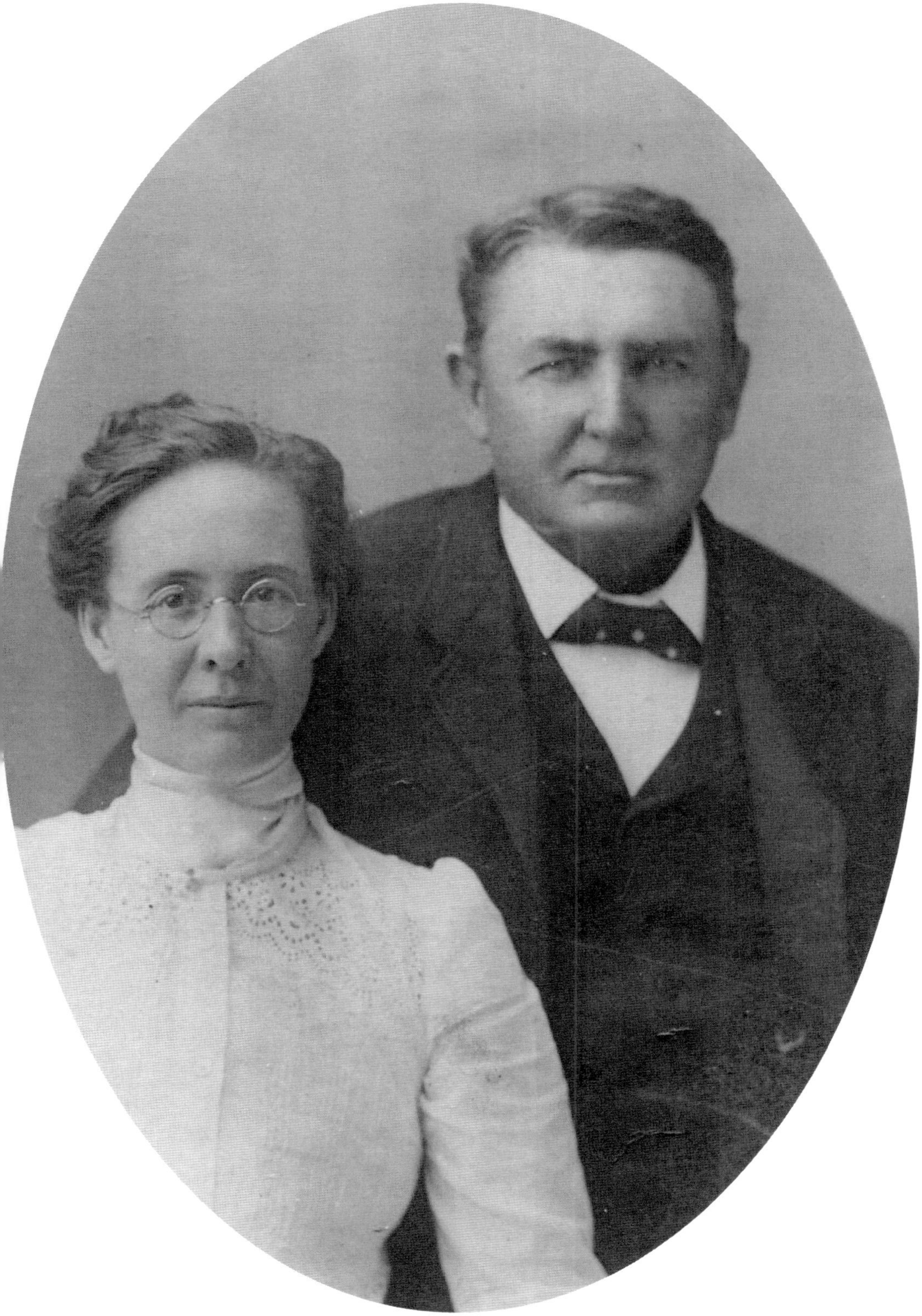

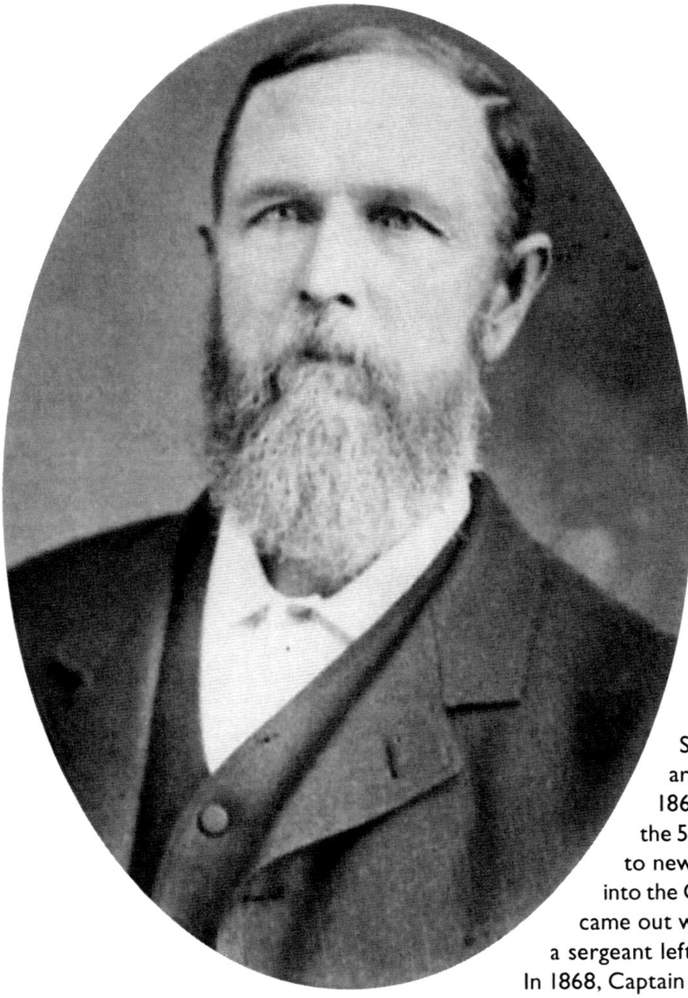

Milton Stanhope Austin

Born in North Carolina in 1828, Milton Stanhope Austin served in the Confederate army during the Civil War. He enlisted in 1862 when he was 34 years old and served in the 52nd North Carolina Regiment. According to newspaper accounts, he "took his company into the Gettysburg fight with eighty-five guns, and came out wounded himself with only nine men and a sergeant left." He lost his right arm during the war. In 1868, Captain Austin brought his wife Margaret and 10 children to Texas, where they settled in Rockwall. Active in civic affairs, he served as sheriff and tax collector for Rockwall County and was elected as a legislator to the Texas House of Representatives, where he served from 1885 to 1887. He passed away in 1906 and is buried in the McLendon Cemetery in McLendon-Chisholm. (Photograph courtesy of the Texas State Historic Preservation Board.)

CHAPTER TWO

Community Leaders and Elected Officials

Since the city of Rockwall was platted in 1854 and Rockwall County was formed in 1873, hundreds of citizens have stepped forward to perform their civic duties through elected office and community leadership. The list of those who deserve to be recognized could literally fill its own volume. Instead, this chapter concentrates on recognizing those elected officials who served in unique positions or who were long tenured in office.

For example, Lannie Stimpson served an astonishing 53 years in elected office in Rockwall County. Most of those years were served as county treasurer. Derwood Wimpee served 35 years in office, splitting his tenure between county clerk and county judge. Paulette Burks worked in the county clerk's office for a total of 35 years (20 years as the county clerk), and Jim Lofland was deputy sheriff for 29 years. W.J. Price served as sheriff from 1944 to 1976.

Those who held unique positions include Claude Isbell, who was a representative to the Texas Senate and also served as secretary of state; and Ralph Hall, who has represented Rockwall at the local, state, and national levels of government. Fate native Henry Wade served as the Dallas district attorney from 1951 to 1987 and was known internationally for prosecuting Jack Ruby for the murder of Lee Harvey Oswald. Mike Reinhardt, a beloved county judge, secured a Works Project Administration grant for the construction of the 1941 Art Deco courthouse, and James Reese served the community as county judge, county commissioner, justice of the peace, county attorney, and representative to the Texas House.

Others who made unique contributions include Odis Lowe, who supported farmers through his tenure as the agricultural extension agent; and Mickey Barnes, a local justice of the peace who served the community during Rockwall's tenure as the "Marriage Capital of the World."

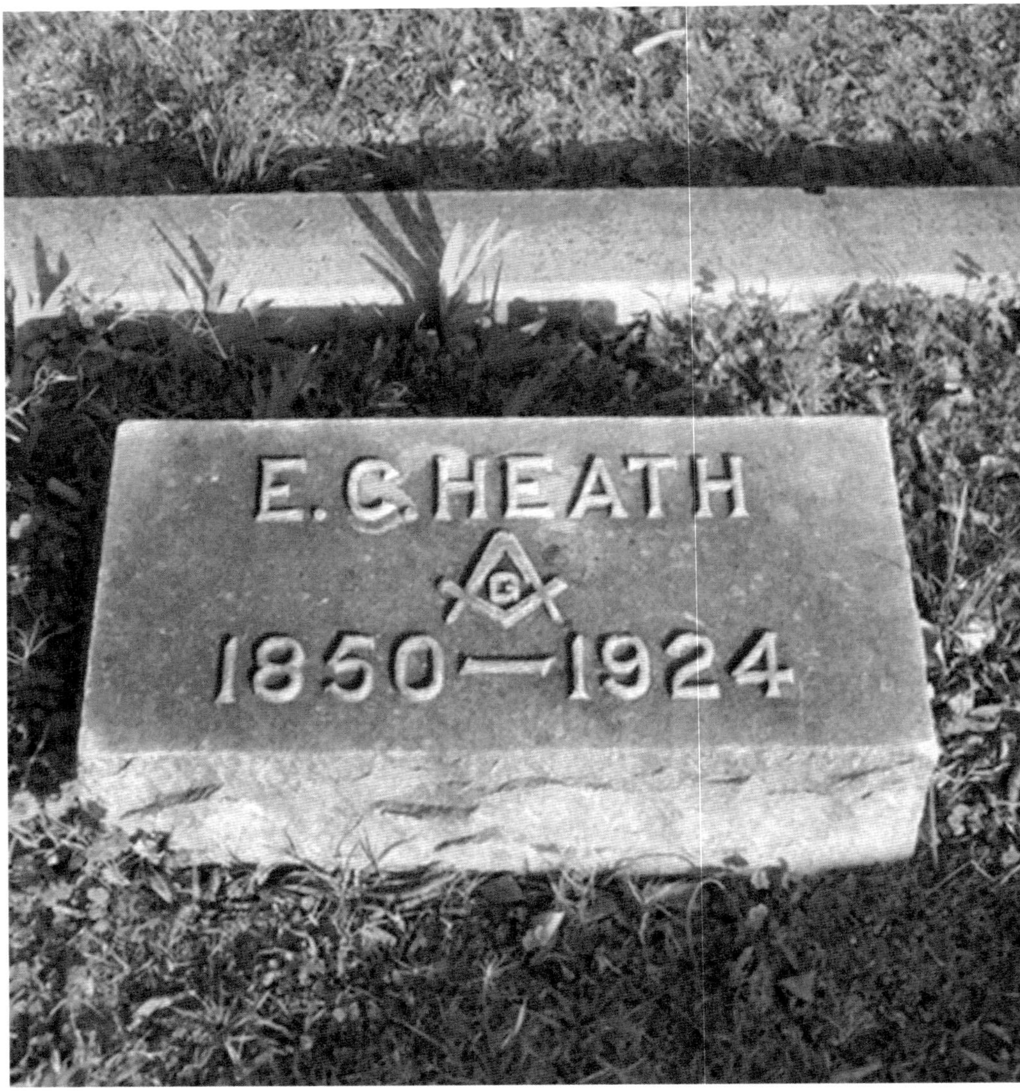

Ephraim Charles Heath

The son of the city of Heath namesake John O. Heath, Ephraim Charles Heath was born in 1850 in the city that bears his family's name. He was elected county judge of Rockwall County upon initial formation of the county in 1882 and held the office until 1886. State records show that when he took office in 1882, the new county was in debt. However, by the end of his tenure, Heath had eliminated the county's debt, lowered the tax rate, and left a cash balance in the county coffers. In 1886, Heath was elected to the Texas State Legislature as representative for the district that held Rockwall County and parts of Dallas and Tarrant Counties. According to his obituary, he was an active supporter of the Prohibition movement and was a candidate on the Prohibition ticket against Gov. James S. Hogg in 1892, but he was defeated. He was successful closer to home, as he led the effort to make Rockwall County the first county in Texas to adopt countywide Prohibition. Legislative biographies from Texas's 20th Legislature state, "He is competent to fill absolutely the highest position to which the people of Texas can raise one of the native born sons of the Lone Star State, for he is a man of the highest talents, most unimpeachable honesty, bold and fearless in his support of men and measures, and a Christian gentleman." (Photograph courtesy of the Texas State Preservation Board.)

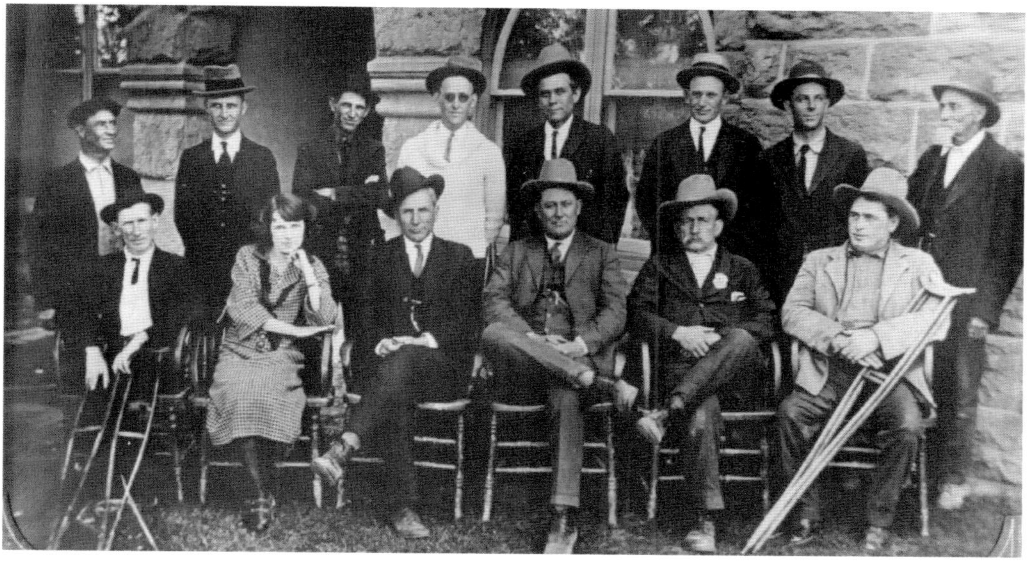

Lannie Stimpson

Dedicating his life to public service, Miles Lannie Stimpson (pictured above in the first row, at left; pictured below in the first row, wearing a white hat) served an astonishing 53 years in elected office in Rockwall County. Born in 1892, he was crippled by polio as a child. At just 19 years old, he was elected Rockwall County treasurer. After serving four years, he was elected tax assessor. In 1920, he was once again elected county treasurer, an office he held until his resignation in 1965. During his tenure, Stimpson also served with many other long-tenured public servants. (Both photographs courtesy of the RCHF.)

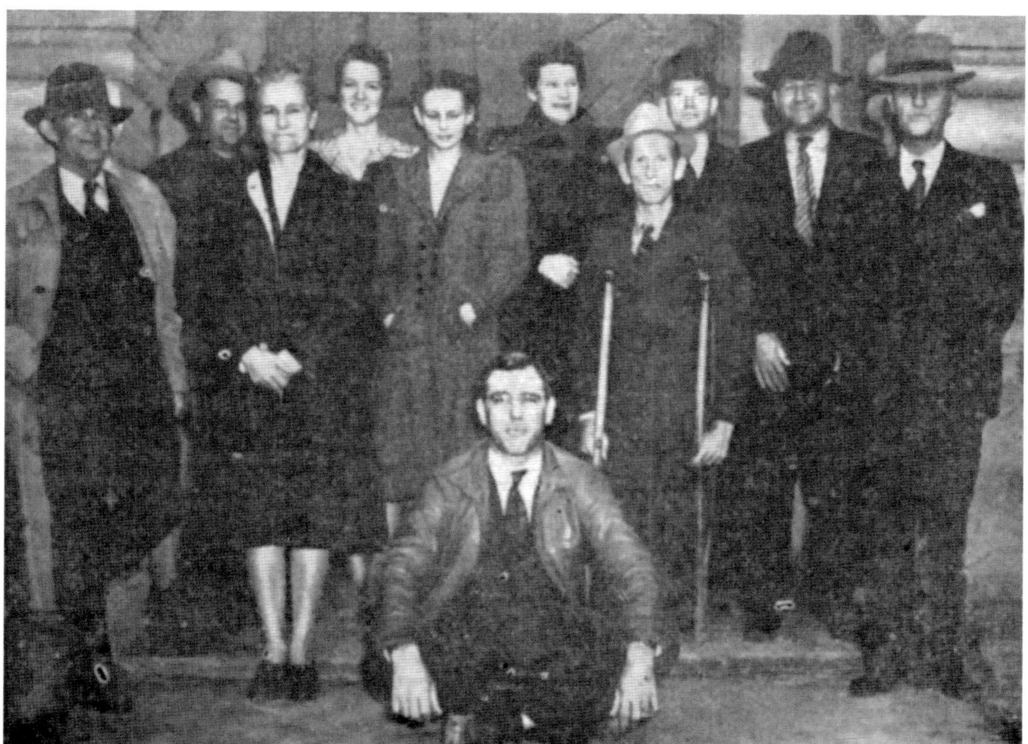

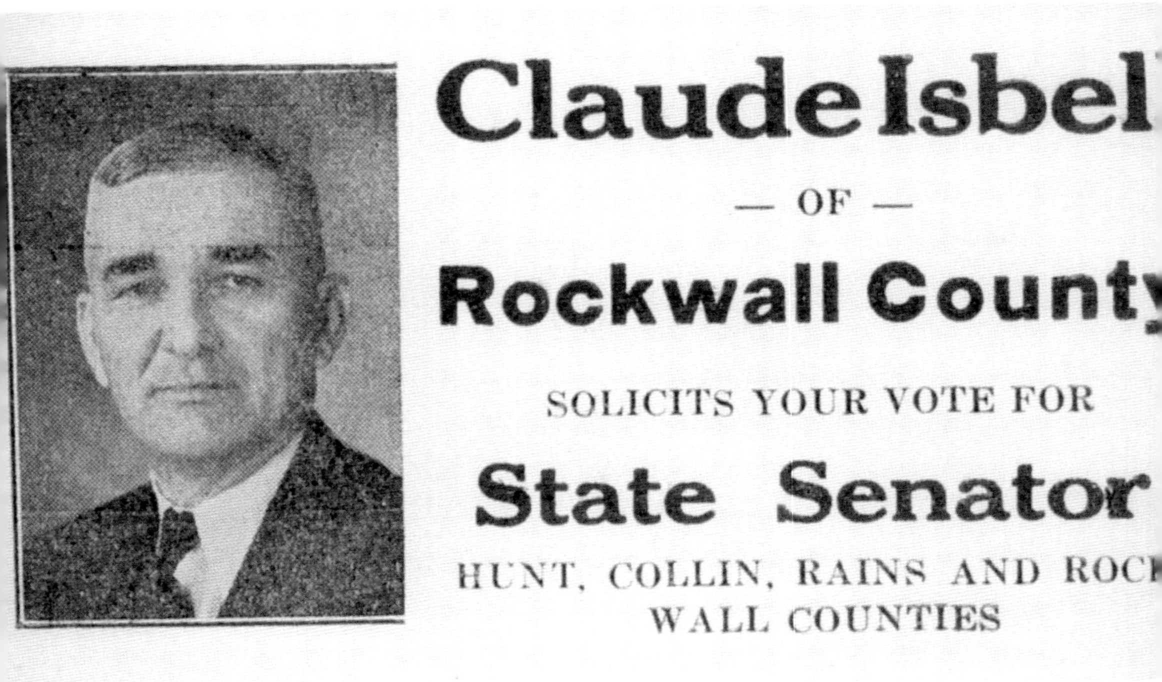

Claude Isbell

Claude Isbell was born in 1884 in Rockwall County and attended Rockwall schools prior to receiving his law degree from Lebanon University in Tennessee. He served as Rockwall County judge from 1927 to 1935. In 1935, he began a six-year tenure in the Texas State Senate. On August 6, 1937, he was honored by serving as Texas's appointed "governor for a day." He served as president pro tempore of the senate prior to resigning his seat to accept an appointment as the assistant securities commissioner in the secretary of state's office. Gov. Coke Stevenson appointed Isbell as secretary of state in 1944, an office he held until 1947. He was the first and—to date—only person from Rockwall County to serve as Texas's secretary of state. He passed away on July 22, 1962, in Austin, Texas. (Above photograph, courtesy of Texas State Preservation Board; opposite page, photograph from author's private collection.)

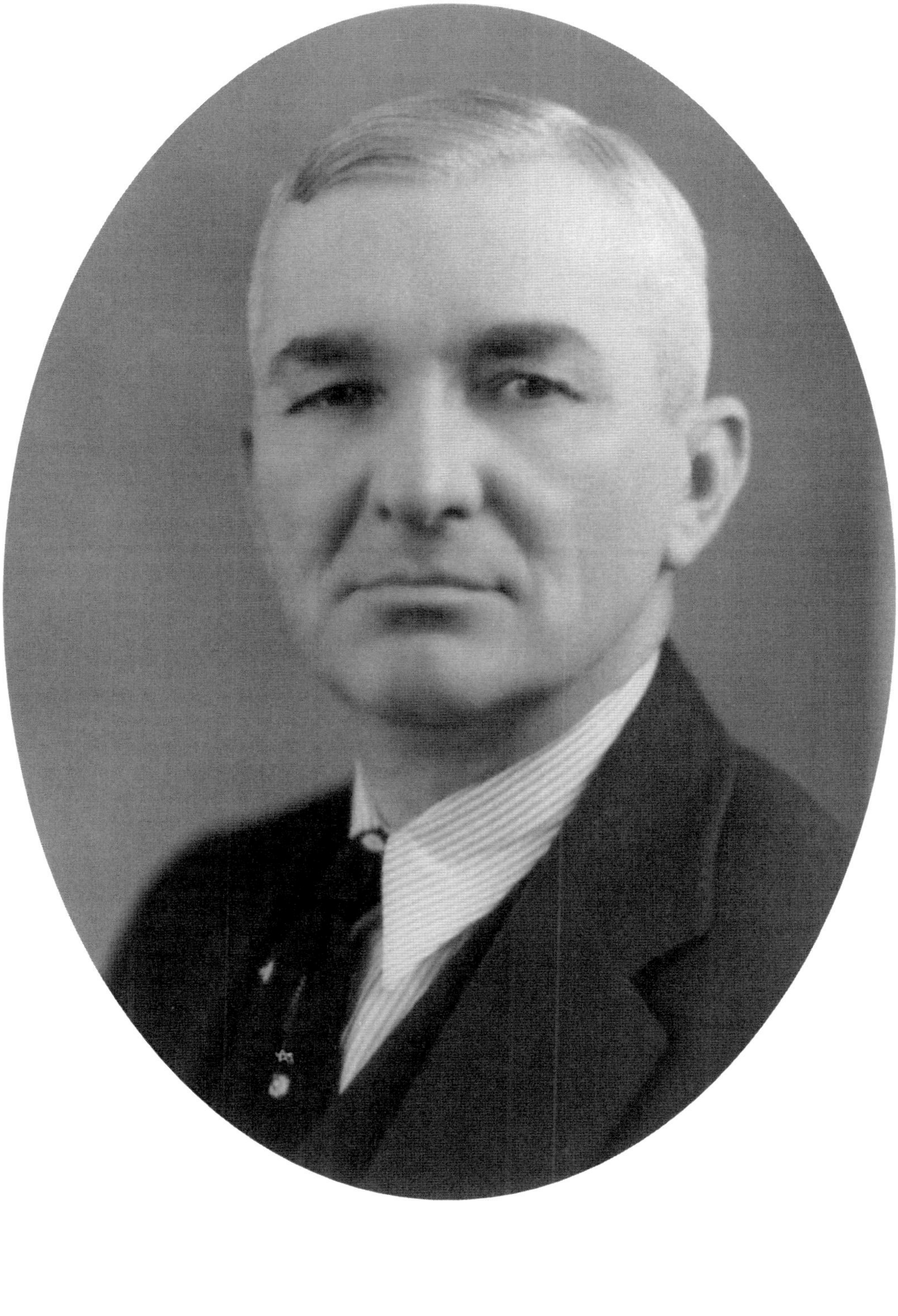

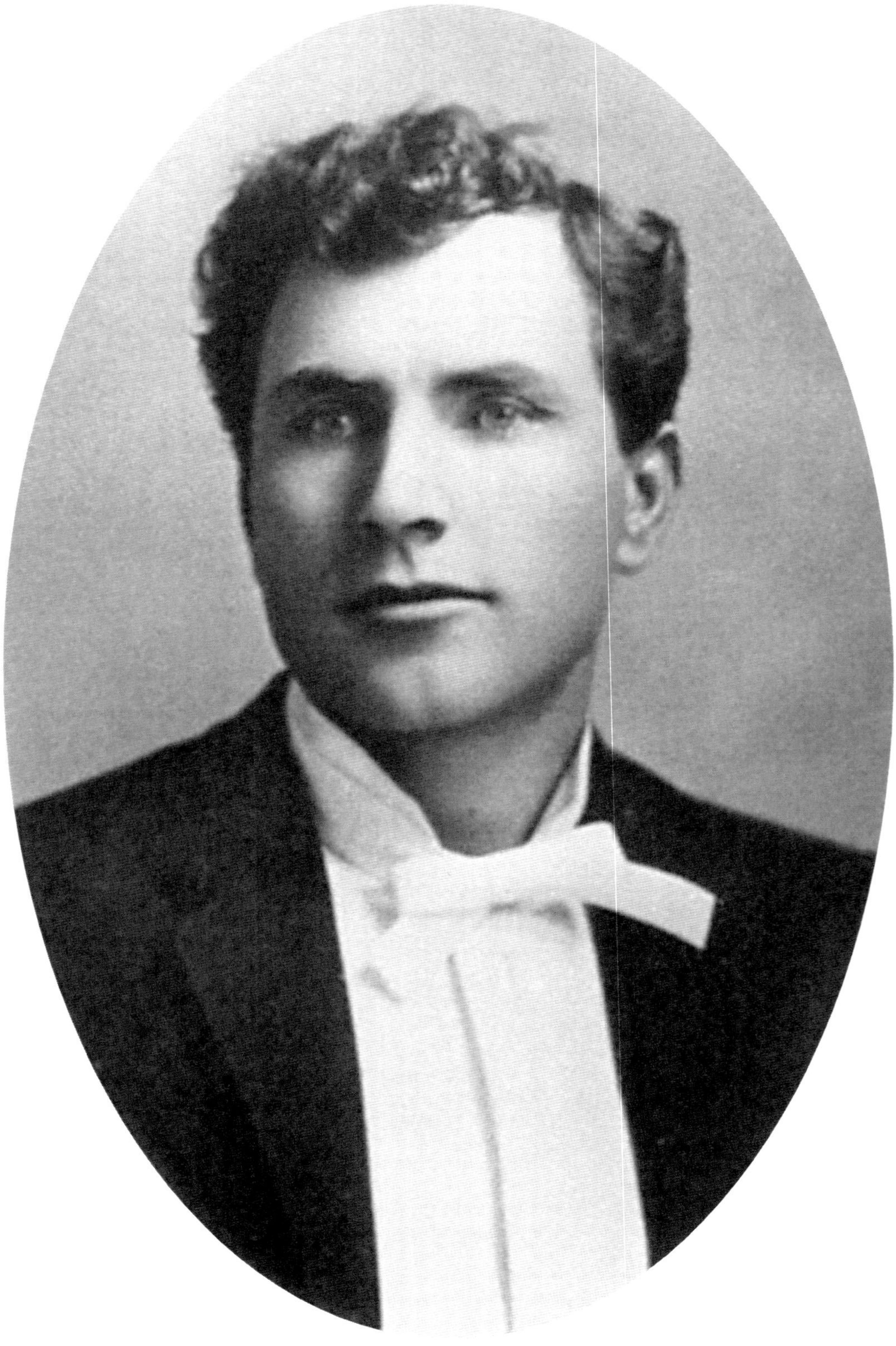

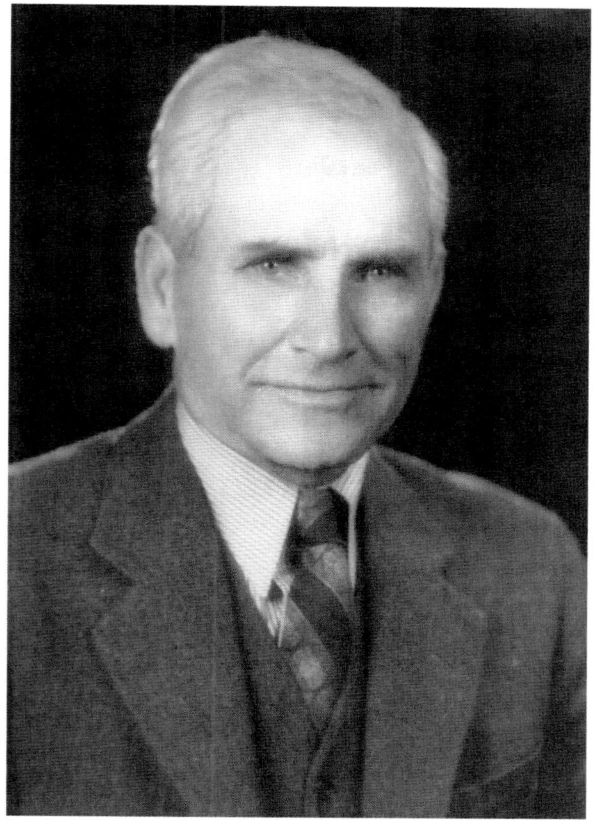

James Reese

James Reese was born in 1866 in a log cabin near the present-day community of Heath. He served the Rockwall County community as county judge for five elected terms as well as county commissioner/justice of the peace, and county attorney. He served in the Texas State Legislature as representative for the Flotorial District composed of Rockwall and Dallas Counties. Judge Reese was a large landowner in Rockwall and Collin Counties, and in 1911 he built a majestic, white-columned home on South Goliad Street, the main thoroughfare into downtown Rockwall. The home was considered Rockwall's first true "mansion" and was moved to a new location on North Goliad Street in the mid-2000s to avoid demolition. (Photographs on both pages courtesy of Texas State Preservation Board and RCHF.)

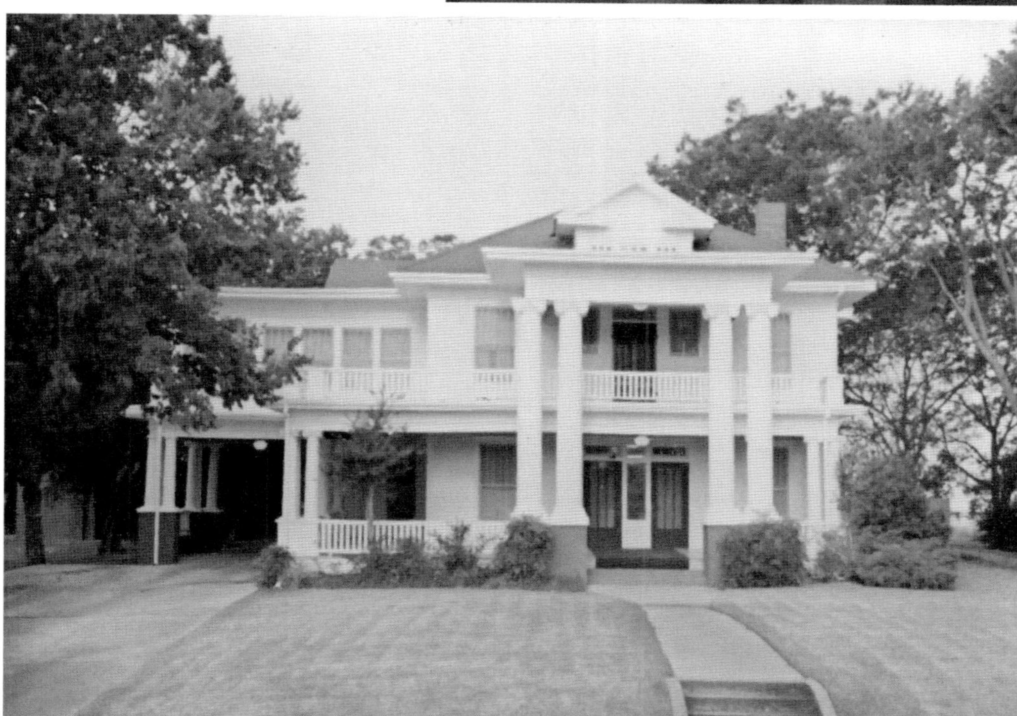

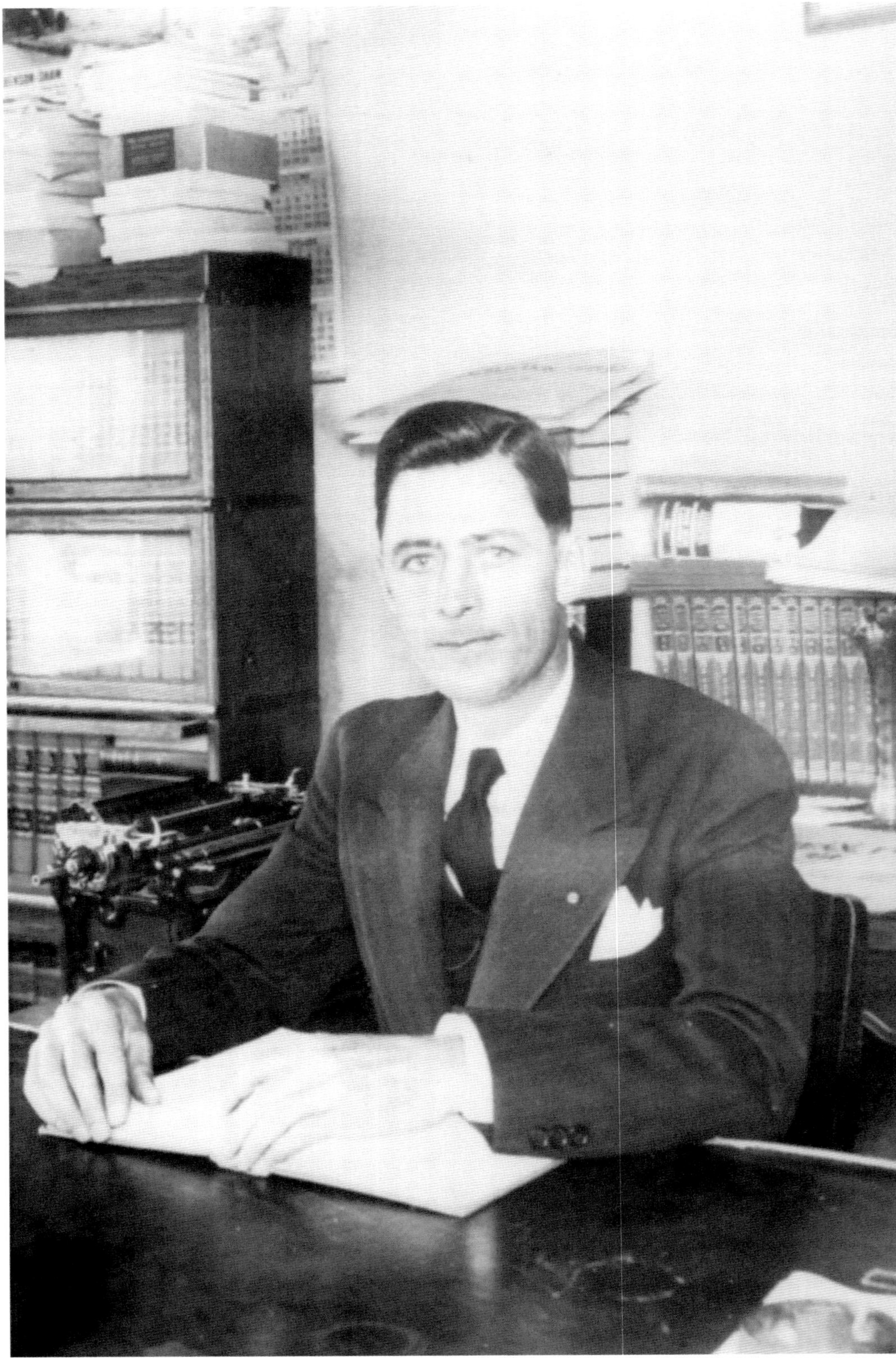

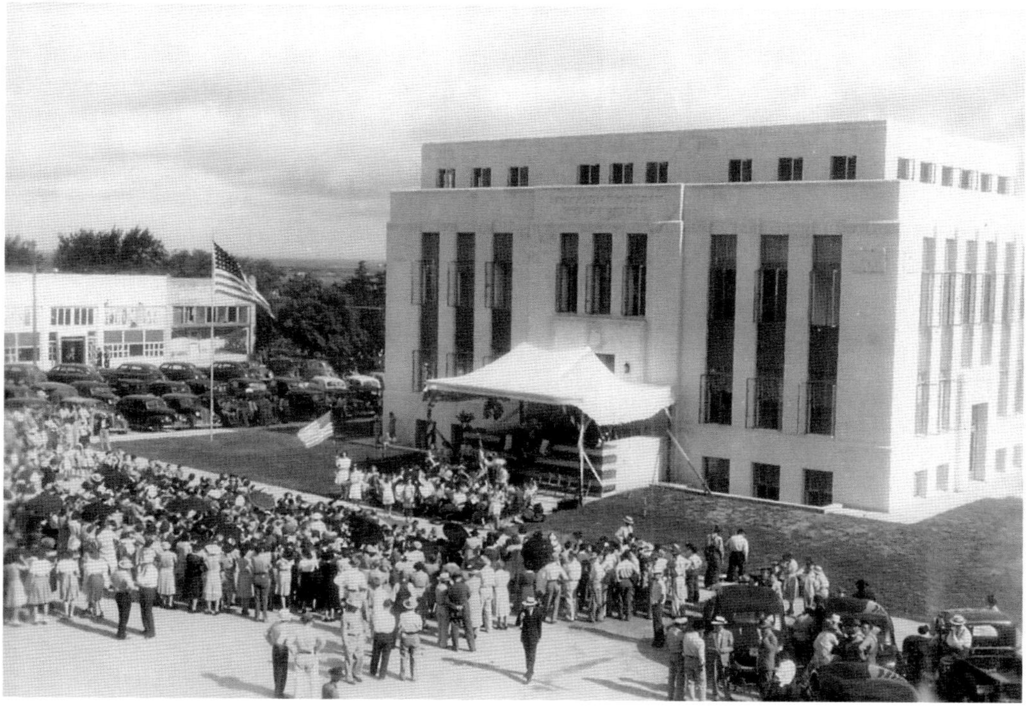

Mike Reinhardt

A revered, astute, and dedicated county judge, Mike Reinhardt was born in Royse City in 1903 to parents who valued education, civic duty, and dedication to church and family. Mike graduated from Royse City High School and attended Southern Methodist University. He received his law degree in 1924 from Cumberland University in Lebanon, Tennessee. He began his law practice in Rockwall County and was elected county judge in 1934. He married Virginia Anderson on Christmas Day in 1937. In the late 1930s, when Rockwall's county courthouse began showing signs of wear, Judge Reinhardt worked with other county officials to begin planning the construction of a new and modern structure. In 1940, he traveled to Washington, DC, to procure a Works Project Administration grant that would pay $52,000 of the full courthouse construction cost of $92,000. On January 19, 1940, he was awarded the grant. While still in Washington, he contracted acute pneumonia that night and passed away in the early morning hours of January 20th in a Washington hospital. At the time of his death, Judge Reinhardt and his wife had one child and she was expecting another. His brother-in-law, Carl Miller, was appointed as county judge to complete his unexpired term and oversee the construction process of the new courthouse, which served as a tribute to Judge Reinhardt. Inspired by the Art Deco buildings that had been constructed at Dallas's Fair Park for the 1936 Centennial Exhibition, Rockwall's new courthouse was intended to reflect a modern and forward-thinking county. Now known as the historic downtown courthouse, Mike Reinhardt's vision still stands as a memorial to his service to the county, as well as a recognized and rare example of Art Deco courthouses in the state of Texas. (Photographs on both pages courtesy of Mary Sue Reinhardt Smith, Pat Stodghill, and the RCHF.)

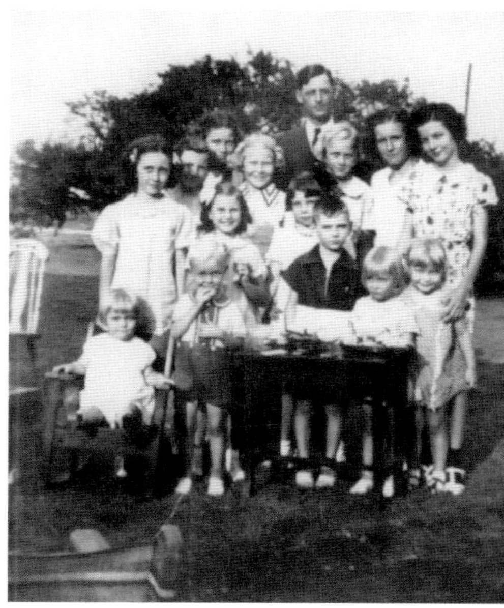

Ralph M. Hall

Ralph Hall has represented Rockwall County at the local, state, and national levels of government. He was born in Fate, Texas, and attended Rockwall County schools. In 1942, he joined the US Navy and served as a lieutenant (senior grade) aircraft carrier pilot during World War II. In 1951, he received his law degree from Southern Methodist University. In addition to being active as a lawyer and businessman in Rockwall County, Hall served as county judge from 1950 to 1962, as a member of the Texas Senate from 1962 to 1972, and as a US congressman from 1980 until 2015. On December 25, 2012, Congressman Hall became the oldest-serving member of the US House of Representatives in recorded history. Ralph and Mary Ellen Murphy married in 1944 and were wed for nearly 65 years; she passed away in 2008. (Photographs on both pages courtesy of Ralph M. Hall.)

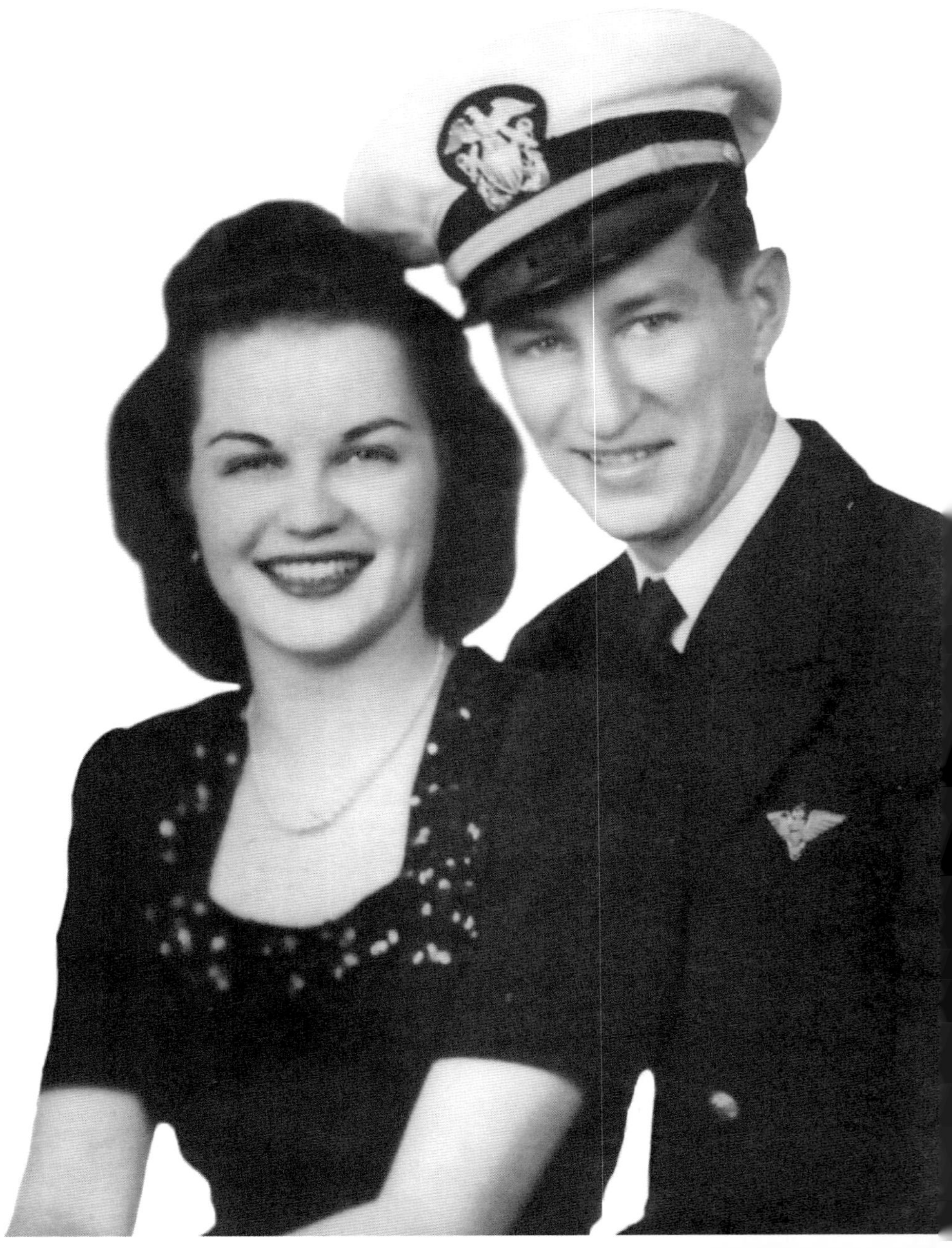

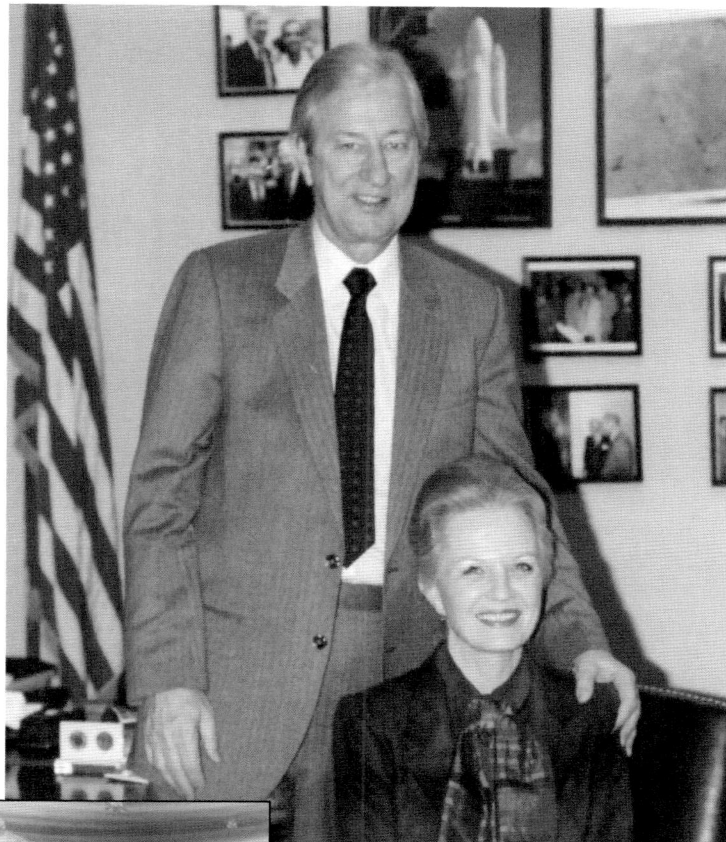

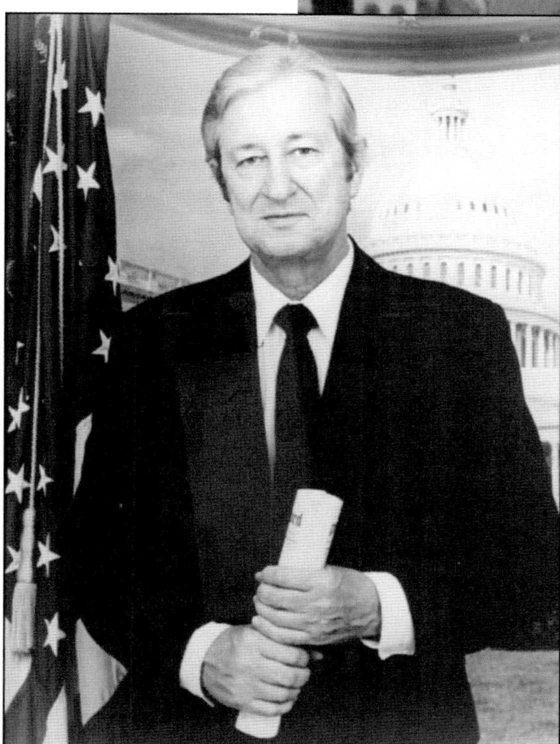

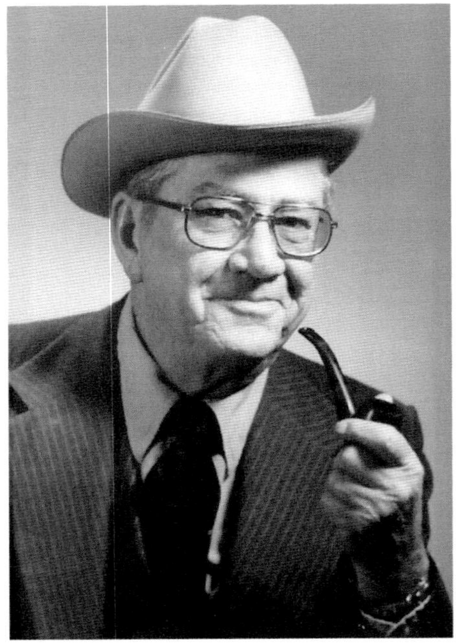

W.J. Price

After serving as deputy sheriff for five years, William Jasper Price—known locally as W.J.—was elected sheriff in 1944. He held the office for 32 years, an unprecedented tenure. In the mid-1950s, W.J. was elected president of the Texas Sheriff's Association and helped clarify and rewrite much of the state's legislation regarding law enforcement and county government. (Photograph courtesy of the RCHF.)

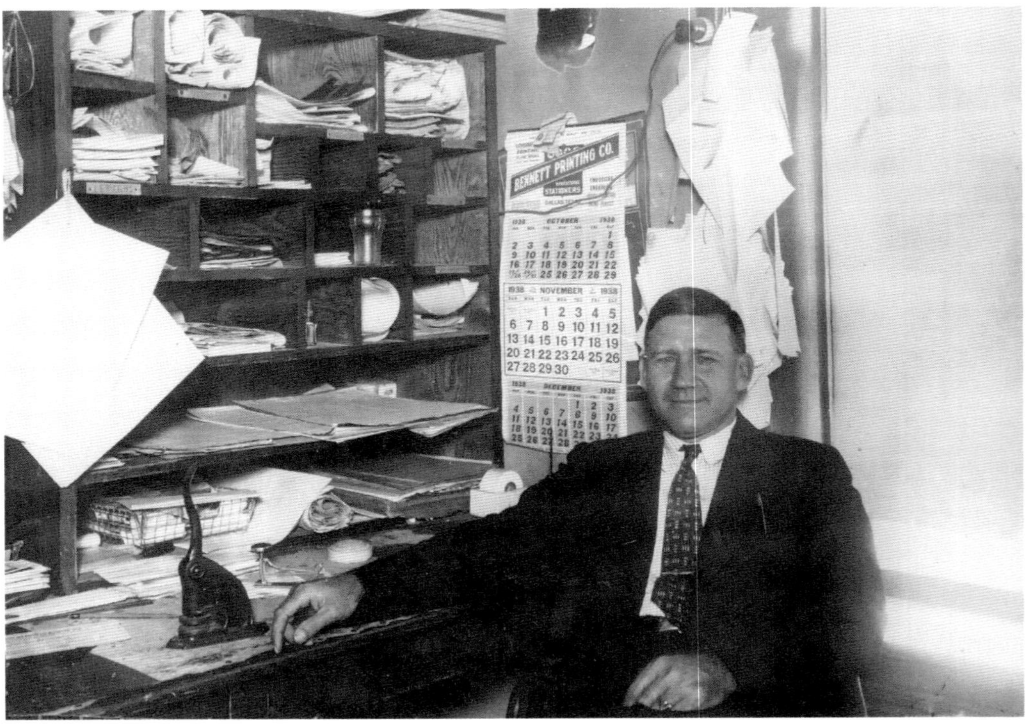

Jim Lofland

James Thomas "Jim" Lofland served as deputy sheriff of Rockwall County for 29 years. His main duties included overseeing the business aspects of the sheriff's office and serving as tax collector and assessor for the county. A native of Heath, Jim also maintained his family farm and, prior to serving as deputy sheriff, worked as a bookkeeper at the Heath gin and in banks in both Heath and Rockwall. (Photograph from author's private collection.)

Henry Wade

Best known for his long-tenured service as the criminal district attorney for Dallas and for leading the prosecution in the Jack Ruby case, Henry Wade was actually a small-town boy who grew up in Rockwall County in a family as one of 11 children. He graduated as valedictorian of his 1933 senior class at Rockwall High School and went on to graduate with highest honors from the University of Texas School of Law. Prior to serving as Dallas district attorney, he was Rockwall county attorney, a special agent with the FBI, and an officer in the Navy during World War II. After leaving the Navy, he joined the Dallas County District Attorney's Office as a felony prosecutor. He served as Dallas County's district attorney from 1951 to 1987. (Photograph courtesy of the family of Don Stodghill.)

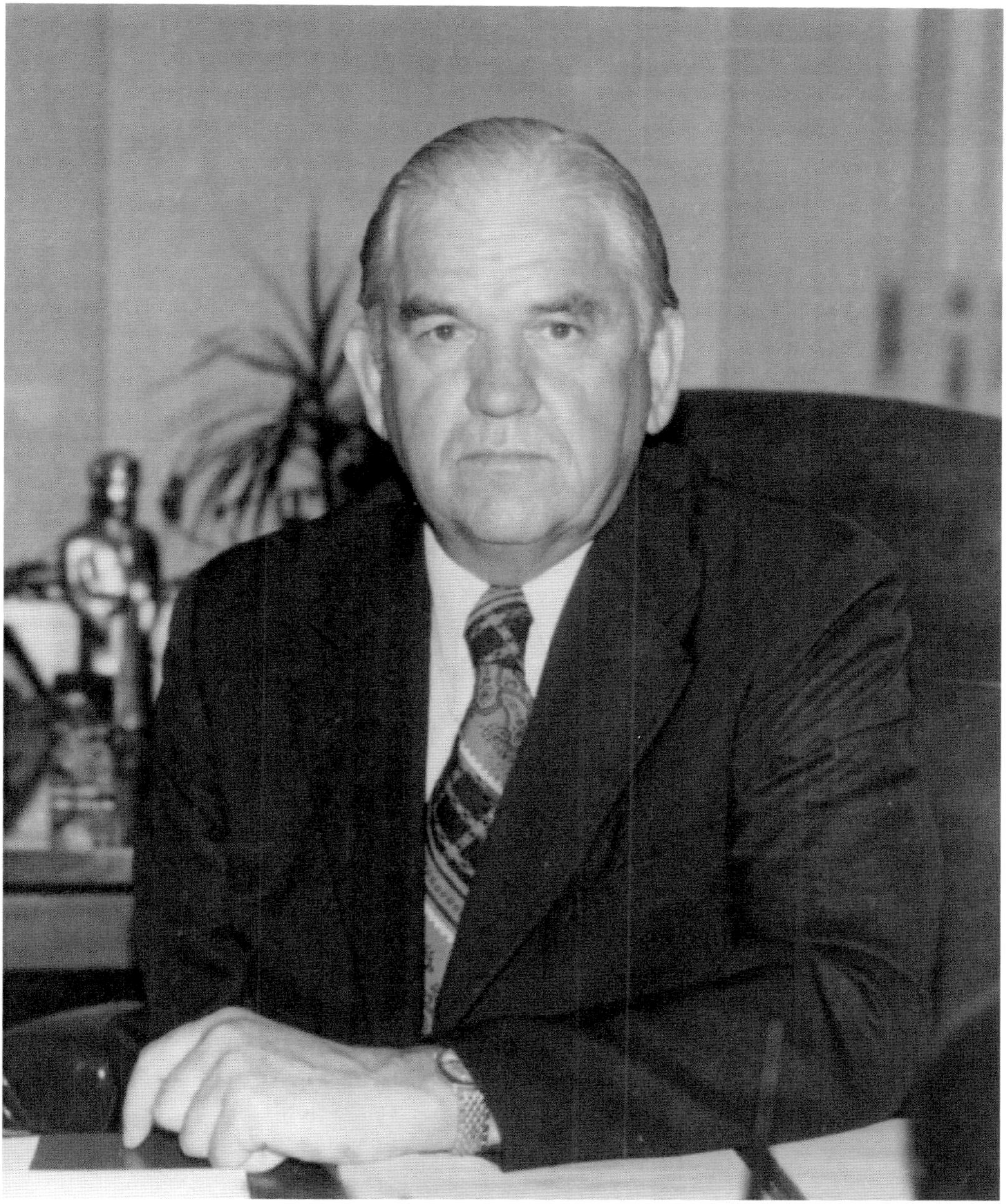

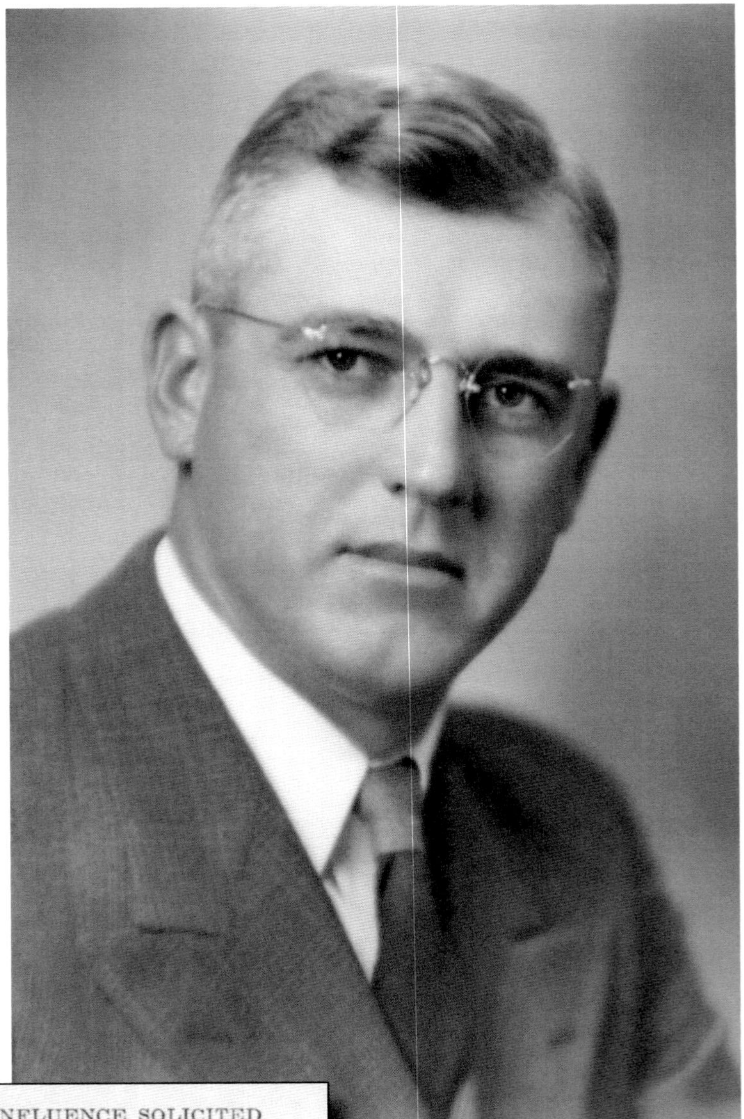

Jack Pullen
Jack Pullen was elected as sheriff, tax assessor, and collector of Rockwall County in 1936. Due to his father's death, he chose not to run for reelection after his fourth term. His full attention and all of his time would be devoted to the Pullen farm. In 1938, Jack married Dorothy Smith, the daughter of a pioneer family from Fate. (Photograph courtesy of the Pullen family.)

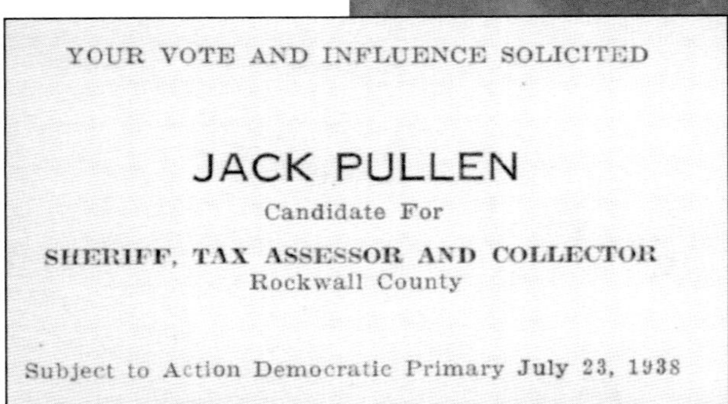

YOUR VOTE AND INFLUENCE SOLICITED

JACK PULLEN

Candidate For

SHERIFF, TAX ASSESSOR AND COLLECTOR
Rockwall County

Subject to Action Democratic Primary July 23, 1938

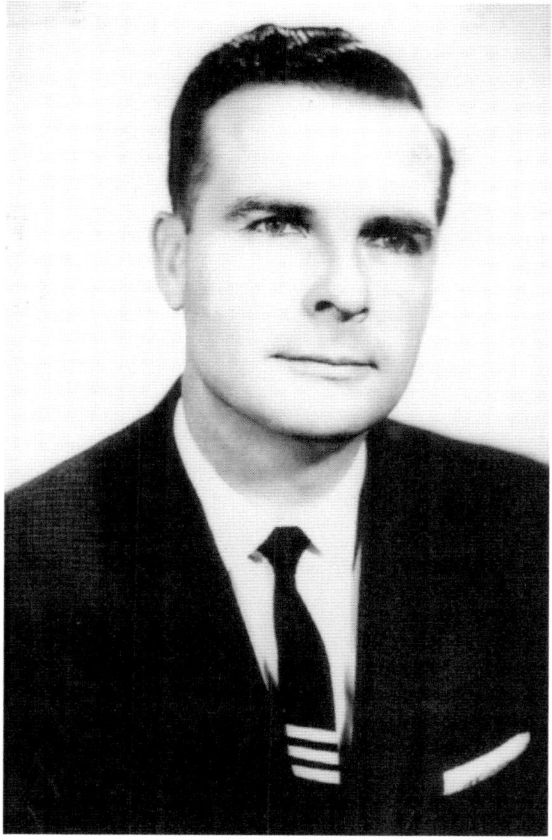

Derwood Wimpee

A World War II veteran and a long-tenured public servant, Martin Derwood Wimpee served 14 years as Rockwall's County Clerk (1947–1963) and 20 years as county judge for Rockwall County (1963–1982). In addition to his local service, Judge Wimpee was elected president of the North and East County Judges and Commissioners Association, served as president of the County Judges and County Commissioners Association of Texas, and served two terms as president of the Texas Association, which consisted of all counties. (Photographs courtesy of the Wimpee family.)

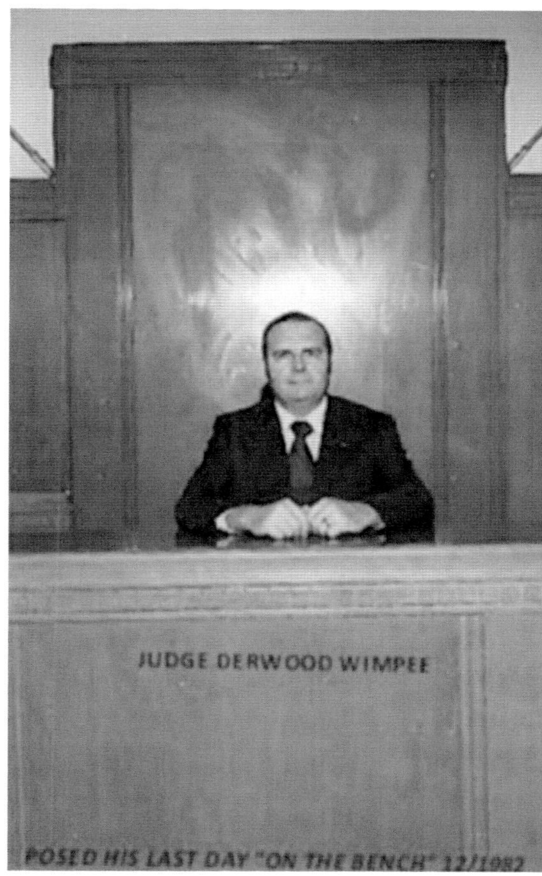

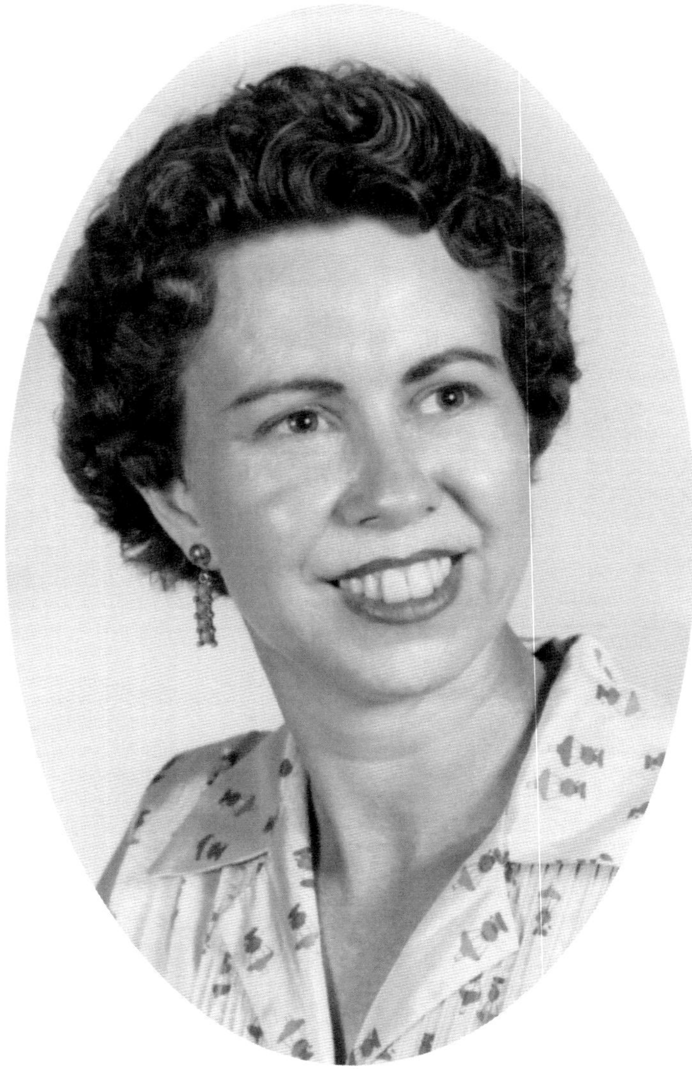

Mildred "Mickey" Barnes

Appointed to fill the unexpired term of her late husband, Mildred Barnes first took office in 1952 and served 14 years as justice of the peace. Reporters described her as "a brown-eyed brunette who beautifies the bench," but she also had a reputation for knowing her job. In a 1962 edition of the *Greenville-Herald Banner*, an article noted, "Barnes is a recognized and competent justice of the peace. There's more than one fella between Rockwall and Greenville who knows it doesn't pay to violate the law in Rockwall County after a session in Mrs. Barnes' court." She was also instrumental in gaining Rockwall the title of "Marriage Capital of Texas," agreeably getting out of bed many times on weekends to marry amorous couples. In her first two years as justice of the peace, she performed more than 2,000 wedding ceremonies. She had a lighted sign in her front yard that proclaimed that a justice of the peace lived on the premises. Since marriage fees were money earned in addition to a JP salary, judges usually set their own prices, but Mrs. Barnes let her clients pay whatever they could afford. Although most of the couples were happy with the all-night availability (which included blood tests and a small fee for the license provided by other area locals), Barnes did receive a few unpleasant letters from less-than-happy mothers. The practice was discontinued in the mid-1950s, and Mrs. Barnes moved on to another profession. (Photograph courtesy of Beverley Mummey.)

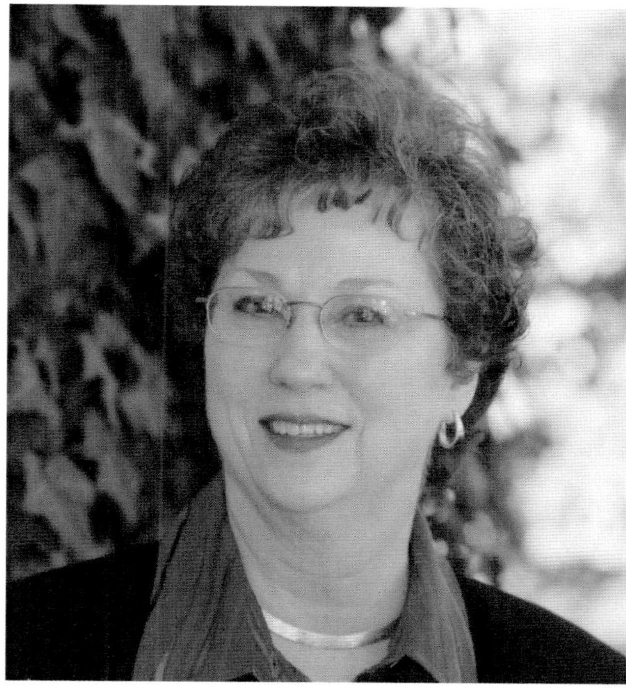

Paulette Burks
In 1969, Paulette Burks started as a part-time employee in the Rockwall County Clerk's Office, eventually taking on a full-time position. When the county clerk retired in 1985, Burks became a candidate for office and won the election. At the time of her retirement in 2006, she had been employed in the Rockwall County Clerk's Office for a total of 37 years—21 of those as the top elected official. (Photograph courtesy of the Burks family.)

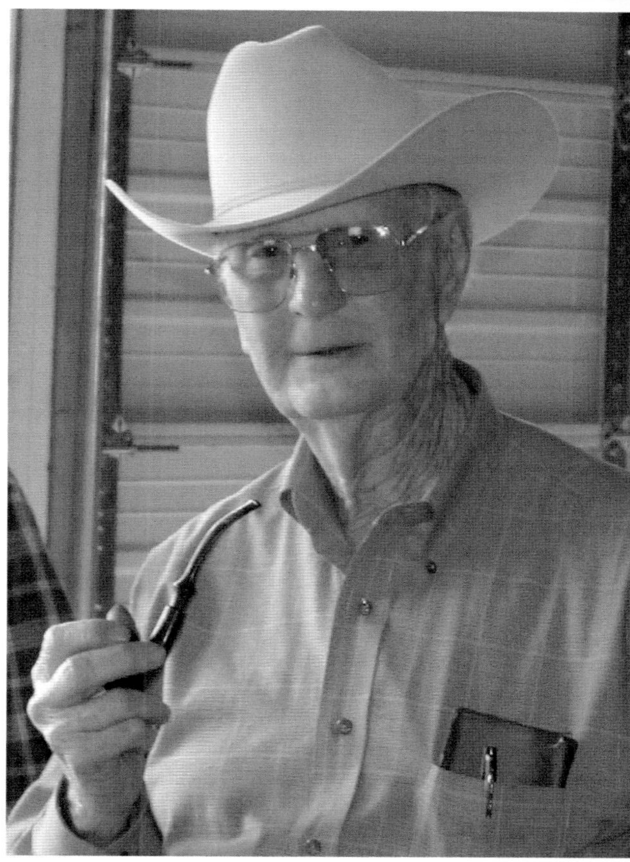

Odis Lowe
Although Odis Lowe has been a part of the Rockwall community since 1946, when he returned from service in the Army, his tenure from 1969 to 1982 as Rockwall County agricultural extension agent gave him the opportunity to directly affect the local economy and make a lasting impact on area farmers and aspiring youth. Having been in farming and ranching for many years, his expertise was vital during a time when Rockwall was shifting from an agrarian-based economy to one more affected by its location as a suburb of Dallas. Throughout the years, he has also been a staunch supporter of youth-based agricultural programs and continues to support these efforts in his retirement. (Photograph courtesy of Lynn Fate.)

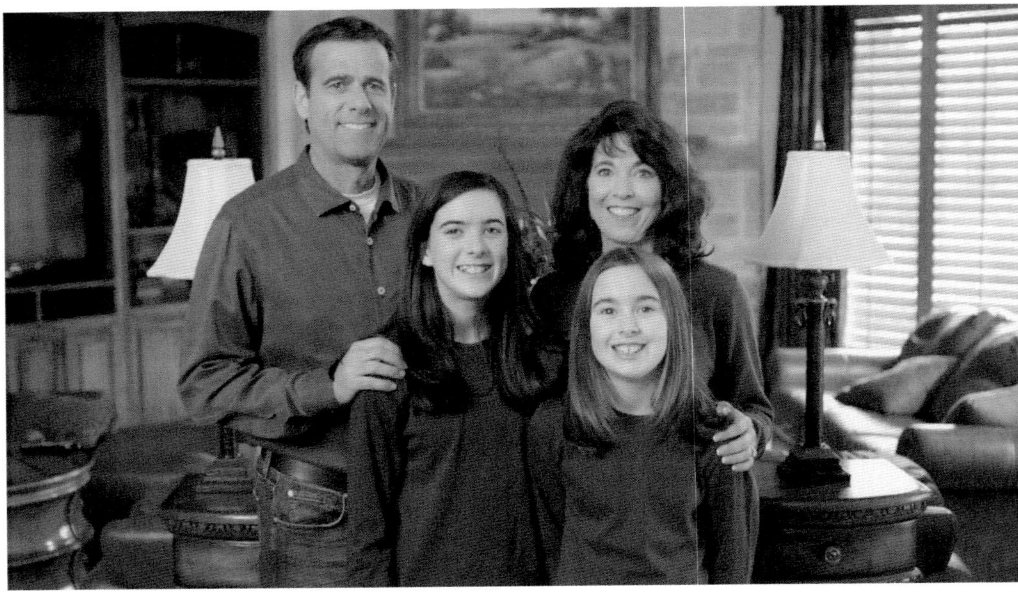

John Ratcliffe

John Ratcliffe is the current Congressman-elect for the 4th District of Texas. In the George W. Bush administration, he was appointed as the chief of anti-terrorism and national security for the Eastern District of Texas and later as the US attorney for the Eastern District of Texas. John's political record also includes eight years as the mayor of Heath, Texas. John and his wife, Michele, have been married for 24 years and reside in Heath with their two daughters. John was sworn in as a member of the 114th US Congress on January 6, 2015. (Photographs courtesy of John Ratcliffe.)

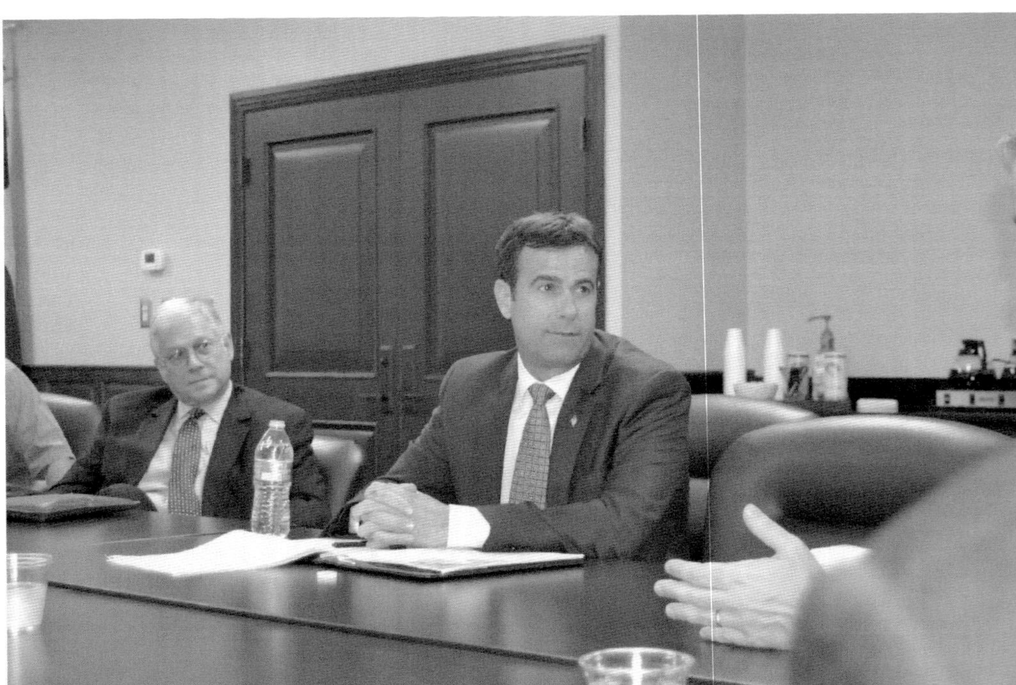

CHAPTER THREE

Hometown Heroes

Every community has its own personal hometown heroes—those people who have championed a cause, fought for a belief, achieved an individual goal, or been honored for a talent or passion. Rockwall is no different. Since the earliest settlers arrived in the 1840s, Rockwall residents have been leaving their mark in unique ways. This chapter celebrates a sampling of citizens—both current and former—who fulfill this criteria.

Rockwall is fortunate to have many residents who are inspired to action by the needs of others. Robert Reeves's vision of providing assistance to Rockwall County residents resulted in the formation of Helping Hands, the area's largest provider and supporter of families in need. With the guidance of Helping Hands executive director Margo Nielsen and an army of dedicated volunteer leaders led by Claudette Johnson, Helping Hands has grown to include a health clinic, a food pantry, a thrift store, and an assistance referral program. In addition, local nonprofits such as the Rockwall Rotary Club, Soroptomists International, the National Charity League, and the Rockwall Women's League have all gained legendary status through their efforts to provide support and volunteer assistance to the community.

Rockwall also has a long list of residents who have been recognized for their unique talents throughout the years. Rockwall High School graduate Carlton Massey played football for the University of Texas and was named an All-American, the only player from Rockwall County thus far to earn this honor. Heath native Pat Stodghill was named Poet Laureate of Texas in 1978 by the Texas State Legislature in recognition of her successful poetic career. Jason Castro and Amber Carrington, both with recent ties to Rockwall, have enjoyed success on national voice competitions.

Personal crusades have also inspired Rockwall residents to achieve what once were considered unattainable goals. In a time of segregated schools, Gloria Williams fought tirelessly to be able to complete her education. Although she had to overcome seemingly insurmountable obstacles, Williams became the first Rockwall student of African American heritage to receive her high school diploma. In another example, the 1963 Yellowjacket football team—comprised mainly of farm boys—became the ultimate Cinderella story as they captured the AA State Championship in a stunning, come-from-behind victory. These hometown heroes represent just a small example of the many residents who, through the years, have provided inspiration to all of Rockwall.

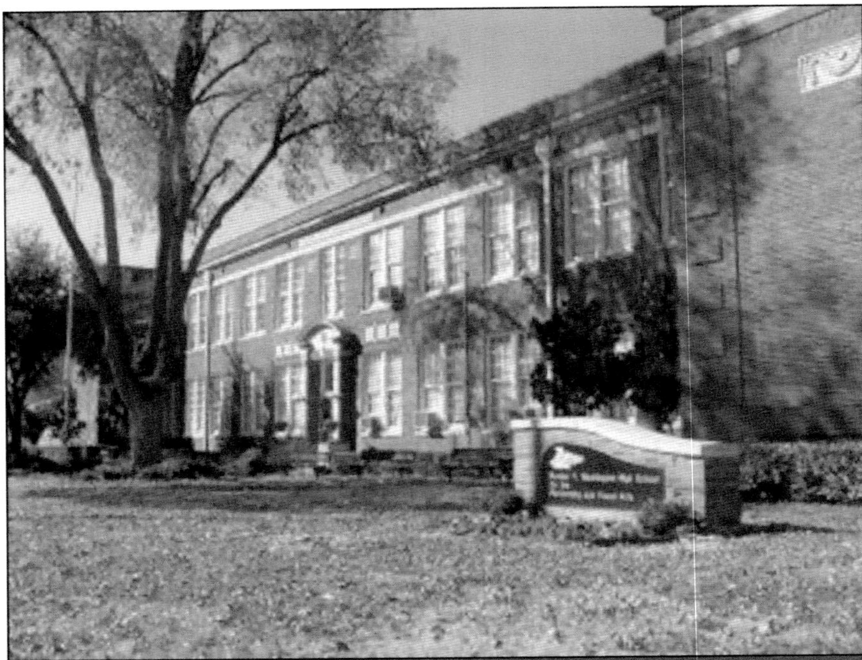

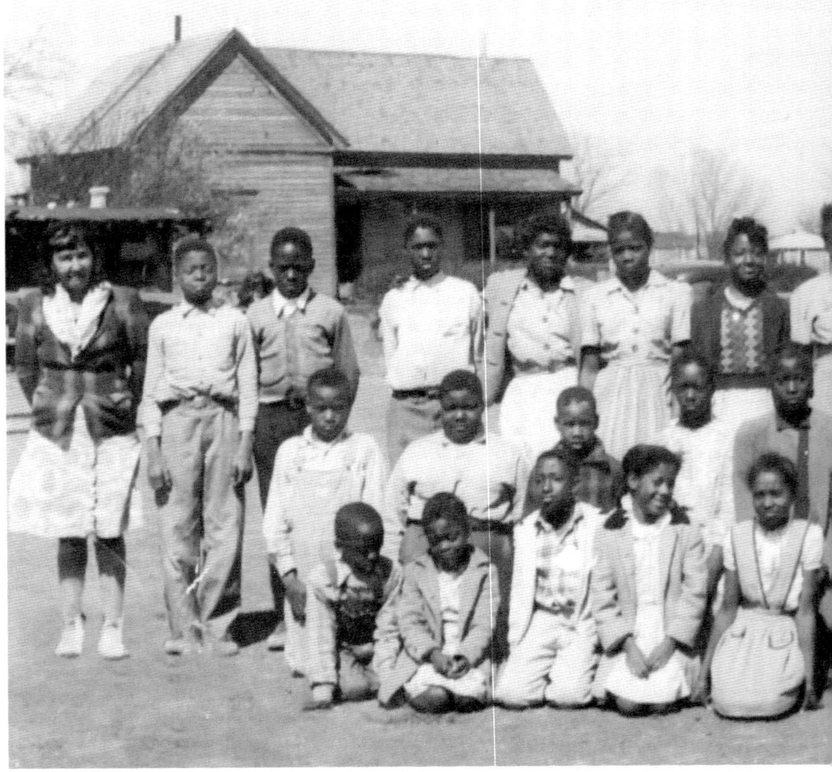

Gloria Williams

In the segregated school system of the 1940s, Rockwall's educational opportunities for African American students only reached the ninth-grade level, but Gloria Williams (pictured third row, fifth from left) was determined to earn her high school diploma. The nearby community of Garland had a 10th grade for African American students, but in order to attend, Gloria had to gain permission from the Garland school principal and the Rockwall school superintendent. She also had to find the money to pay the round-trip fare to Garland on a Continental Trailways bus that came through Rockwall each morning and evening. She was granted that permission with a plea so moving that Rockwall ISD superintendent of schools J.A. Wilkerson actually paid her bus fare out of his own pocket. After completing the 10th grade, Garland's African American students were bused to Dallas's Booker T. Washington High School for the 11th and 12th grades. This meant that Gloria then had to take two buses every morning: the Continental Trailways bus in Rockwall and then a Garland school bus—and the same two buses home again each evening. By this time, Superintendent Wilkerson had retired due to health concerns, and Gloria's family had to pay her bus fare. By the fall of 1949, money was tight, so Gloria wrote to a school official to request early graduation. She was told that if she doubled her core courses and continued to make passing grades, she would be awarded her diploma in January instead of June. In January 1950, Williams graduated from Booker T. Washington High School (pictured above) with triple honors. (Photographs on both pages courtesy of the RCHF.)

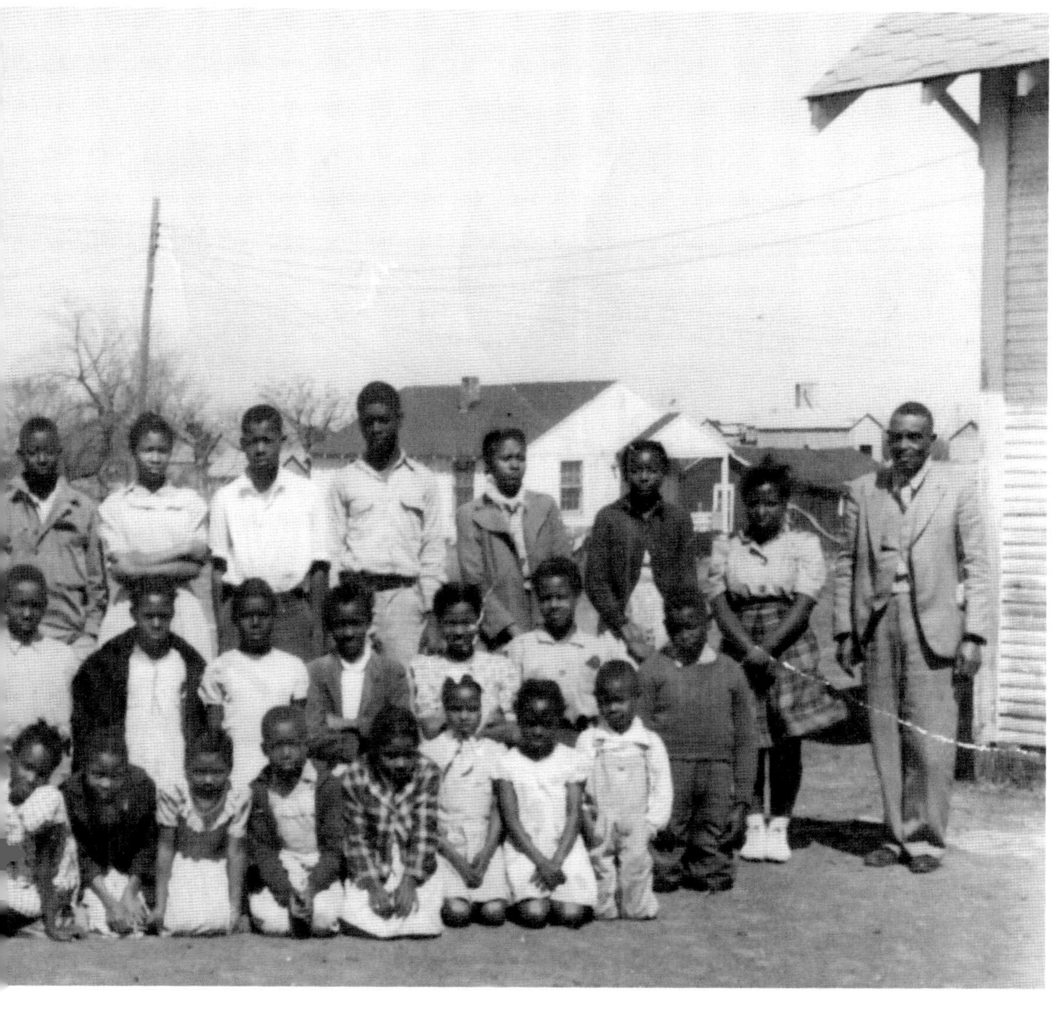

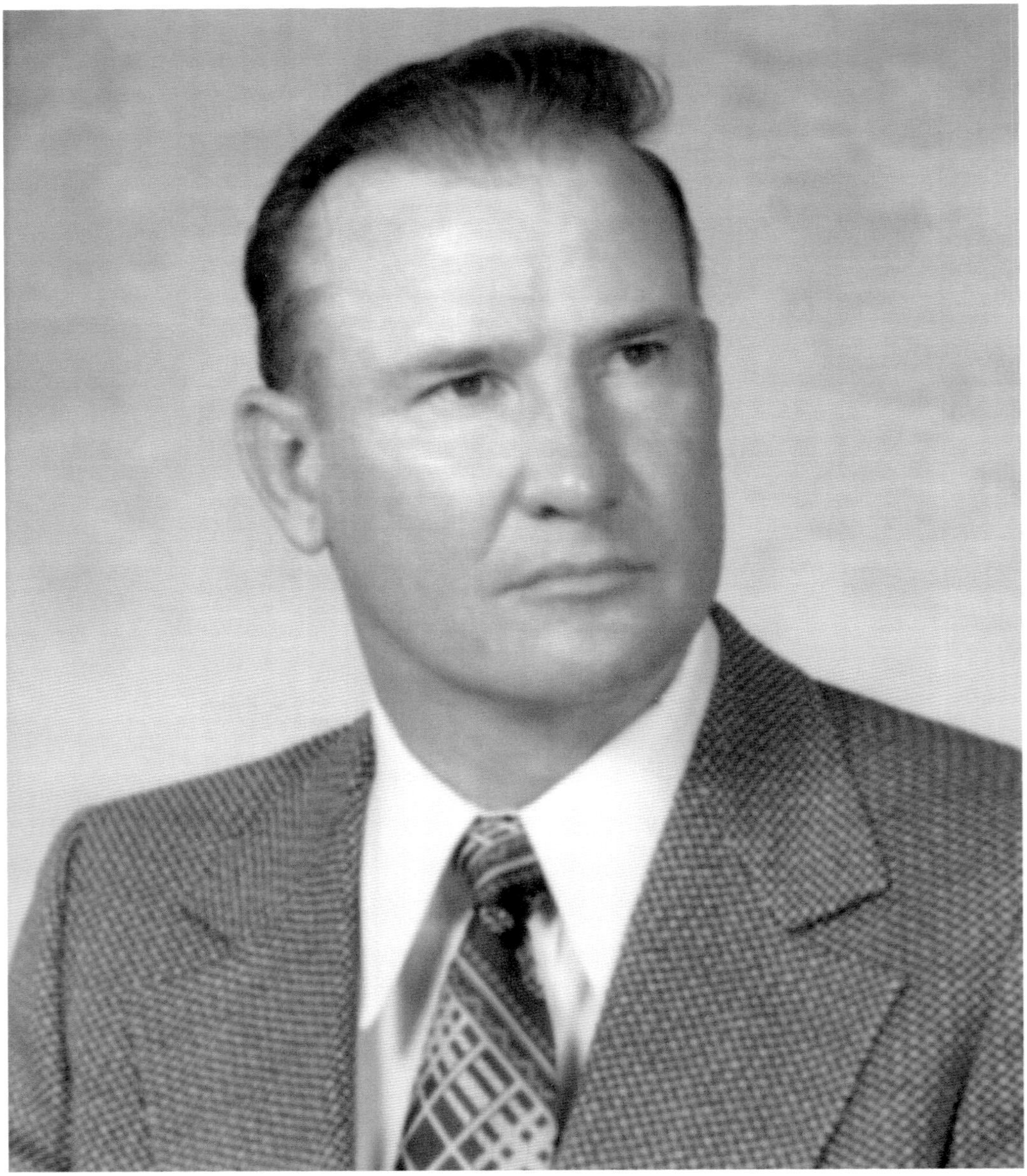

Carlton Massey

Carlton Massey moved with his family to Rockwall in 1943 and graduated from Rockwall High School in 1949. In the fall of that year, he started college at Southwestern University, where he played on the football team and was named All Texas Conference End. In 1951, he transferred to the University of Texas at Austin, where he became a star player on the Longhorn football team and earned the title of All Southwest Conference End in both 1952 and 1953. In 1953, he was named an All-American Football Player, the only All-American thus far from Rockwall County. After graduating from the University of Texas, he played professional football for the Cleveland Browns, beginning his pro career in the fall of 1954. In his rookie year, he was in the starting lineup of the Browns World Championship Team and played in the All-Pro Game. He played for the Browns in 1956 and was then traded to the Green Bay Packers, where he played in 1957 and 1958. He was inducted into the University of Texas Longhorn Hall of Fame in 1975. (Photographs courtesy of the family of Don Stodghill.)

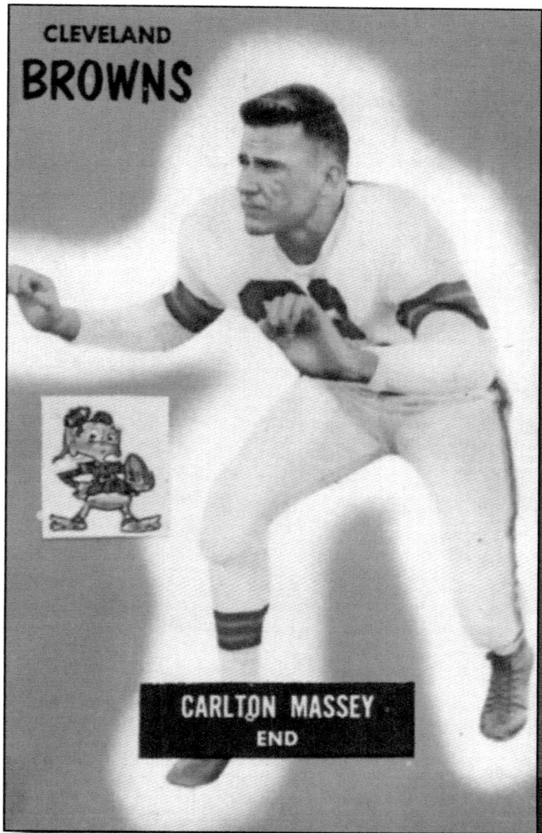
CLEVELAND
BROWNS
CARLTON MASSEY
END

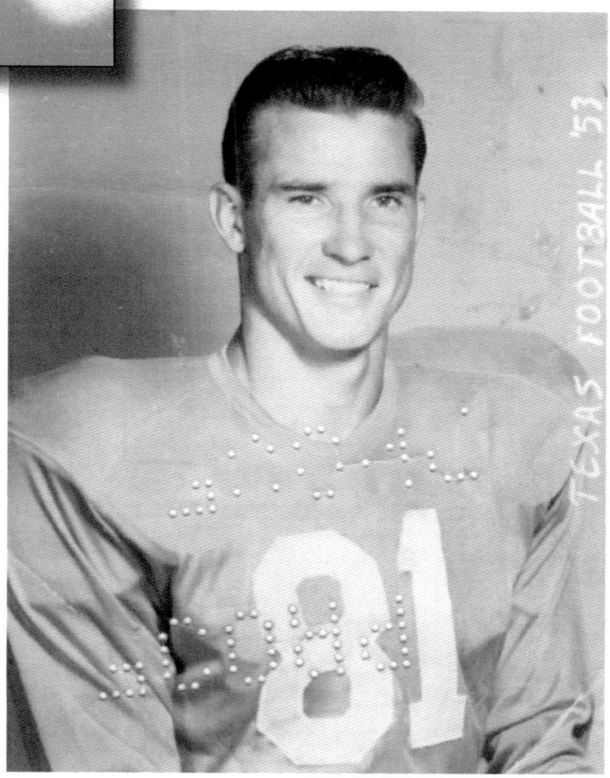
TEXAS FOOTBALL '53
81

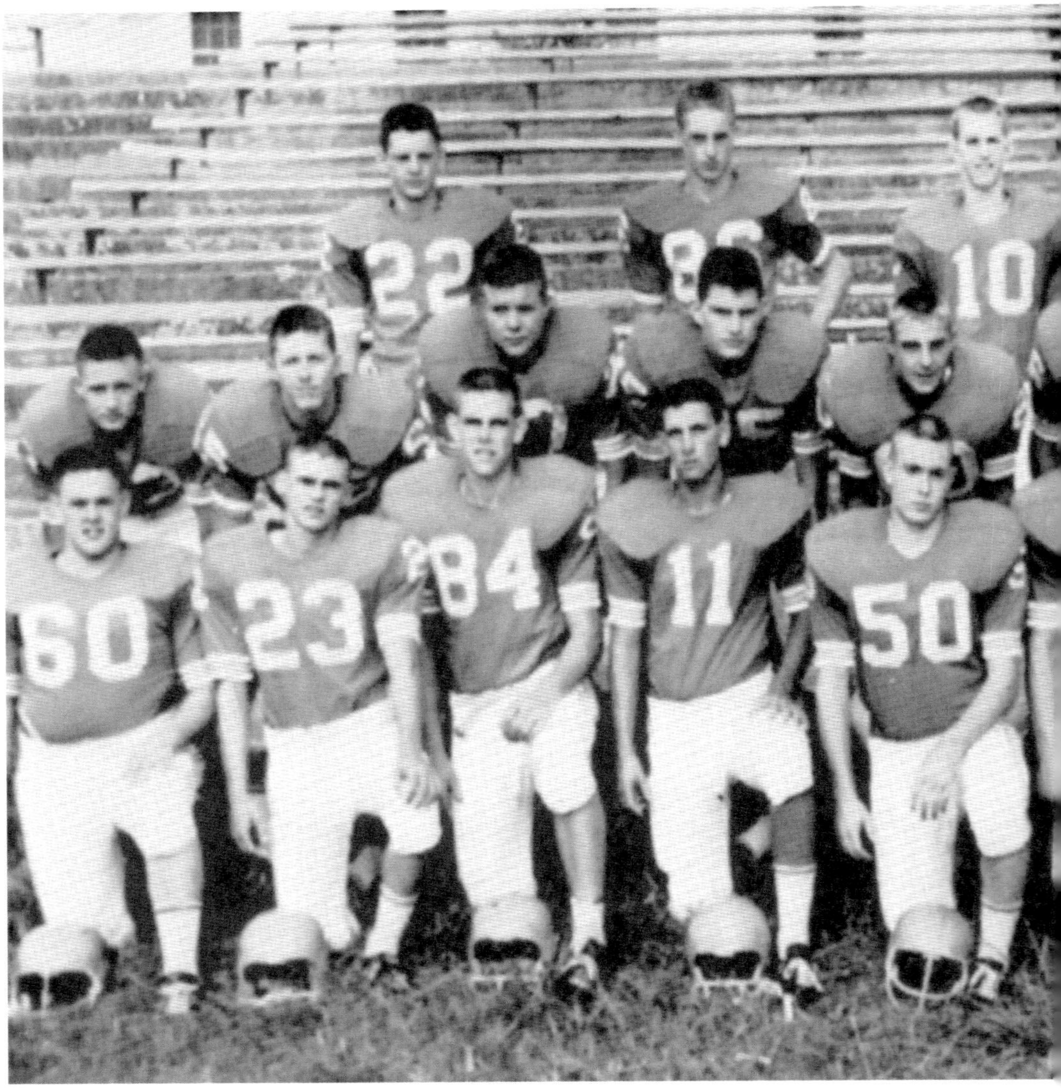

1963 Yellowjacket State Championship Football Team
In freezing rain, just four days prior to Christmas, the 1963 Yellowjacket football team took to the field at Baylor Stadium in Waco to play for the AA State Football Championship against John Foster Dulles. Despite the cold, a caravan of buses and cars traveled to Waco filled with fans ready to cheer on the Jackets. The crowd endured a scoreless game until late in the third quarter, when Dulles scored a touchdown but missed the extra point. With just moments left in the fourth quarter, the score remained 6-0 with Dulles in the lead and Rockwall fans losing hope. With a fourth-and-five situation and Rockwall in its own territory, there was less than a minute left to play. Many Rockwall fans had already left for the warmth of their cars or the waiting buses. Quarterback Kenny Terry threw down the field to Marc Noel, who miraculously caught the ball and staggered to the end zone, avoiding multiple tackles and staying upright on a treacherously icy field. With Dulles fans already poised on the sidelines to rush the field in victory, Yellowjacket kicker Jackie Anderson put the ball through the uprights and secured a Rockwall victory. The final score was Rockwall: 7, Dulles: 6, and the Yellowjackets earned the title of 1963 AA State Champions. The 1963 State Championship Football Team was the first inductee into Rockwall ISD's newly formed Athletic Hall of Honor in 2013. (Photographs courtesy of RISD.)

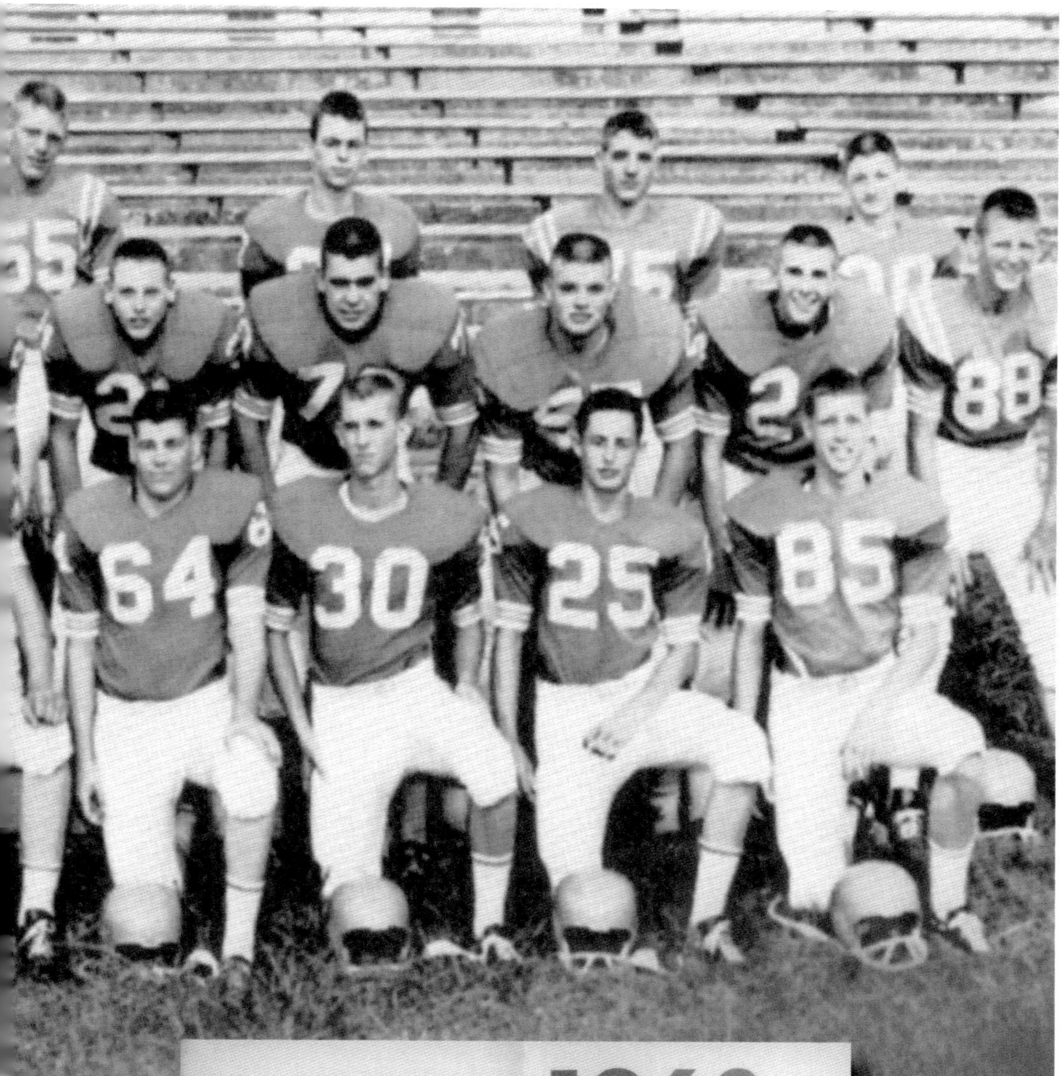
64
30
25
85
88

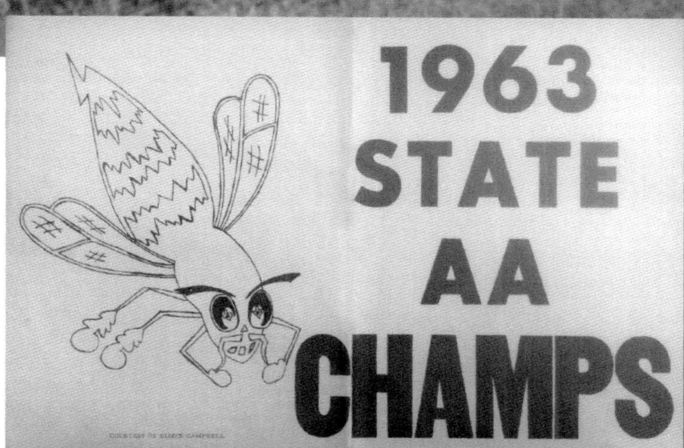
1963
STATE
AA
CHAMPS

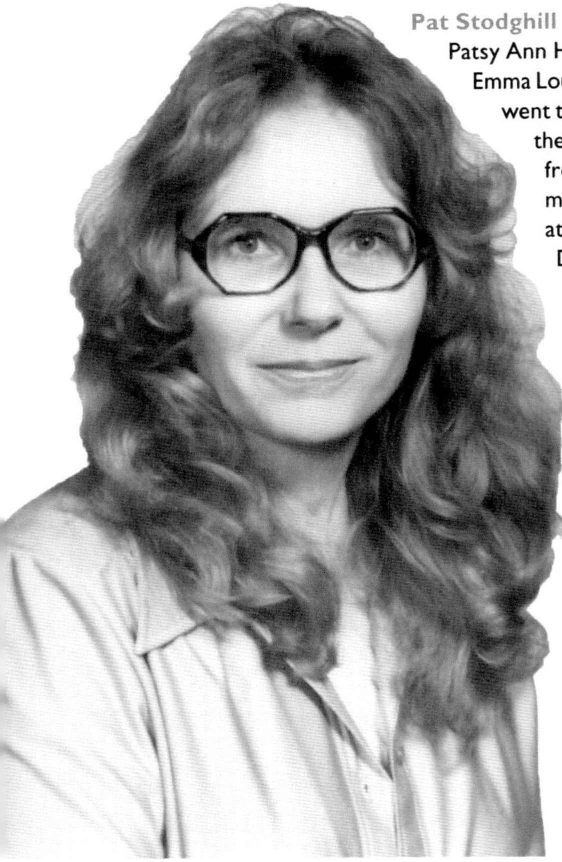

Pat Stodghill

Patsy Ann Hall was born in Heath, Texas, to William Curtis Hall and Emma Lou (Lofland) Hall. She first attended school in Heath and then went to Rockwall High School, where she was a cheerleader and the valedictorian of her class. She received a bachelor's degree from North Texas State University and went on to earn a master of arts degree in English from the University of Texas at Austin. In 1959, Pat married her high school sweetheart, Donald R. Stodghill. The couple had two children, Steven Hall and Sheri Sue. Pat worked as an educator for over 33 years, teaching classes in both the Dallas and Rockwall Independent School Districts, at the Yavnah Academy, and for Southern Methodist University. She also taught courses in poetry and literature as part of the gifted and talented program and was literary consultant for RISD. In addition to her accomplishments as a teacher, Pat has been writing poetry since childhood. Her poems have been awarded many state, national, and world prizes, and her work has been published in numerous anthologies. She is the author of two volumes of poetry (*Mirrored Images* and *Kaleidoscope Pieces*) and a children's book (*Jake's Snapping Catastrophe*). Pat served as president of the Poetry Society of Texas—the first woman ever elected to the position—for five years, and as president of the National Federation of State Poetry Societies. In 1978, she was appointed Poet Laureate of Texas by the Texas State Legislature. (Photograph courtesy of the Stodghill family.)

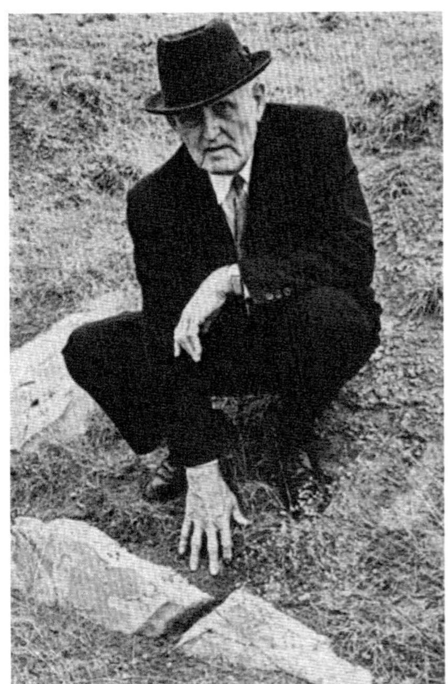

Dr. James Glenn

Although his first calling was as pastor of the First Presbyterian Church in Rockwall, Texas, Dr. James Glenn was also an active member of the chamber of commerce and a well-known civic leader. He was especially interested in the origins of the rock wall, for which the city and county were named. In 1950, after extensive study, he published a report titled "Photographic Essay on the System of Rock Walls at Rockwall, Texas," which is still used today as a reference on the history of the rock wall. (Photograph courtesy of the RCHF.)

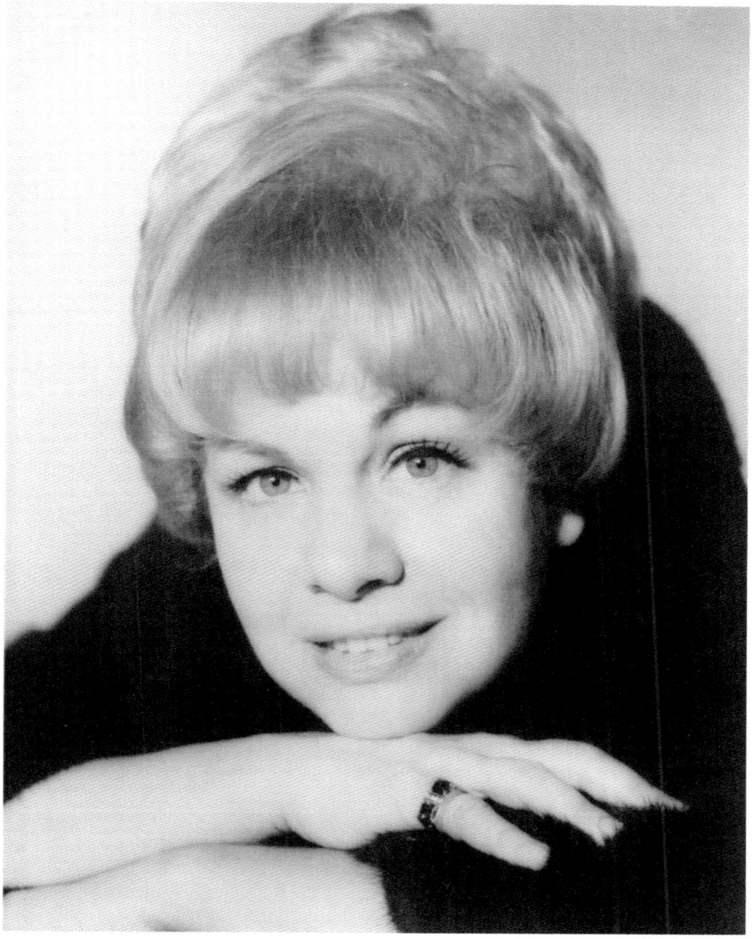

Ruth Peck

When Ruth Peck was seven years old, her mother took her from their home in New Jersey to New York to see the musical *Babes in Arms*, and she was instantly mesmerized by music and the theater. Ruth commuted to New York for voice and drama studies from the time she was 16 years old. Upon graduation from Battin High School in New Jersey, she furthered her studies at The New School and with private drama and vocal teachers and coaches in New York City. She devoted her beginning years in theater to volunteering at the American National Theatre and Academy working toward establishing a national theater in America. She auditioned for Richard Rodgers and Oscar Hammerstein and joined the cast of *Annie Get Your Gun*. Further supporting herself by working in the business end of theater, her positions included executive secretary for the Olney Theatre in Olney, Maryland; on the production of *The Country Girl* in the office of producer Dwight Deere Wiman; in the newsroom and office of NBC commentator Kenneth Banghart; and as executive secretary to MGM agent Peter Witt. Upon marrying Oscar Peck, a trucking executive, she moved to Houston, Texas, where she became active in local theater and music. Ruth appeared in productions at the professional Houston Music Theatre and as a soloist with the Houston Symphony, and she founded a talent agency and a drama workshop. She moved to Dallas and appeared in roles at the Country Playhouse and was also under contract to a West Coast agent, performing leading roles throughout the United States. Ruth has appeared with and worked alongside many of the stars of 20th-century Hollywood and Broadway, including Olivia de Havilland, Ginger Rogers, Ann Blythe, Rita Moreno, and Buddy Ebsen. Ruth also brought her incredible talent and experience to Rockwall, where she was instrumental in developing a number of arts programs throughout the community. She cofounded the Greater Rockwall Philharmonic Orchestra and was an organizer and supporter of its production arm, Rockwall Musicfest. The orchestra was established in 2004 to give talented, young students the opportunity to play side by side with professional musicians in a full orchestral setting. The Labor Day weekend concert at Rockwall's Harbor has become a much-anticipated, end-of-summer event for the community. Ruth has used her skills to inspire both students and adults to embrace musical theater, and she has actively and enthusiastically supported the arts throughout the Rockwall County area. (Photograph courtesy of Ruth Peck.)

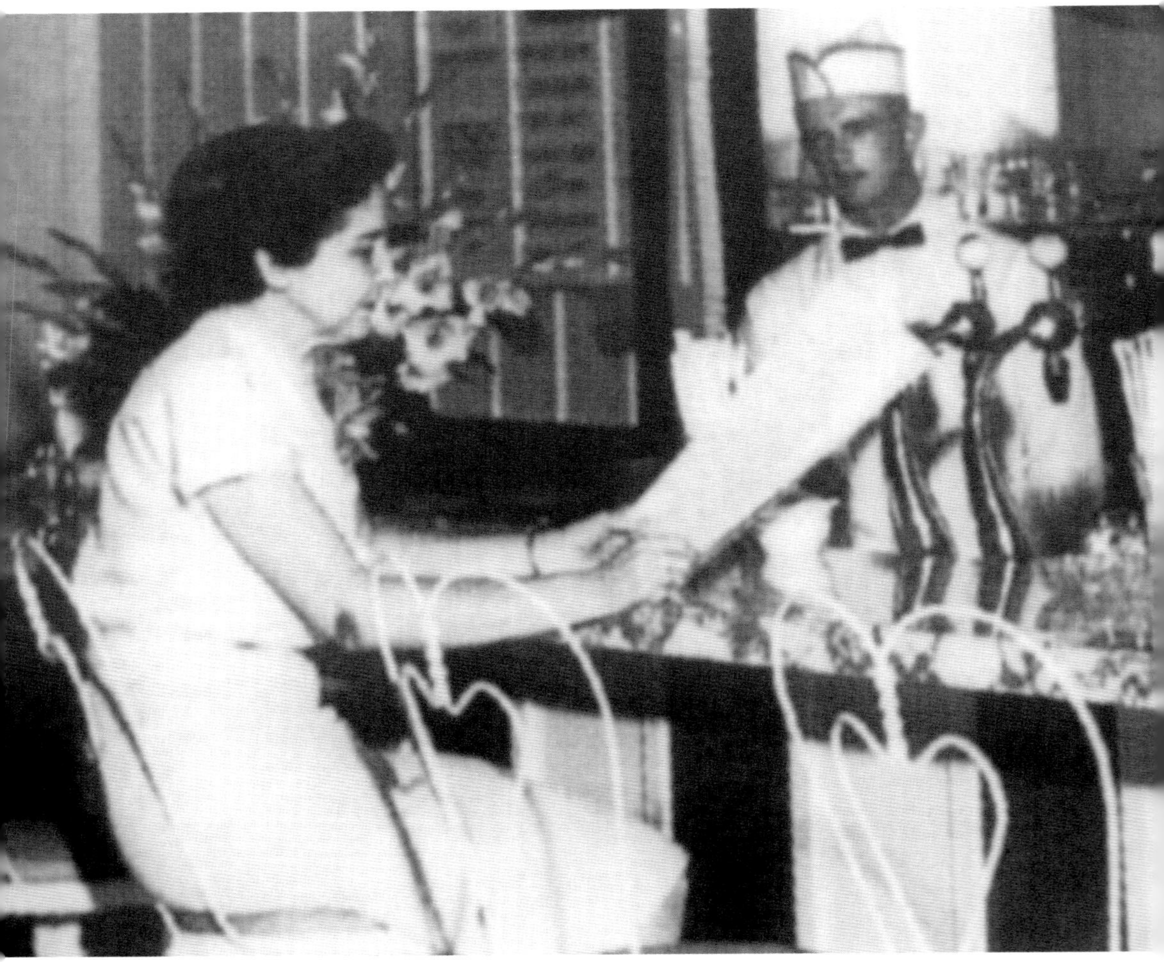

Eloise Cullum

Founding member of what eventually became the Tom Thumb family chain of grocery stores, Eloise Cullum was a longtime Rockwall resident. She was also a charter member of the Rockwall Soroptomists International, a nonprofit organization that describes itself as "a global volunteer movement working together to transform the lives of women and girls." Eloise's Closet, a Soroptomist project that provides business clothes to women in need, was founded in 2009 and named in her honor. (Photograph courtesy of the RCHF.)

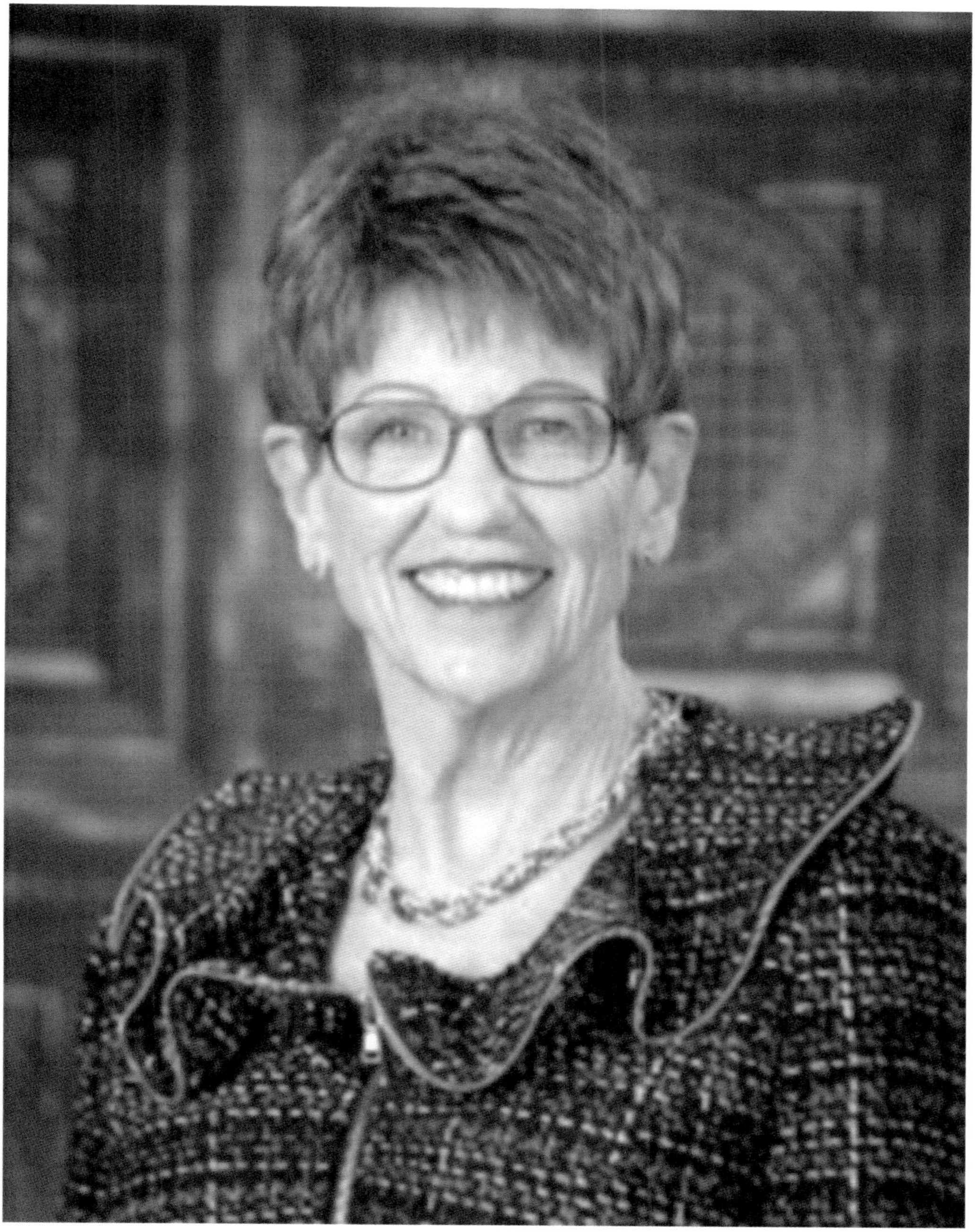

Leigh Plagens
In addition to teaching French for 37 years (the last 22 at Rockwall High School), Leigh Plagens has devoted herself to serving her community. She has volunteered her time for countless organizations, including the Rockwall County Friends of the Library, the Rockwall County Historical Foundation, the Friday Study Club, the Rockwall Noon Lions, the Rockwall ISD Educational Foundation, the Rockwall County Juvenile Board, the Rockwall Literary Club, the Rockwall Area Retired Teachers Association, and the Rockwall County Republicans, among others. She currently serves on the Rockwall Independent School District Board of Trustees. (Photograph courtesy of RISD.)

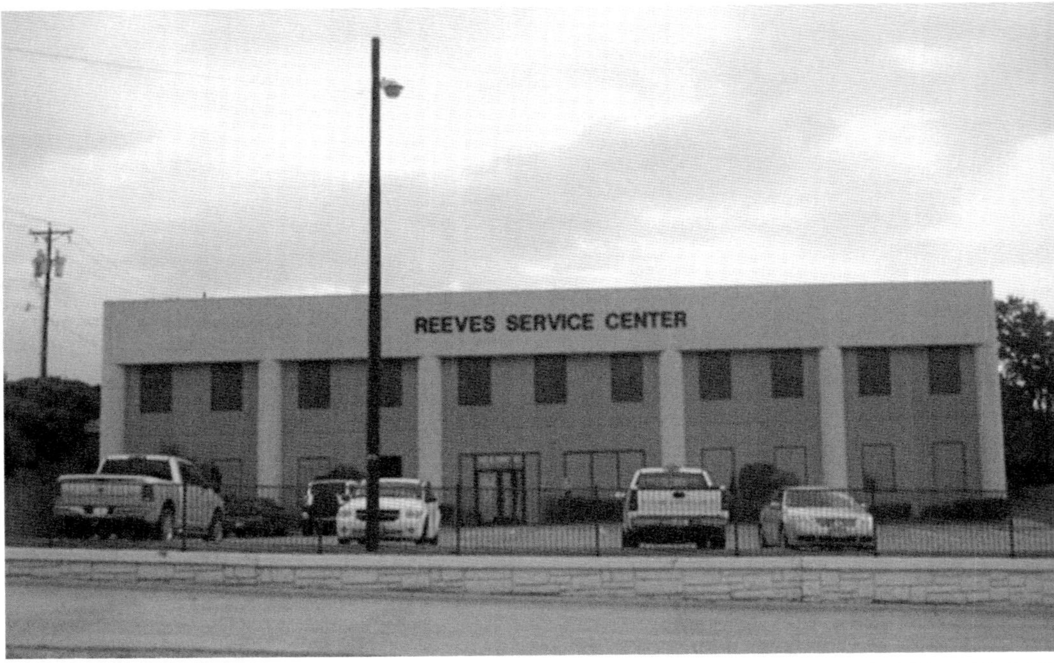

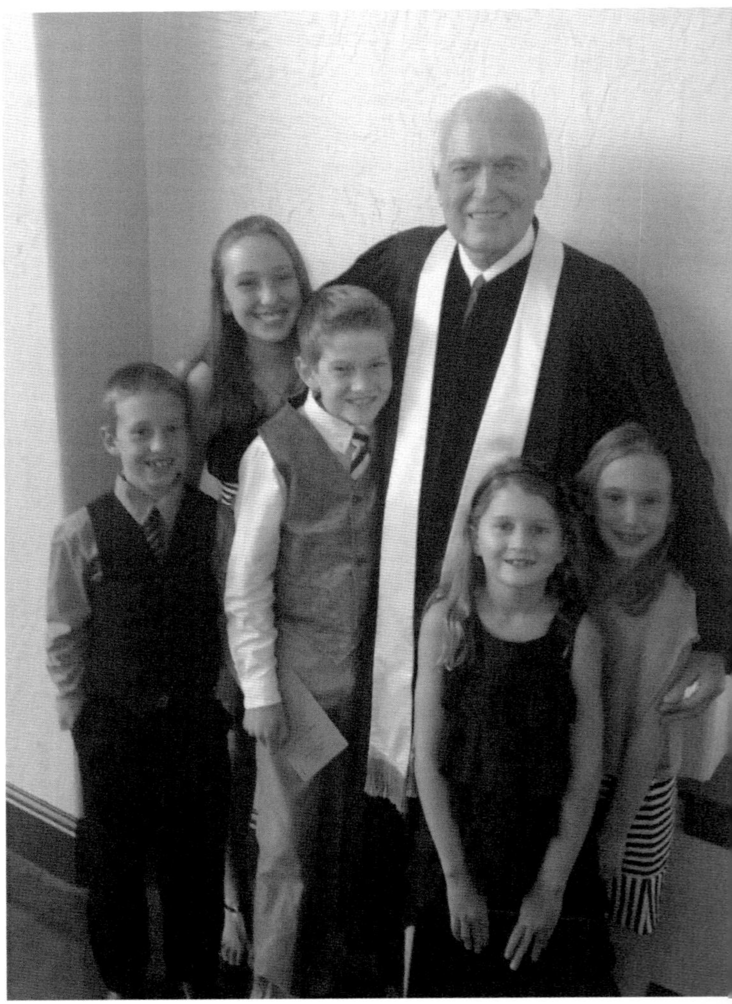

Robert D. Reeves
In 1976, Rockwall County's largest family assistance entity, Helping Hands, was founded by volunteers under the leadership of Robert Reeves, who was pastor of the First Presbyterian Church of Rockwall. Claudette Johnson was one of these volunteers who was instrumental in this effort from the earliest days of the project. Starting with a simple Christmas collection for items for needy children, Reeves's vision to help Rockwall County families now includes a health clinic, food pantry, assistance program, and thrift store, among other services. (Photographs courtesy of Helping Hands.)

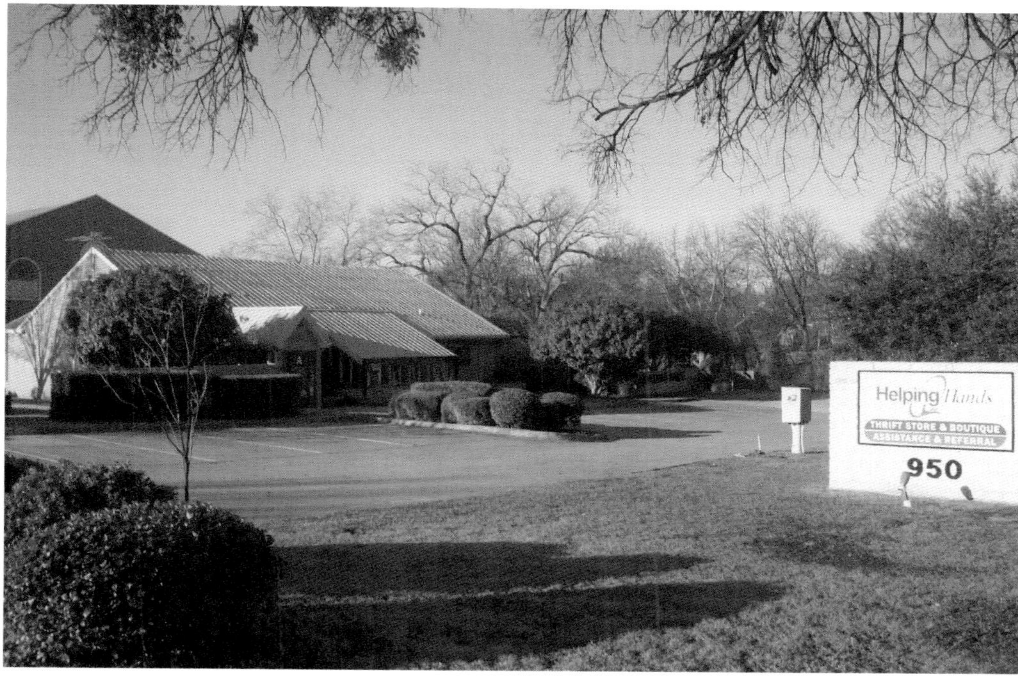

Margo Nielsen

Although Margo was born in Florida, when she and her husband moved to Rockwall in 1985 she embraced the community wholeheartedly and was soon using her background in social work to help identify and serve those who were in need in Rockwall County. In August 1989, she was selected as the first executive director of Helping Hands. In August 2014, Margo celebrated 25 years in this position. It is estimated that Helping Hands assists more than 10,000 people each year through its food pantry and assistance and referral programs. In addition to her work with Helping Hands, Margo served on the Rockwall City Council for seven years. (Photographs courtesy of Helping Hands.)

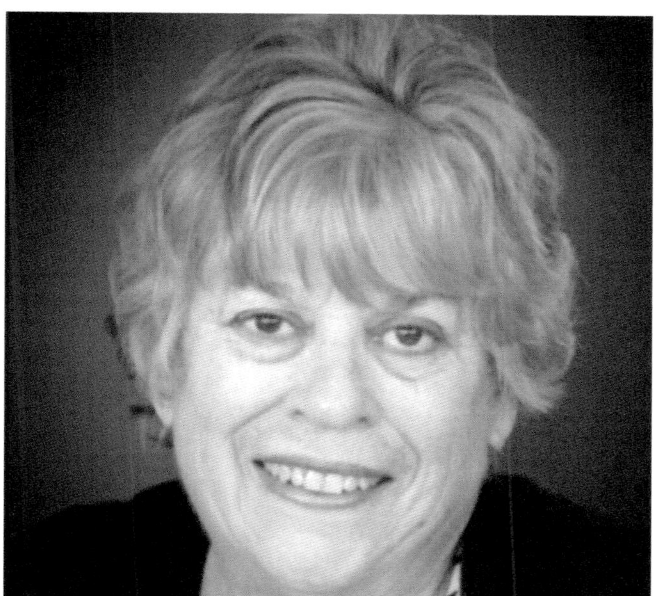

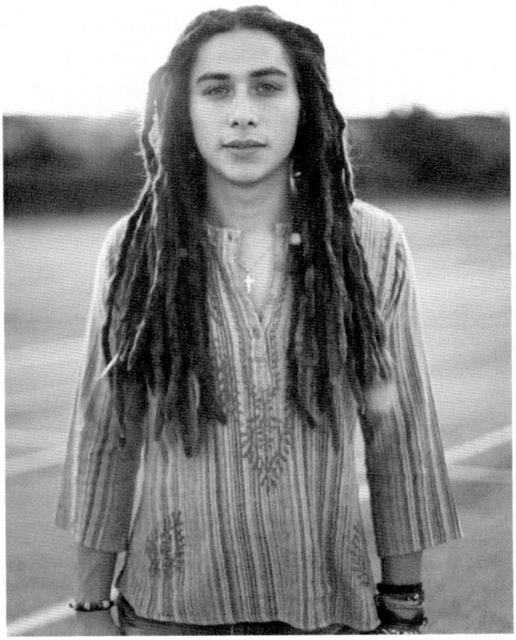

Jason Castro

A former resident of Rockwall, Jason Castro was born in Dallas and raised in Rowlett. Known for his distinct acoustic, folk style, Castro was the fourth-place finalist on the seventh season of *American Idol*. During his tenure on the show, Castro sang in three languages and showed his musical versatility by playing both the guitar and the ukulele. (Photograph courtesy of Jason Castro.)

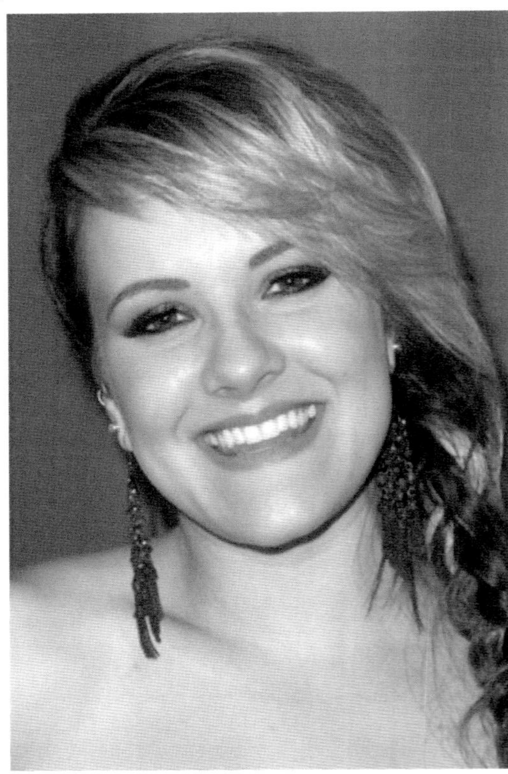

Amber Carrington

A talented singer and songwriter, Amber Carrington was a semifinalist on season four of the nationally televised show *The Voice*. Having moved to Rockwall when she was nine years old, Amber attended Rockwall schools, graduating from Rockwall High School in 2011. She honed her talents through performances at local and regional venues and participated in a number of contests that foreshadowed her success on *The Voice*. Currently, Amber lives in Nashville. (Photograph courtesy of the Carrington family.)

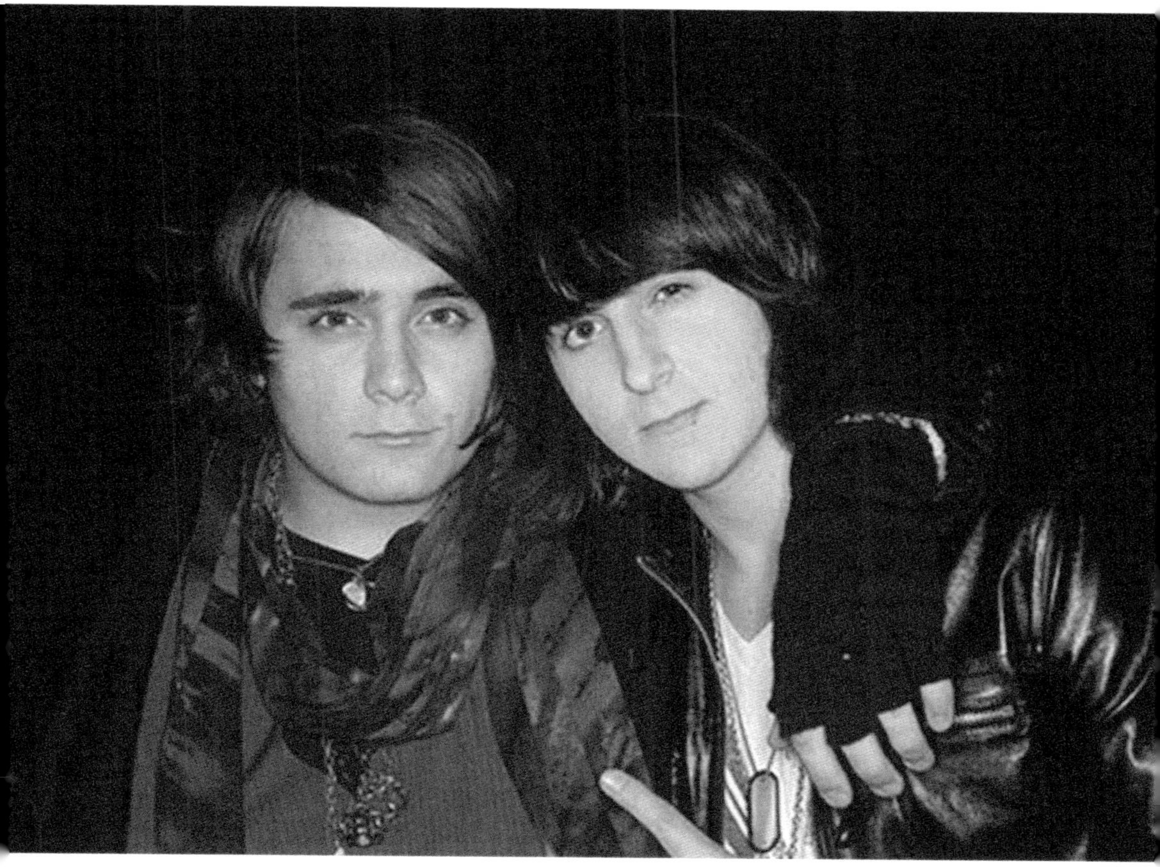

Mitchel and Mason Musso
The Musso brothers are versatile entertainers who grew up in the Rockwall County vicinity. Although he has many acting credits, Mitchel is probably best known for his portrayal of Oliver Oken on the Disney Channel series *Hannah Montana*. In addition, he is a musician and a singer-songwriter. His older brother, Mason, is also a vocalist, guitarist, and songwriter who is best known as the lead singer for the alternative rock group Metro Station. (Photograph courtesy of the Musso family.)

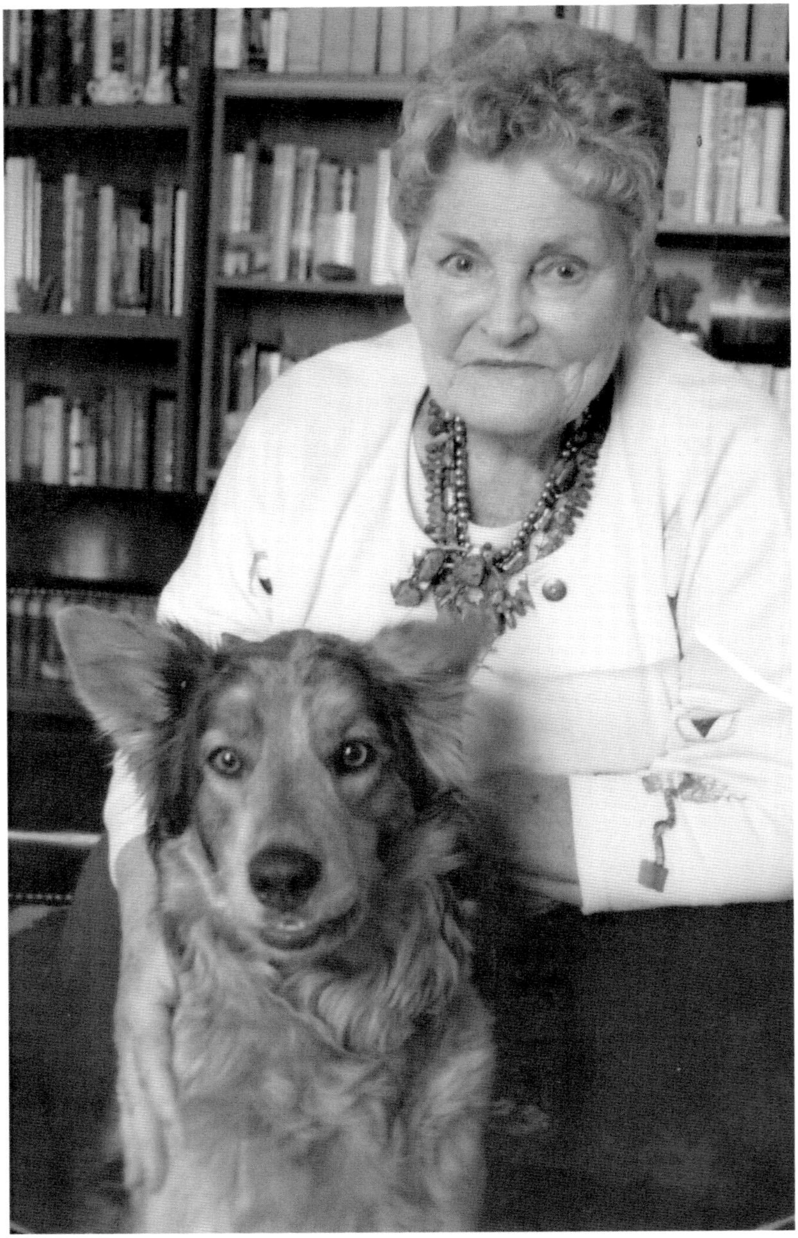

Barbara Montgomery

A professor, author, and activist, Barbara Montgomery is a longtime Rockwall County resident who has done important and prolific work in the political arena and in the fields of education, history, and the arts. Montgomery (shown with her dog, Indie) has long been associated with the Dallas Community College District, for which she designed and taught courses, primarily in history. She was municipal judge for the City of Heath from 1978 to 1988 and established the court for that municipality. She has served as the Rockwall County Democratic chairman on the State Democratic Executive Committee and was a candidate for the US House of Representatives in 1978. She has also devoted her time to several local organizations, including the Rockwall County Historical Foundation and the NAACP of Rockwall County. (Photograph courtesy of Barbara Montgomery.)

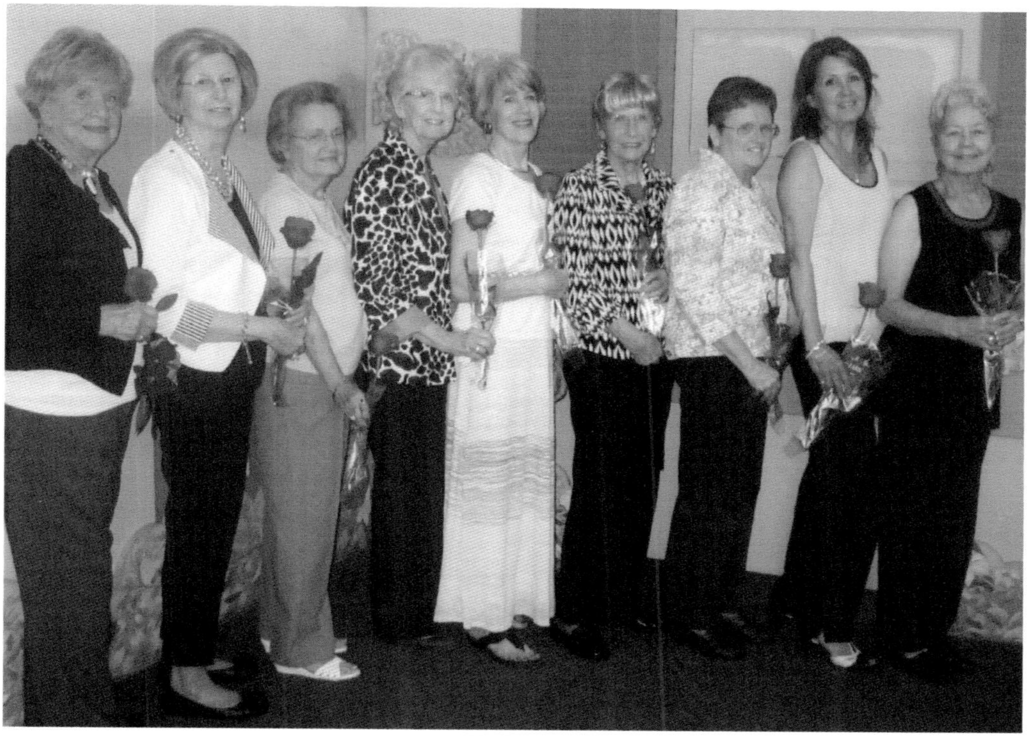

Friday Study Club
Organized in 1919, the Friday Study Club is the longest tenured social club in the Rockwall community. Created as a social, cultural, and civic club for women, the organization initially centered its programs on the study of art, literature, and music. Conceptualized by Mrs. Hugh Lofland, the club was formed by 25 charter members and still meets today. Members of the Friday Study Club pictured here include, from left to right, Ruth Peck, Becky Cecil, Nancy Hill, Ruth Willis, Carolyn Duckworth, Martha Baker, Kathy Melston, Peg Pannel Smith, and June Frawley. (Photograph courtesy of the Friday Study Club.)

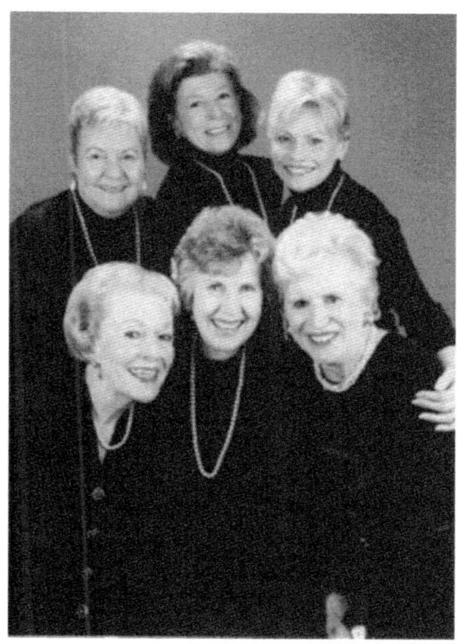

Rockwall Women's League
The Rockwall Women's League was chartered in Rockwall in November 1973 with 50 charter members. According to its by-laws, the league's purpose is "to unite and promote the Rockwall area through service to the community by initiating and supporting civic, study, and social events." Patsy Hendrickson served as the first president of the organization, whose work through the years has included volunteering throughout the community. In addition, through its fundraising efforts, the Rockwall Women's League has been able to award hundreds of thousands of dollars in scholarships to the students of Rockwall County. From left to right are (first row) Lynn Houston, Randa Hance, and Lee Albright; (second row) Bobbie Johns, Patsy Hendrickson, and Alma Williams-Howard. (Photograph courtesy of the Rockwall Women's League.)

National Charity League

With origins that can be traced back as far as 1925, the National Charity League was officially incorporated in 1947 as a mother-daughter organization dedicated to philanthropic, social, and cultural purposes. Although termed a "national" organization, for many years the only chapters existed in California—at least until Ann McNabb's family moved to Rockwall, Texas. Having been involved with NCL in California with her oldest daughter, McNabb's move to Texas meant that her younger daughter Amy would miss that experience. To prevent this, in 1981 McNabb and nine other mothers requested the addition of a Texas NCL chapter. In 1983, the National Charity League officially welcomed its 23rd chartered chapter, naming it the Lone Star Chapter. It was the first NCL chapter in Texas and the first outside California. Today, the Lone Star Chapter boasts more than 350 members. Pictured on the opposite page from left to right are Amy McNabb Van Vleck; daughter Victoria Van Vleck; and mother Ann McNabb, founder of the first Texas chapter of the National Charity League. (Photographs courtesy of Ann McNabb and Amy Van Vleck.)

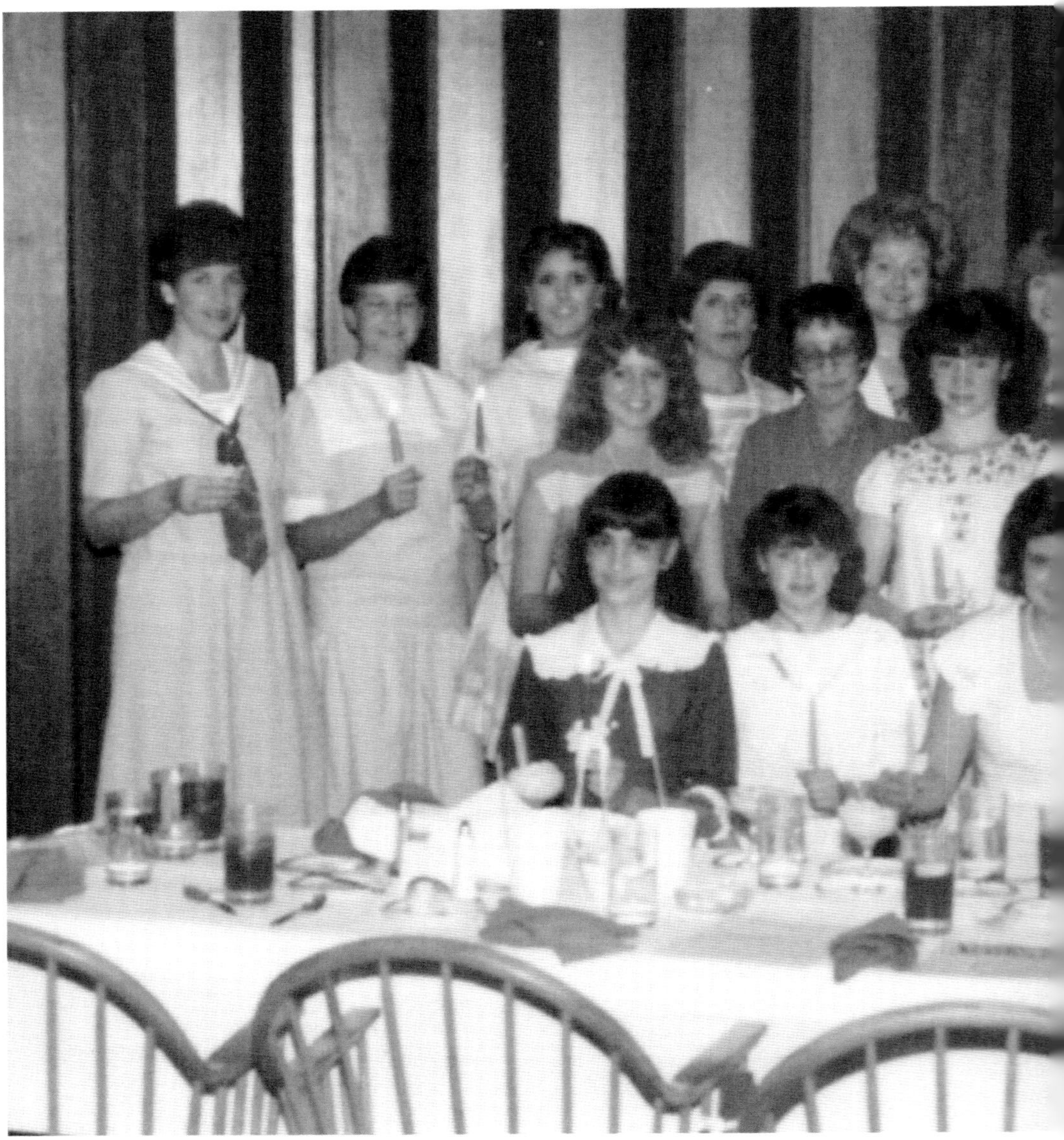

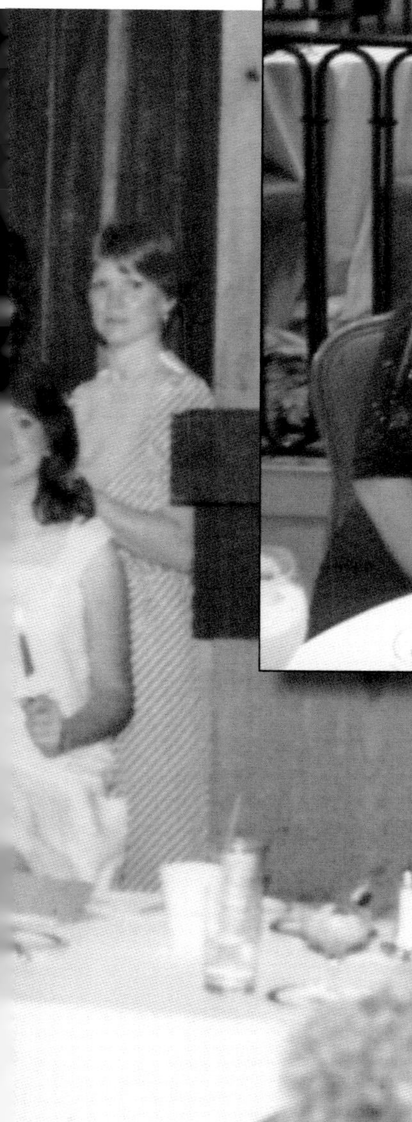

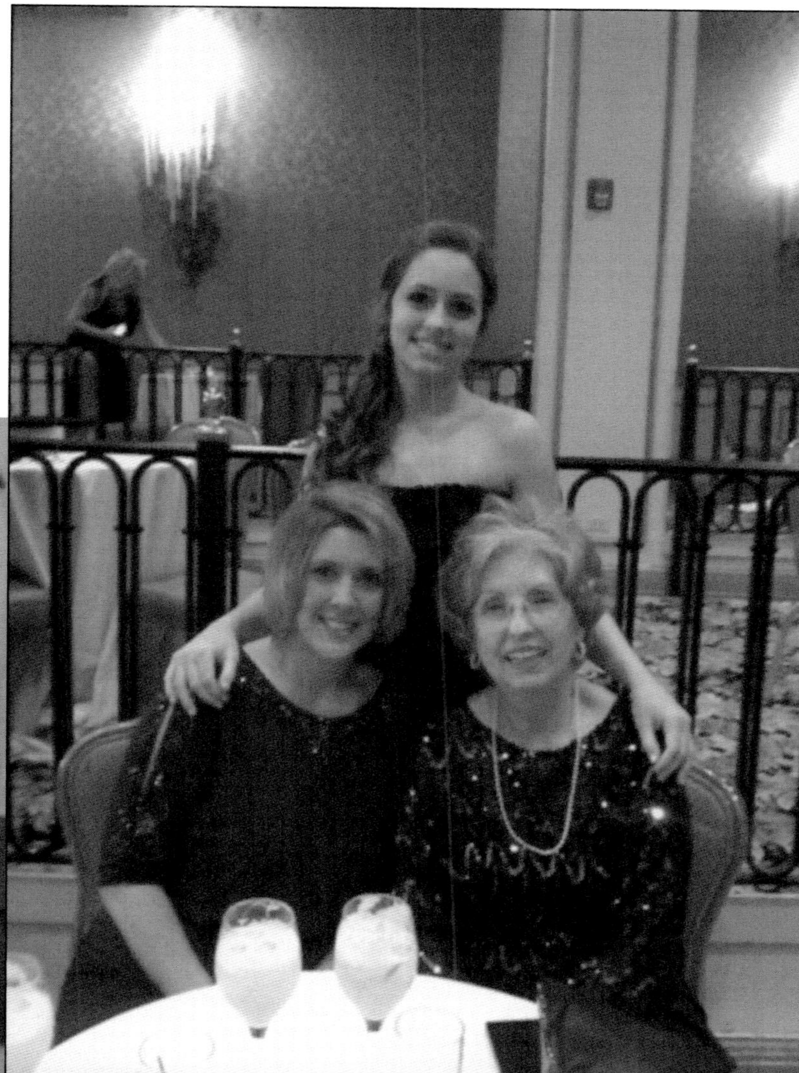

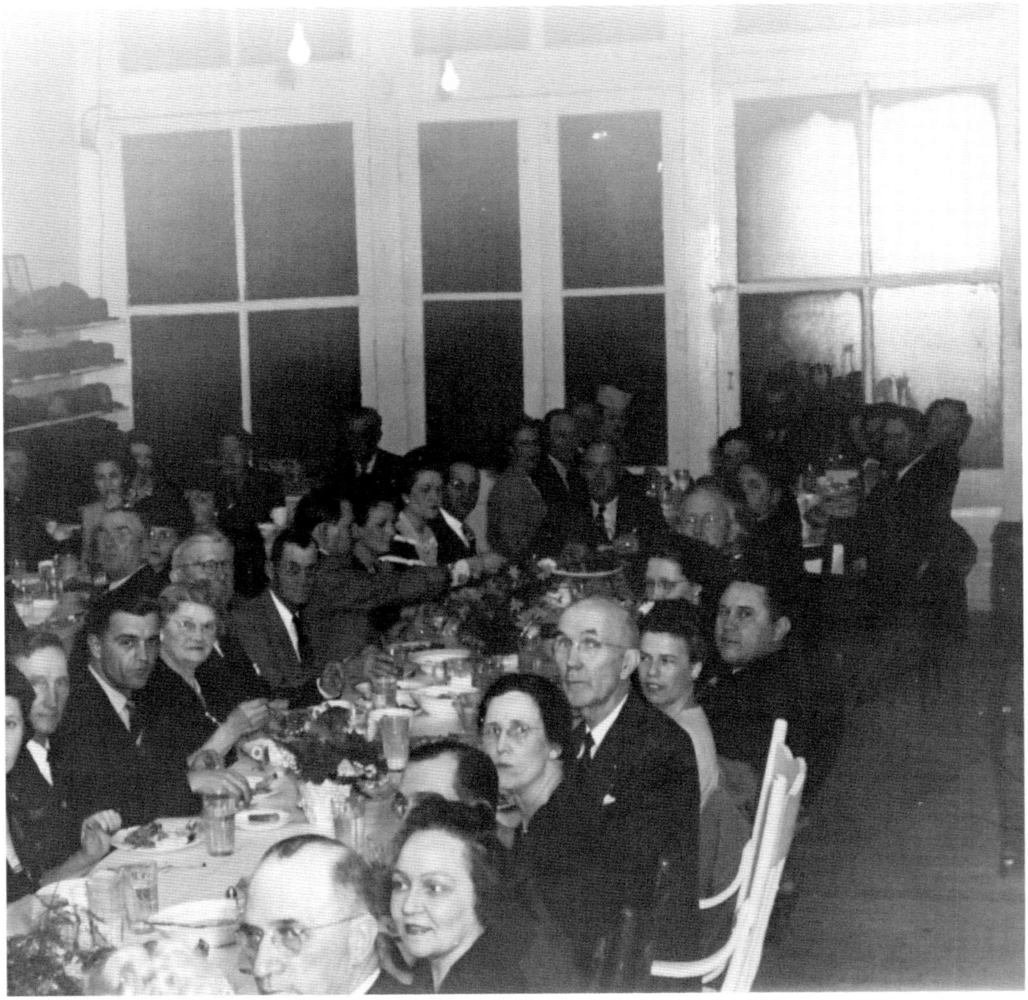

Rockwall Rotary Club

The Rockwall Rotary Club was organized on April 6, 1939, with 20 charter members. Part of Rotary International, the club is one of thousands worldwide that provide both local and international support to multiple civic and health-oriented projects. The membership is comprised of local business professionals who have a desire to serve their communities. The Rockwall Rotary Club has also furthered the goal of Rotary International by supporting the formation of additional Rotary Clubs in the Rockwall County area. Pictured above is a Rockwall Rotary Club dinner from the late 1940s. Pictured from left to right are (left side of the table) Henry Rochelle, Charles Atkins, Mrs. A.L. Atkins, and A.L. Atkins; (right side of the table) Joe White, Laurene Stokes, Bob Stokes, Evelyn Wallace, J.O. Wallace, Mrs. Fred Ellis, and Fred Ellis. (Photograph courtesy of the family of Don Stodghill.)

CHAPTER FOUR

Educators and School Namesakes

The first schools in the area were country schools usually built on land donated by a local farmer. These were one-room schoolhouses with all grades taught by one teacher. In the Rockwall area alone, there were at least 60 of these country schools. They had names such as Happy Home, Friendship, Locust Grove, Prairie View, Elm Grove, and Griffith League.

By 1855, Rockwall also had some schools located in the city. In 1878, with a growing population and the need for more organized education, the city constructed the first free public school. By 1885, a larger facility was needed and the second public free school was built. In 1908, a large, three-story brick building was constructed on Fannin Street to house the Rockwall Public Schools, which served grades 1 through 11. In 1925, a stand-alone, two-story brick high school was built on Clark Street. Rockwall High School graduated its first class in 1926.

For the next two decades, school enrollment and facilities stayed somewhat static. In the 1940s, several outlying community schools merged with Rockwall schools to form the Rockwall Independent School District. However, in the 1960s, nearby Dallas took notice of the small suburb of Rockwall. Families began to move to the area, thus beginning the transformation of Rockwall from an agrarian community to a bedroom community located just in the shadow of Dallas.

As more people moved to town, the need for additional schools became evident. Starting in the mid-1960s with a new Rockwall High School, Rockwall ISD began a building program for facilities that is still active today. While the names of the early country schools mostly reflected their locations, today's schools honor local educators who have spent years serving the children of Rockwall. Examples include Dorothy Smith Pullen, who spent 32 years of her 40-year career teaching second grade; Howard Dobbs, who was a coach, science teacher, principal of Rockwall Elementary School, and an active civic leader; Doris Cullins, who served the district for 42 years as both teacher and principal; and Jimmy Williams, who served as the RISD superintendent of schools for 17 years.

In addition to schools bearing the names of local educators, other district facilities are named to honor those who served the district in various capacities. Wilkerson-Sanders Memorial Stadium honors former coach and superintendent J.A. Wilkerson, as well as Harvey Sanders, a local restaurant owner who volunteered his time to help coach Rockwall football teams. The Mickey Florence Multi-Purpose Athletic Facility is named to honor a former Yellowjacket head coach and assistant superintendent for the district. Thanks to the foresight of district leaders, the schools in the Rockwall communities bear significant names that reflect the rich educational history of the area.

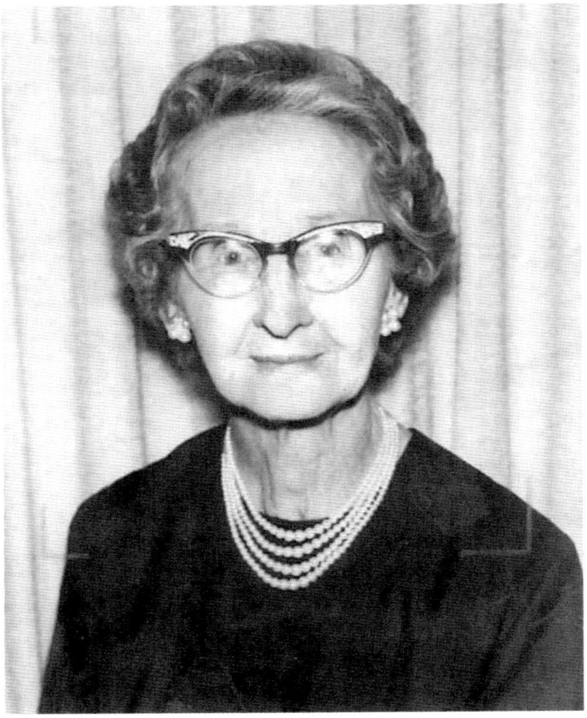

Amanda Rochell

Born into a pioneer Rockwall family, Amanda Lofland Rochell attended Rockwall schools and Wells College. She graduated from the College of Industrial Arts and taught homemaking in Highland Park and Hill Country schools. She married George Calvin Rochell in 1919. The couple settled in Rockwall, where they lived for the rest of their lives. Mrs. Rochell was a strong supporter of education and cultural development. Her daughter, Elizabeth Rochell Cameron, was also a schoolteacher. Elizabeth and her husband, Raymond Cameron, donated the land for Amanda Rochell Elementary School. (Photograph courtesy of Elizabeth Rochell Cameron.)

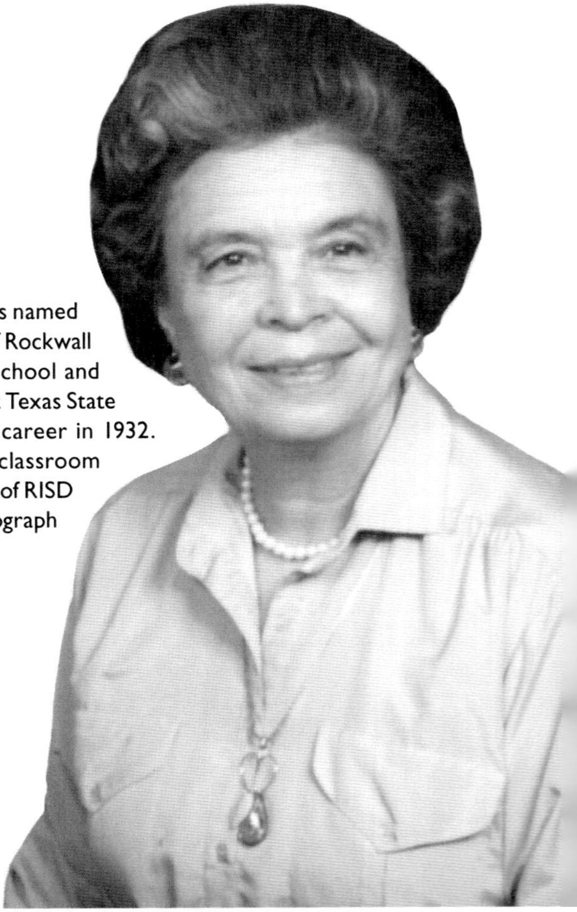

Virginia Reinhardt

Rockwall's third modern-era elementary school is named in honor of Virginia Reinhardt, a lifelong resident of Rockwall County. After graduating from Rockwall High School and receiving science and education degrees from East Texas State University, Mrs. Reinhardt began her teaching career in 1932. Although she did take some time off from the classroom throughout her career, her service to the students of RISD encompassed 35 years. She retired in 1981. (Photograph courtesy of Virginia Reinhardt Smith.)

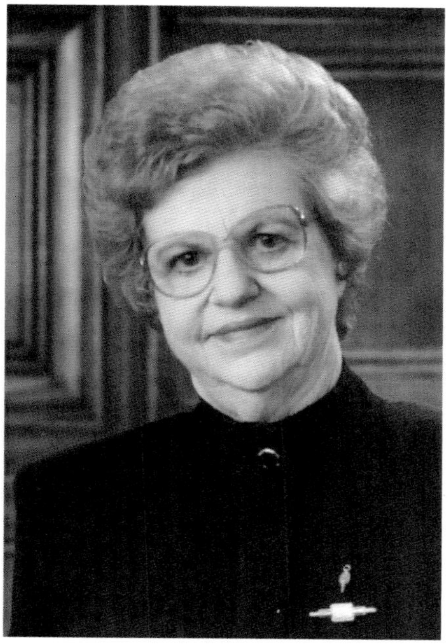

Doris Cullins

Doris Crawford Cullins was born into a pioneer Rockwall County family, graduated from Rockwall High School, and received her bachelor of science and master of education degrees from East Texas State University. Doris Cullins-Lake Pointe Elementary School was named in her honor. She began teaching in 1943 and served more than 20 years in the classroom. She was the first principal of three Rockwall ISD campuses: Rockwall Intermediate School, Amanda Rochell Elementary School, and Virginia Reinhardt Elementary School. She retired in 1987 after a 42-year career in education. In her retirement, Cullins was very active in philanthropic, educational, and civic organizations. She was part of the "Fate Girls," a group of Fate natives who took on the task of preserving the history of the Fate community. (Photographs courtesy of Rockwall ISD.)

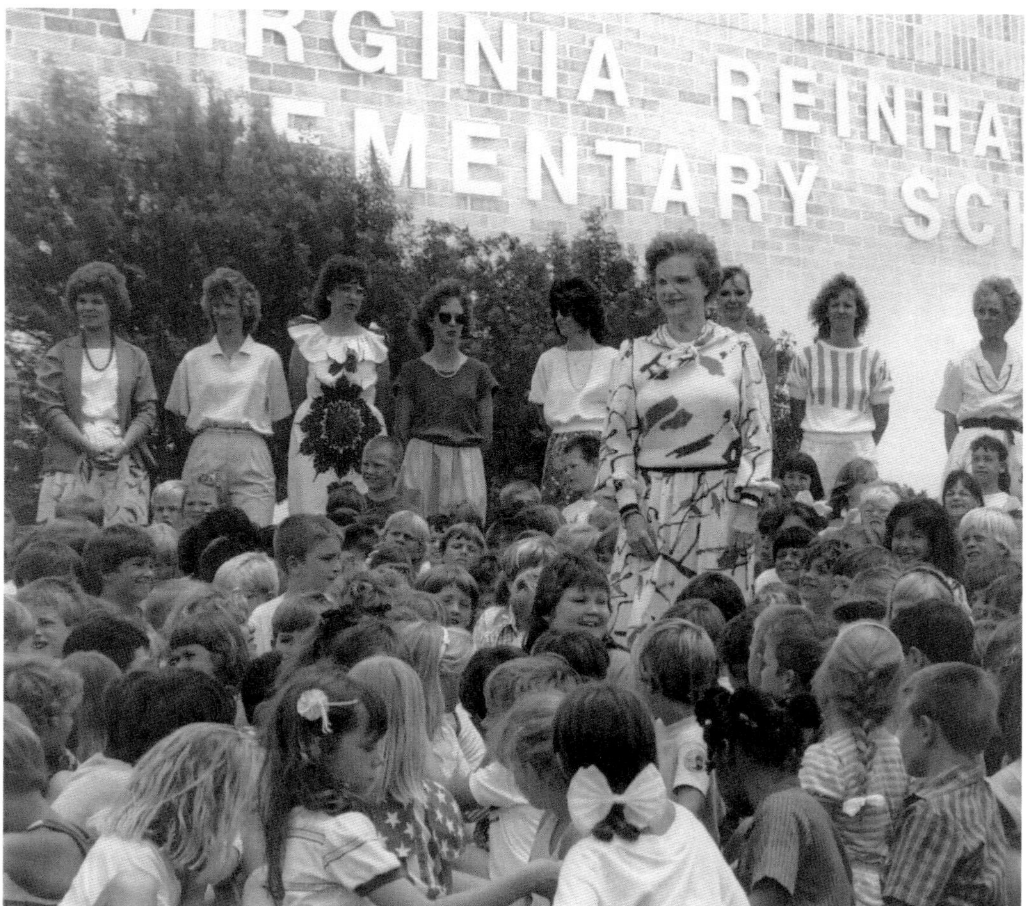

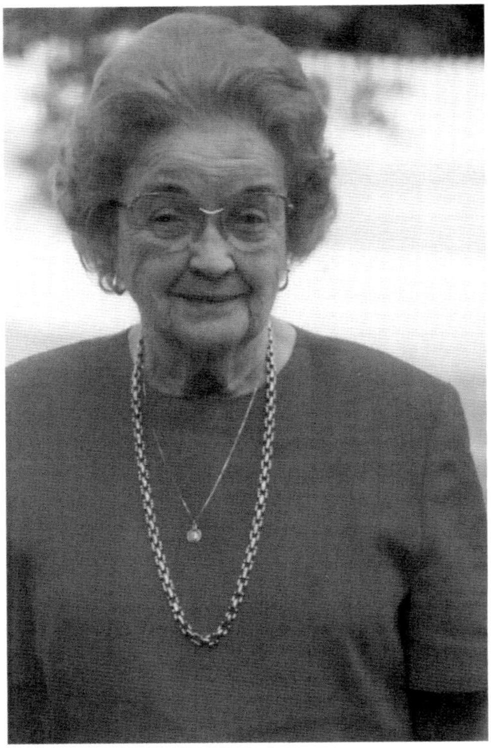

Amy Parks
Rockwall ISD's fifth modern-era elementary school was named in honor of Amy Parks, a lifelong educator who spent 35 years teaching first grade. She attended Rockwall schools, graduated from Rockwall High School in 1928, and received her bachelor of science and master of science degrees from East Texas State University. She began teaching in 1931 and retired from RISD in 1976. (Photograph courtesy of RISD.)

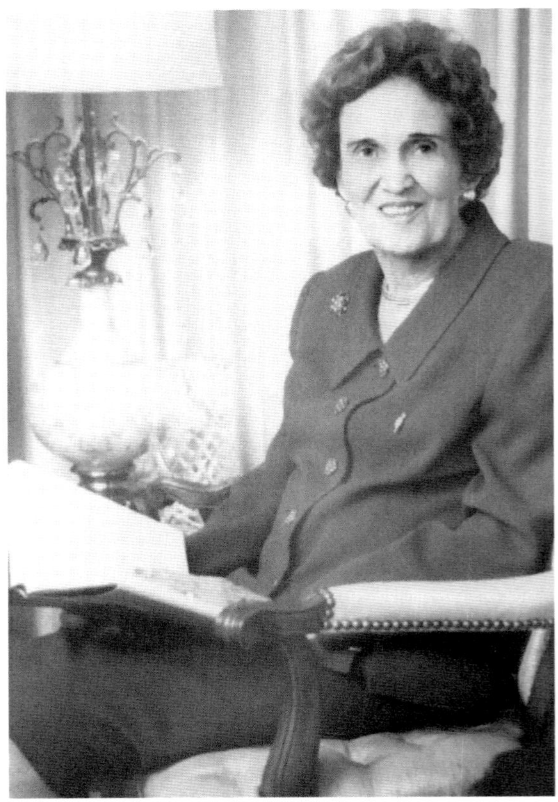

Nebbie Williams
The 43-year educational career of Nebbie Williams began in a one-room schoolhouse in 1928 and ended with her retirement from the classroom in 1971. In addition to teaching in several small county schools, Williams served Rockwall High School as a science instructor; she also taught business and English classes. Her last position was as a fourth-grade teacher at Rockwall Elementary School. (Photograph courtesy of RISD.)

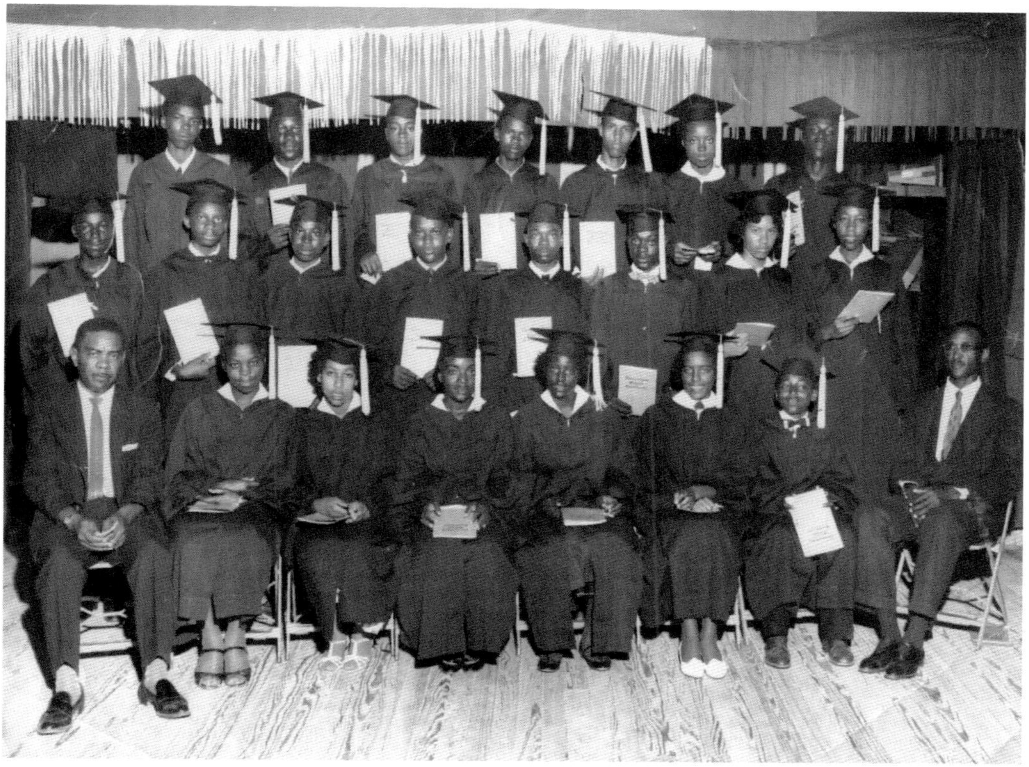

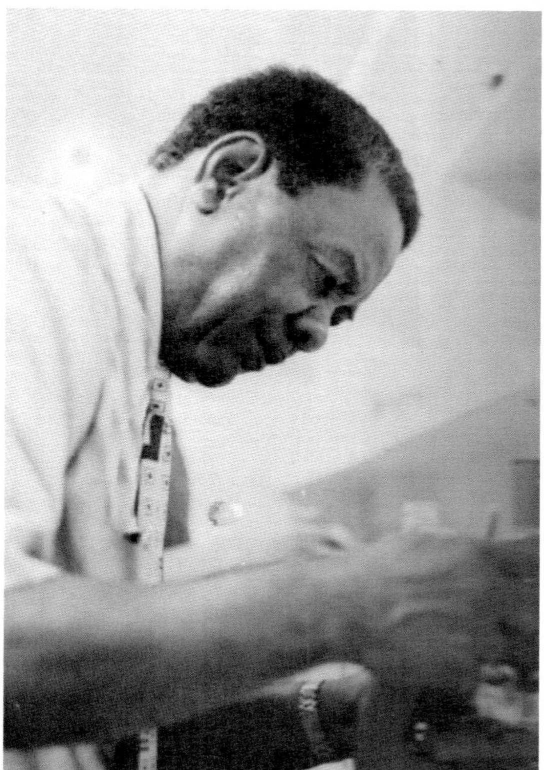

Dorris A. Jones
Born in 1906 in Rockwall County, Dorris Albion Jones's (pictured above in the first row at far left and in the image at left) educational career spanned 50 years. He held administrative and teaching positions in Rockwall and Fate. In a time of segregated schools, Jones served 17 years as principal of Rockwall's Bourn Avenue School for African American students. When Rockwall schools were integrated in the mid-1960s, he taught physics at Rockwall High School. He was highly respected for his professionalism and his dedication to all RISD students. At the dedication ceremony for Dorris A. Jones Elementary School, this quote from Mr. Jones was printed in the program: "The most interesting aspect of teaching science is how everything is somehow concerned with the realm of physics and how far-reaching and complex concepts are derived from simple phenomena. The most rewarding aspect of teaching is to see former students being strong, useful, successful adult products of my efforts." (Photographs courtesy of RISD and RCHF.)

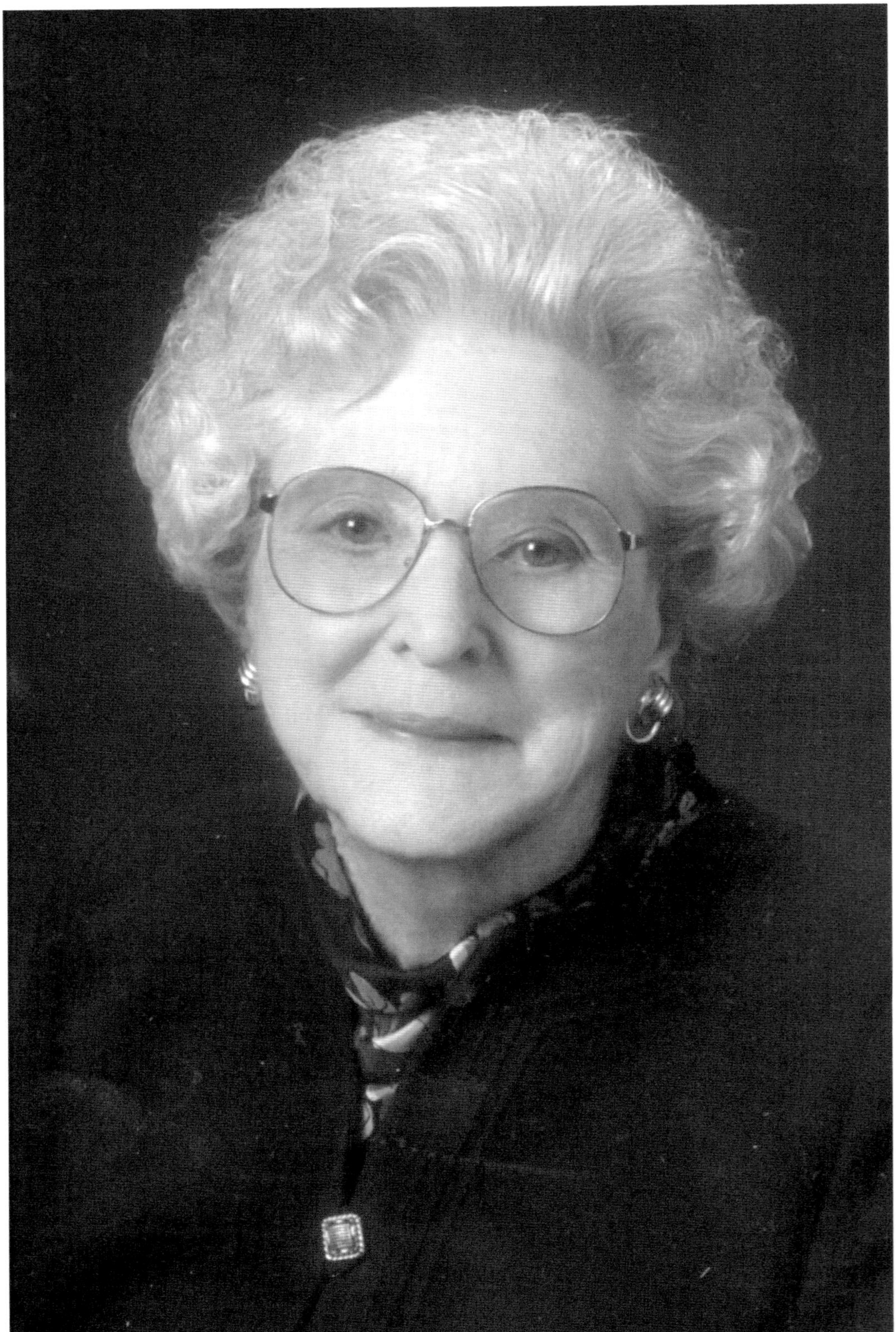

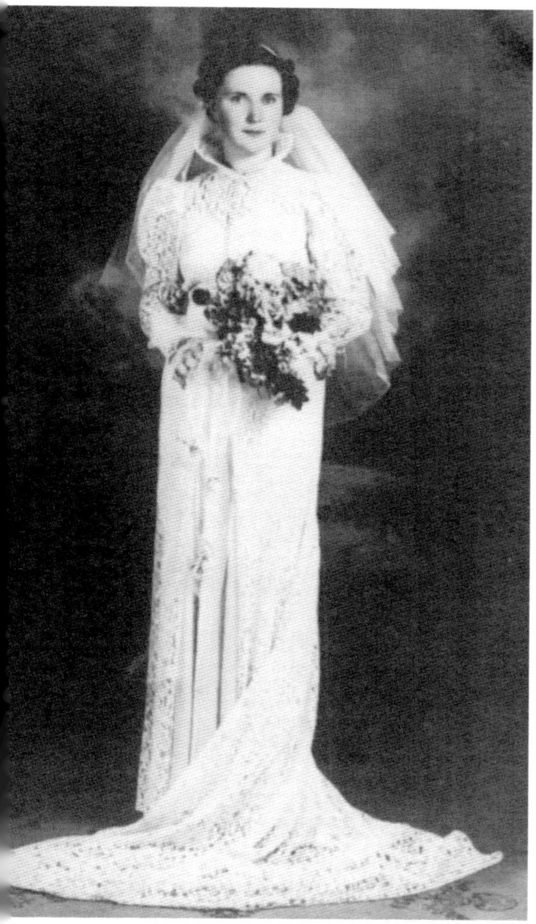

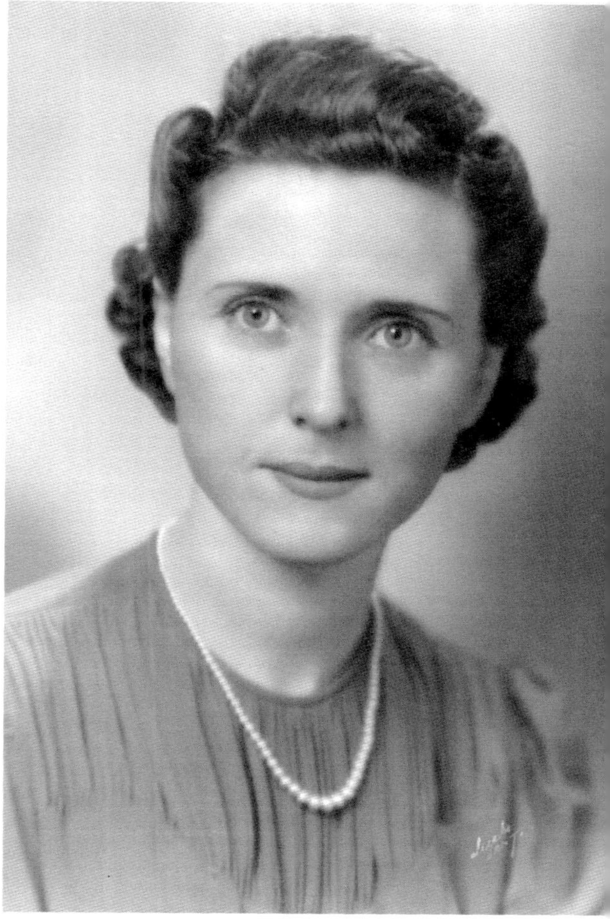

Dorothy Smith Pullen

After spending her entire 40-year teaching career serving the students of Rockwall ISD, the district recognized Mrs. Pullen by naming its seventh modern-era elementary school in her honor. She was born in Fate to Bob and Ada Lucinda Smith. The Smiths were pioneer settlers in the county and were a well-respected farming family. Dorothy grew up attending Rockwall County schools and graduated from Rockwall High School. In 1936, she started her teaching career in the county schools in Blackland and Fate but soon moved to the classrooms of Rockwall Elementary School, where she taught the second grade for 32 years. (Photographs courtesy of the Pullen family.)

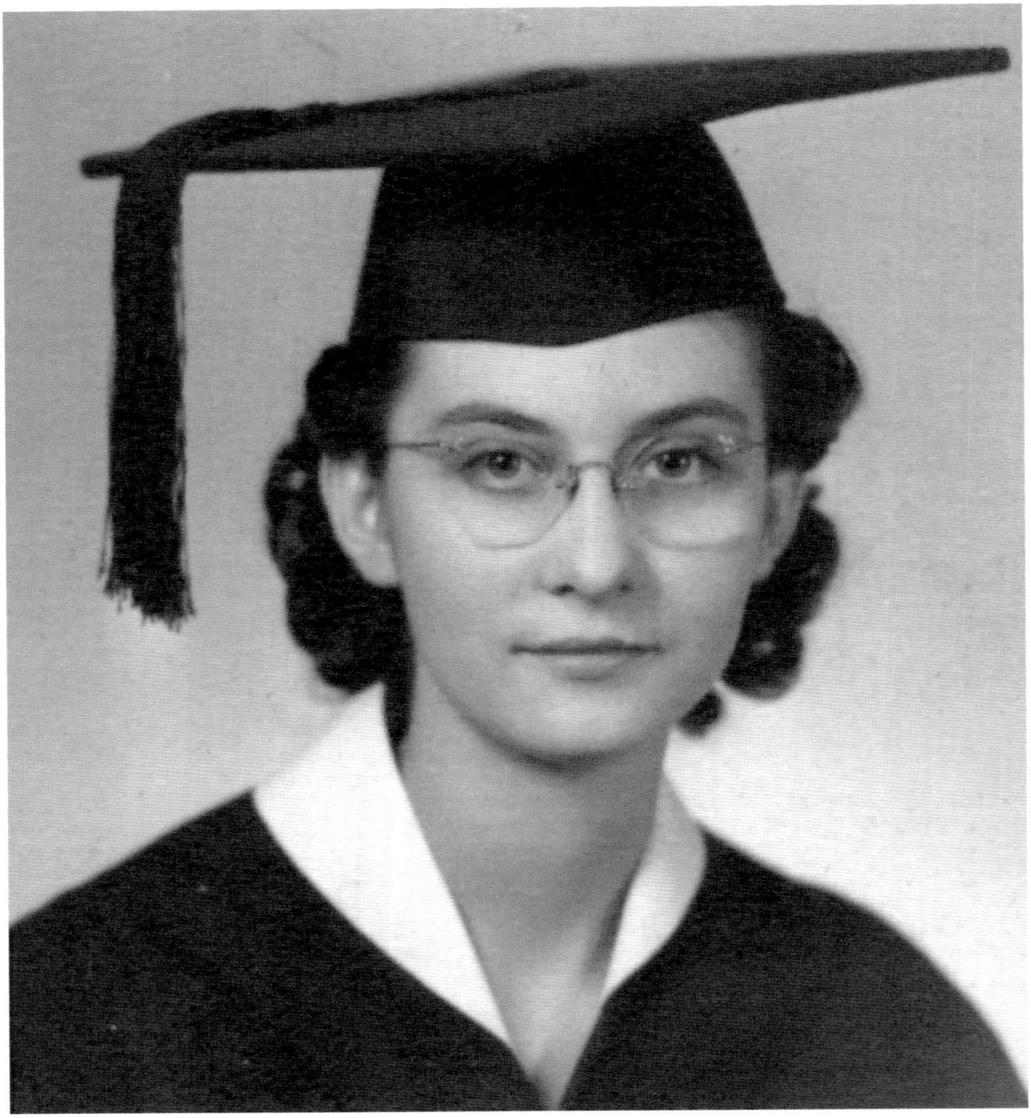

Maurine Williamson Cain

The namesake of Maurine Cain Middle School is a Rockwall County native who served 38 years in the classroom. She was the youngest of five children born to Jim and Grace Williamson (pictured on the opposite page, above). After graduating from Rockwall High School in 1936, she attended Texas Military College in Terrell, Texas, and East Texas State Teachers College in Commerce, where she received her bachelor of science and master of education degrees. On June 8, 1941, Maureen married high school sweetheart Ted Cain. The couple (pictured together on the opposite page, below) had one son, DeWayne. In 1942, after teaching at both Scurry Rosser High School and Quinlan High School, she began teaching in Rockwall County's Locust Grove Community School. Locust Grove was a one-room school, and Cain taught kindergarten through sixth grade simultaneously. Subsequently, she taught at Rockwall Elementary School and later Dobbs Elementary School for the final 34 consecutive years of her career. After retiring in 1987, Cain remained active in both school and community events, often visiting her namesake campus to interact with students. Maurine and Ted were married for over 70 years. Ted passed away in December 2011, and Maurine died in July 2014. (Photographs courtesy of the Cain family.)

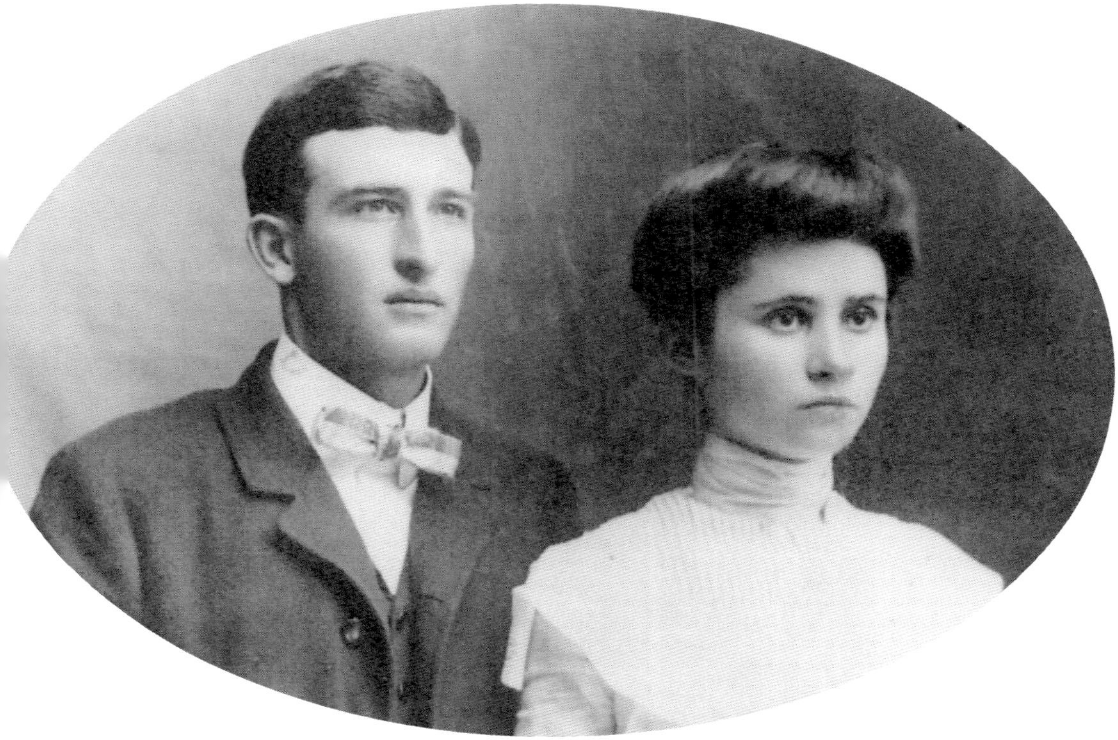

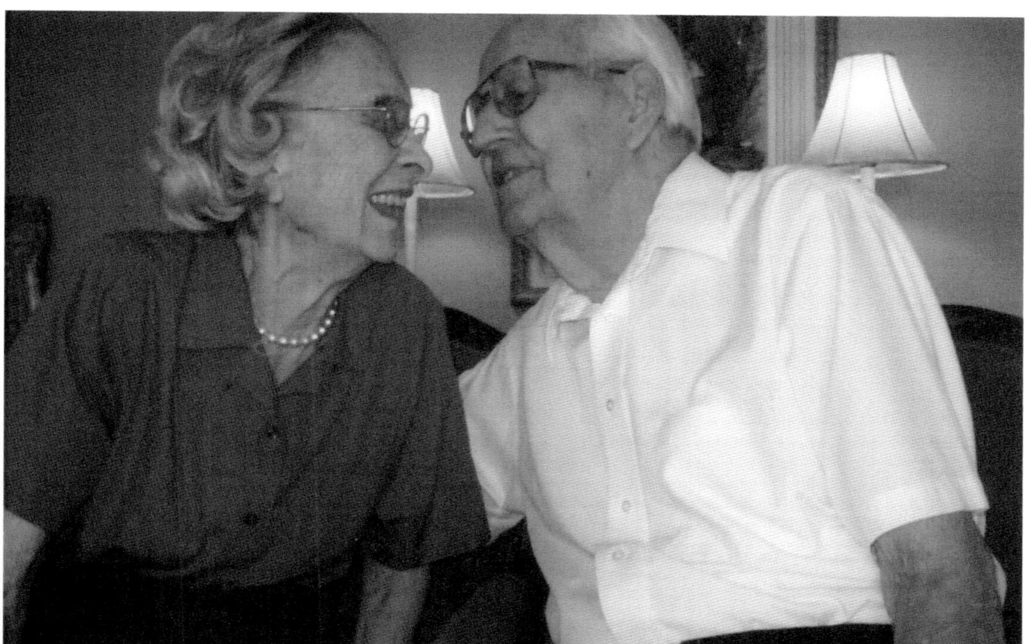

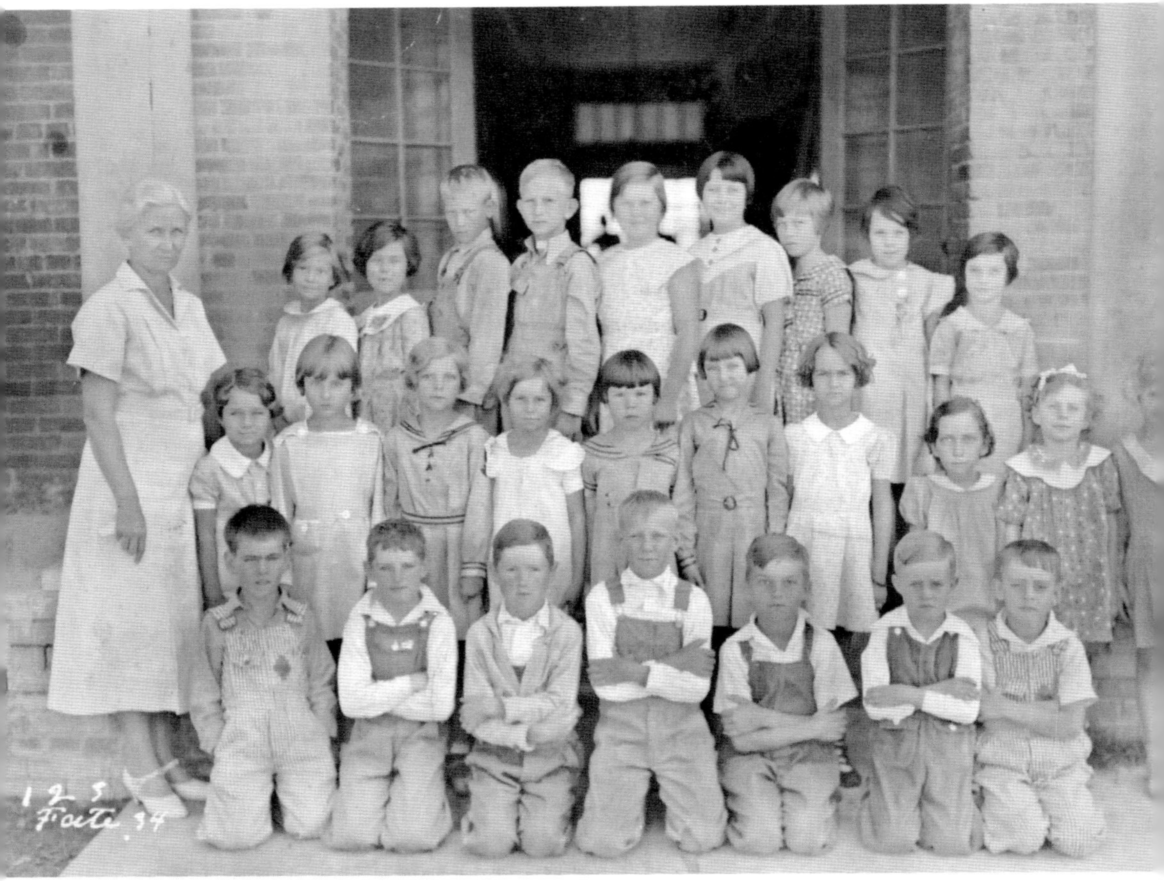

May Vernon

Miss May Vernon, as she was respectfully called, was a dedicated, lifelong educator. She began her teaching career in Fate at the age of 20 and taught for approximately 50 years. Classes began with students reciting the Pledge of Allegiance, the Lord's Prayer and the 23rd Psalm. In addition to the basic curriculum, Miss May made sure her students were adept at penmanship, and she exposed them to art and other culture. Many of her former students swore she had "eyes in the back of her head," as she would often be writing on the blackboard with her back to the class and still be able to single out misbehaving students. In reality, Miss May had some assistance from a framed portrait of George Washington that hung over the board. The glass covering the portrait presented a perfect reflection of the classroom and allowed her to see mischievous students even when she had her back turned to the class. (Photograph courtesy of Billie Stevenson.)

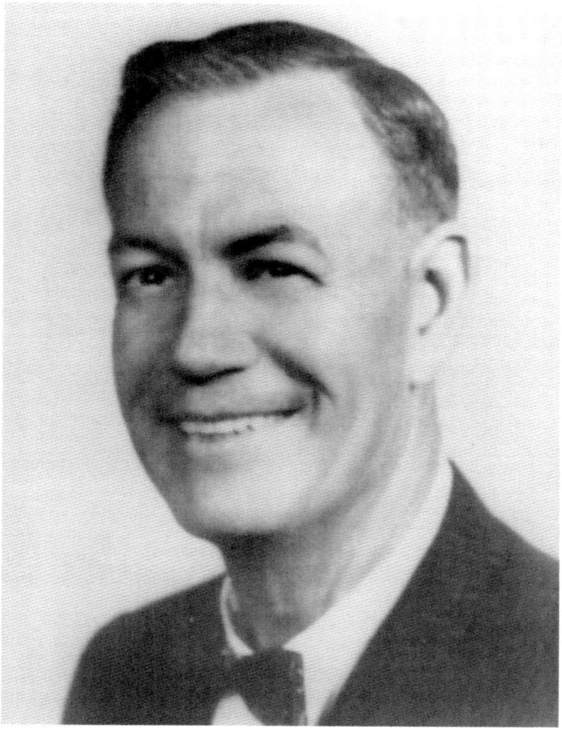

Howard Dobbs

The city of Rockwall's first modern-era elementary school is named after educator and community servant Howard Dobbs, a coach, science teacher, and principal of Rockwall Elementary School. He began the school library by donating some of his personal volumes. In the community, Dobbs was president of the Lions Club, mayor of Rockwall, and a local merchant. (Photograph courtesy of Sharon Shannon.)

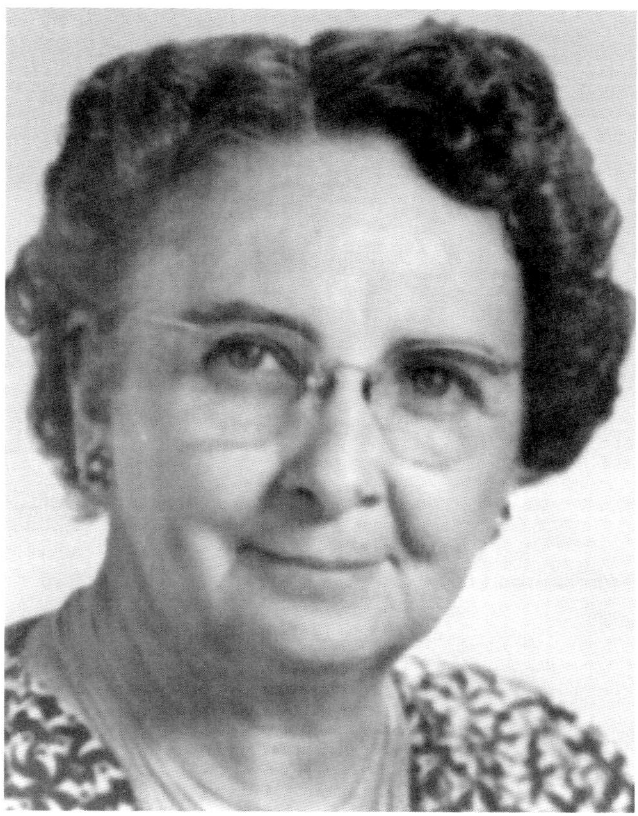

Grace Hartman

A career educator, Grace Hartman taught in Rockwall schools from 1917 to 1959. In addition to enjoying a career as an accomplished teacher, Hartman was instrumental in the formation of the Rockwall County Library in the 1940s. She and her husband, Alfred, were also well known as talented china painters. A display of Hartman china can be seen at the Rockwall County Library. (Photograph courtesy of RISD.)

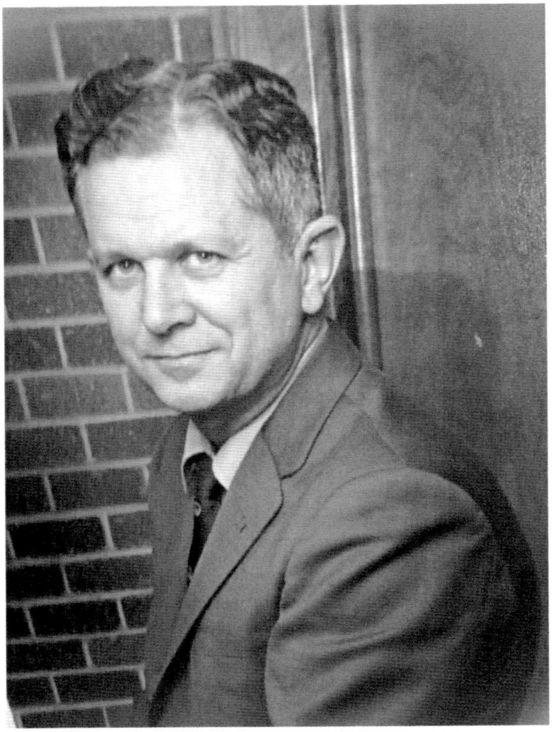

Herman E. Utley

Herman Utley came to Rockwall in 1958 to fill the position of Junior High School principal. He served in that capacity from 1958 to 1963, at which time he began a nine-year tenure as principal of Rockwall High School. He served an additional 10 years as principal of Howard Dobbs Elementary School prior to retiring in 1982. Herman E. Utley Middle School is named in his honor. (Photograph courtesy of Mercedes Utley.)

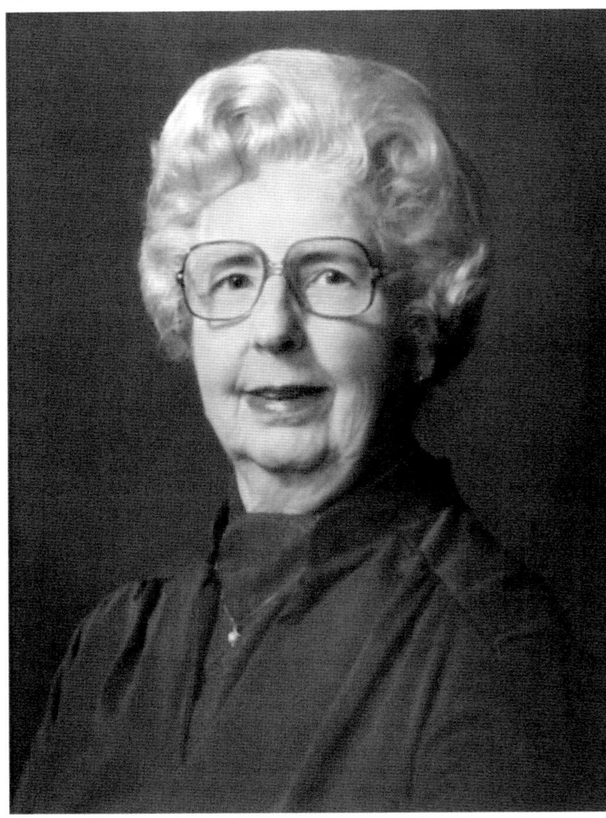

Celia Hays

The child of a pioneer family, Celia Hays's Rockwall roots go back to the early days of settlement in the area. Her grandparents donated the land for the Locust Grove School, a one-room schoolhouse north of the city of Rockwall. Hays graduated from Rockwall High School in 1924 and began her teaching career in a country schoolhouse in Rockwall County in 1926. She retired in 1974 after 42 years in the classroom. After her retirement, she became the librarian for the Rockwall County library, which was then located in a room in the courthouse. She also accrued more than 4,200 volunteer hours at Lake Pointe Medical Center. (Photograph courtesy of Rockwall ISD.)

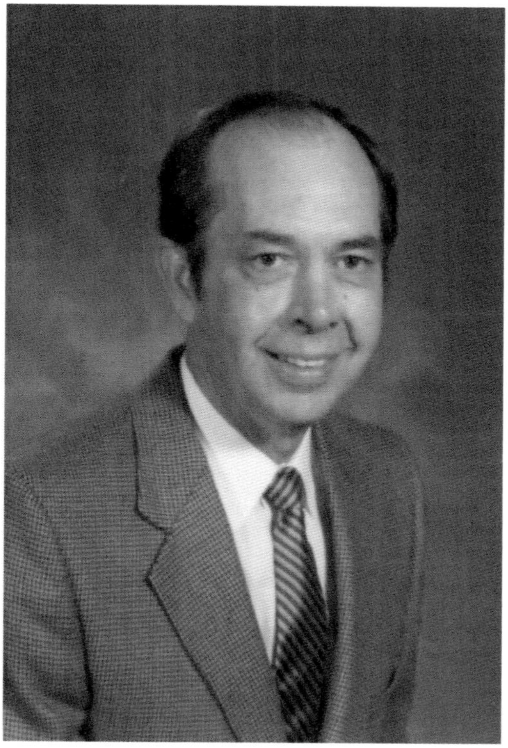

J.W. Williams
In 1969, Jimmy Williams came to Rockwall to serve as principal at the junior high school. Three years later, in 1972, he was promoted to superintendent of schools, a position he held for 17 years. During his tenure as superintendent, enrollment in the district tripled. Williams managed a growing program that provided new facilities as well as new academic and extracurricular opportunities. J.W. Williams Middle School is named in his honor. (Photograph courtesy of Rockwall ISD.)

Sharon Shannon
A gifted and engaging English teacher, Sharon Shannon taught for 29 years in the Rockwall Independent School District. During her tenure, she taught almost 4,000 students, many of whom named her as their most influential teacher. Her colleagues at Rockwall High School voted her campus Teacher of the Year numerous times. Since her retirement, Mrs. Shannon (pictured with husband and former RHS coach Stan Shannon) has served many local organizations, including the Rockwall County Committee on Aging (Meals on Wheels), the Friday Study Club, Delta Kappa Gamma, and the Rockwall Area Retired Teachers Association. (Photograph courtesy of Sharon Shannon.)

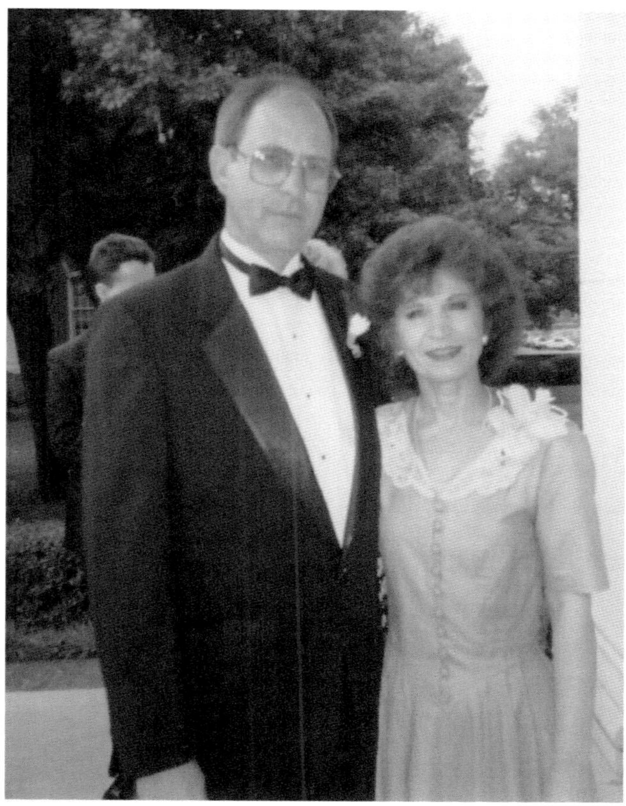

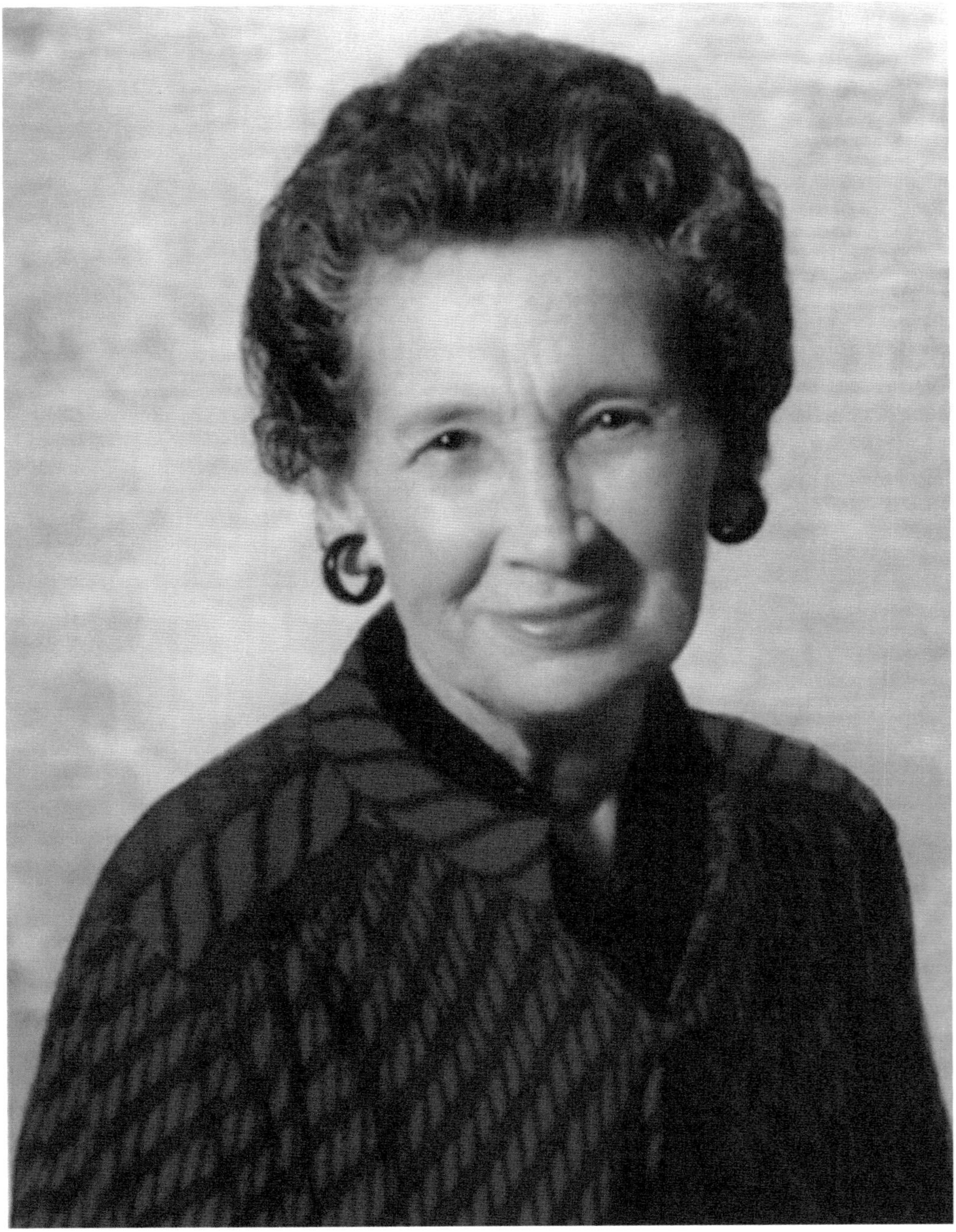

Ouida Springer

The namesake of Rockwall ISD's 10th modern-era elementary school, Ouida Springer served the students of the district for 27 of her 32 years in education. She was born near Waco, Texas, and marriage brought her to Rockwall County in 1940. She began her long association with the school district as a substitute teacher, taking a full-time role in 1952. Mrs. Springer retired in 1979. On the opposite page, Dorothy Pullen (left) and Ouida Springer (right) are pictured on their graduation day from East Texas State University. (Photographs courtesy of the Springer family.)

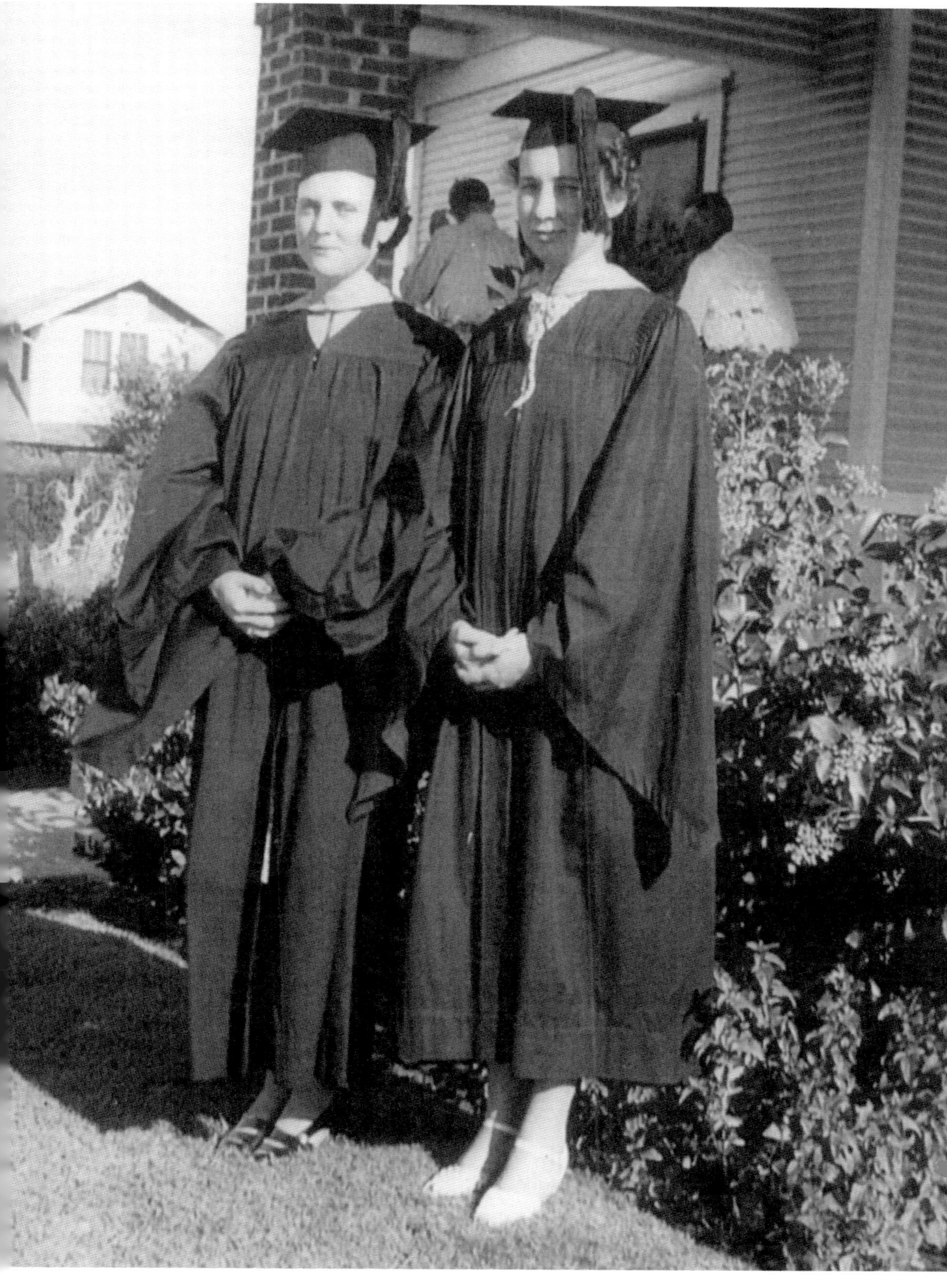

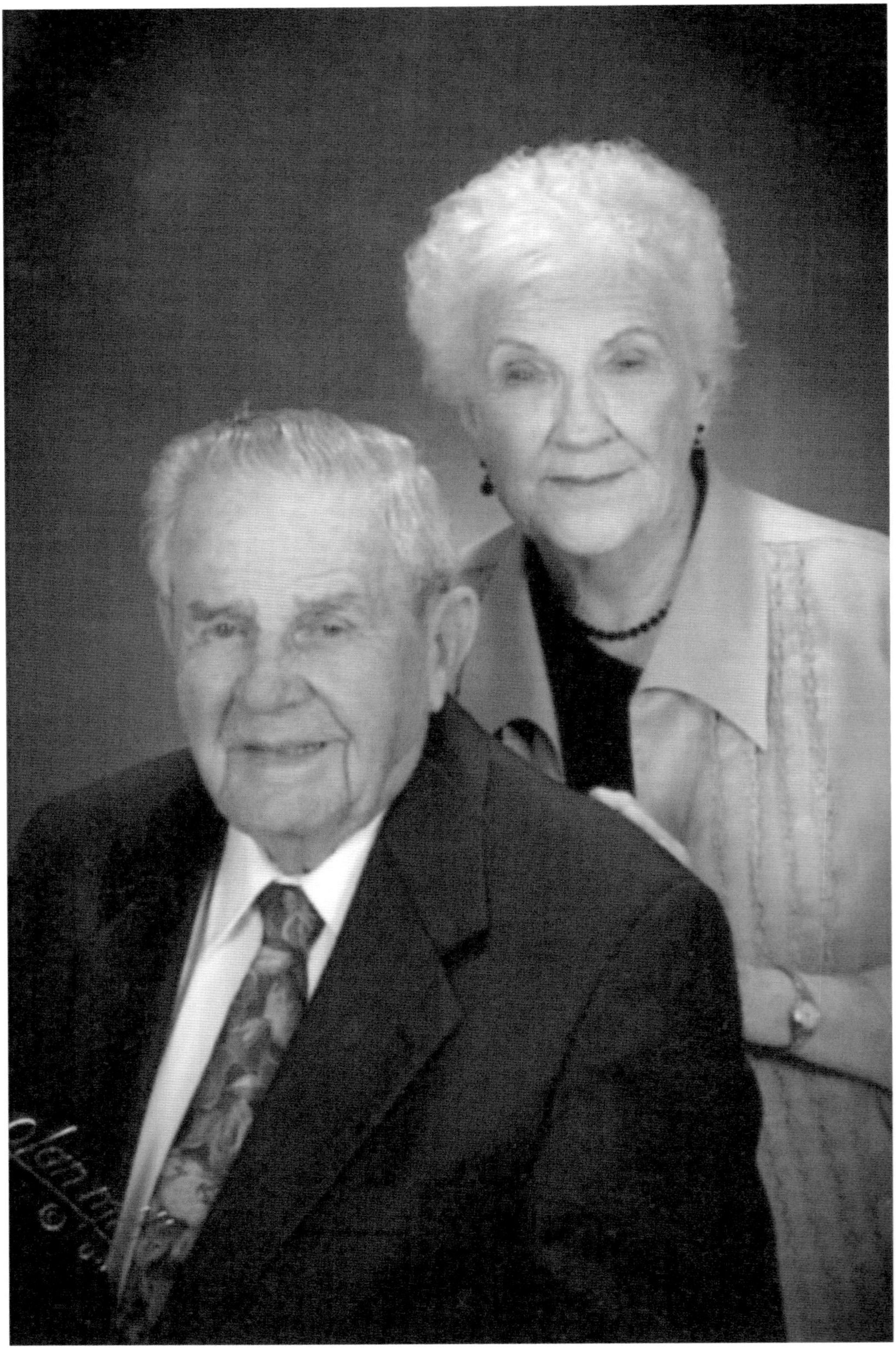

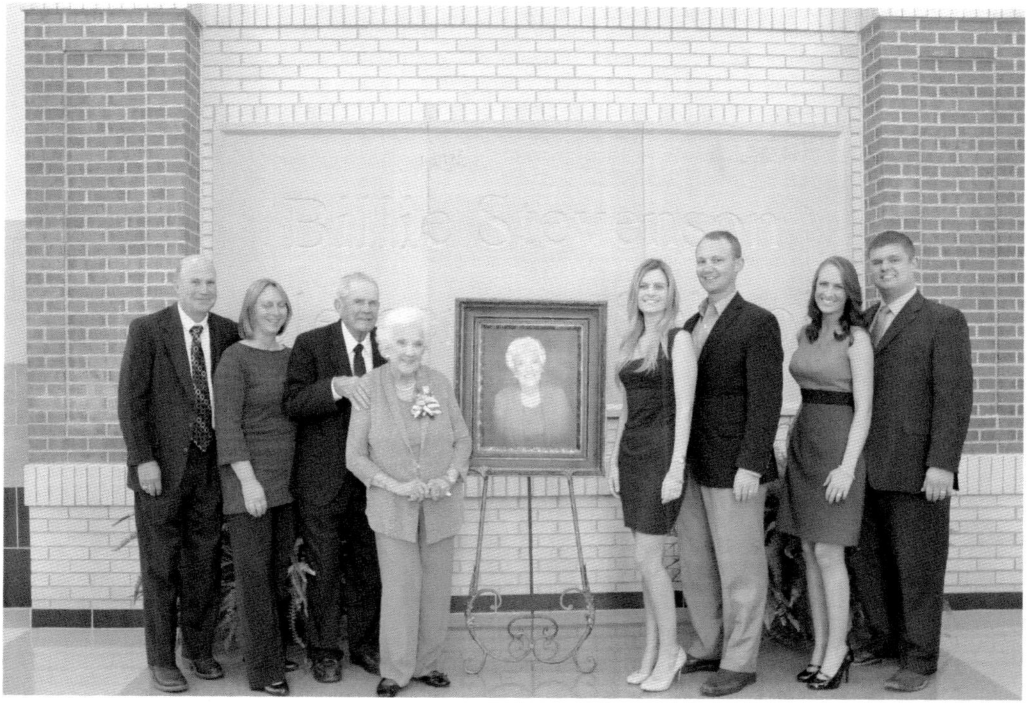

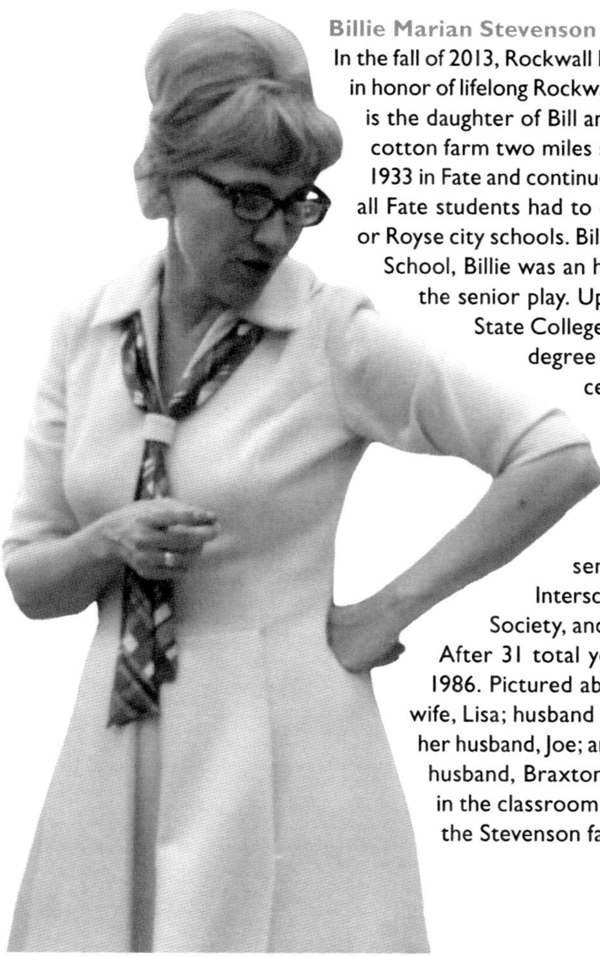

Billie Marian Stevenson

In the fall of 2013, Rockwall ISD opened its 13th elementary school, named in honor of lifelong Rockwall County resident Billie Stevenson. Stevenson is the daughter of Bill and Lockie Garrett and was born in 1927 on a cotton farm two miles south of the city of Fate. She began school in 1933 in Fate and continued there through the sixth grade. At that time, all Fate students had to choose whether to attend Rockwall schools or Royse city schools. Billie Garrett chose Rockwall. At Rockwall High School, Billie was an honor student, a cheerleader, and the lead in the senior play. Upon graduation, she enrolled in North Texas State College at Denton, where she earned her bachelor's degree in business administration and her teaching certificate. She began her teaching career in Lewisville and, in 1960, began a 26-year tenure at Rockwall High School, teaching English, business courses, and office education while sponsoring the cheerleaders, the school yearbook, the junior and senior classes, the senior prom, the student council, University Interscholastic League competitions, National Honor Society, and Office Education Association competitions. After 31 total years in the classroom, Stevenson retired in 1986. Pictured above from left to right are son Allen with his wife, Lisa; husband Bill; Billie; granddaughter Lauren Pluhar with her husband, Joe; and granddaughter Leigha Nottingham with her husband, Braxton. In the photograph at left, Billie is pictured in the classroom in the early 1970s. (Photographs courtesy of the Stevenson family.)

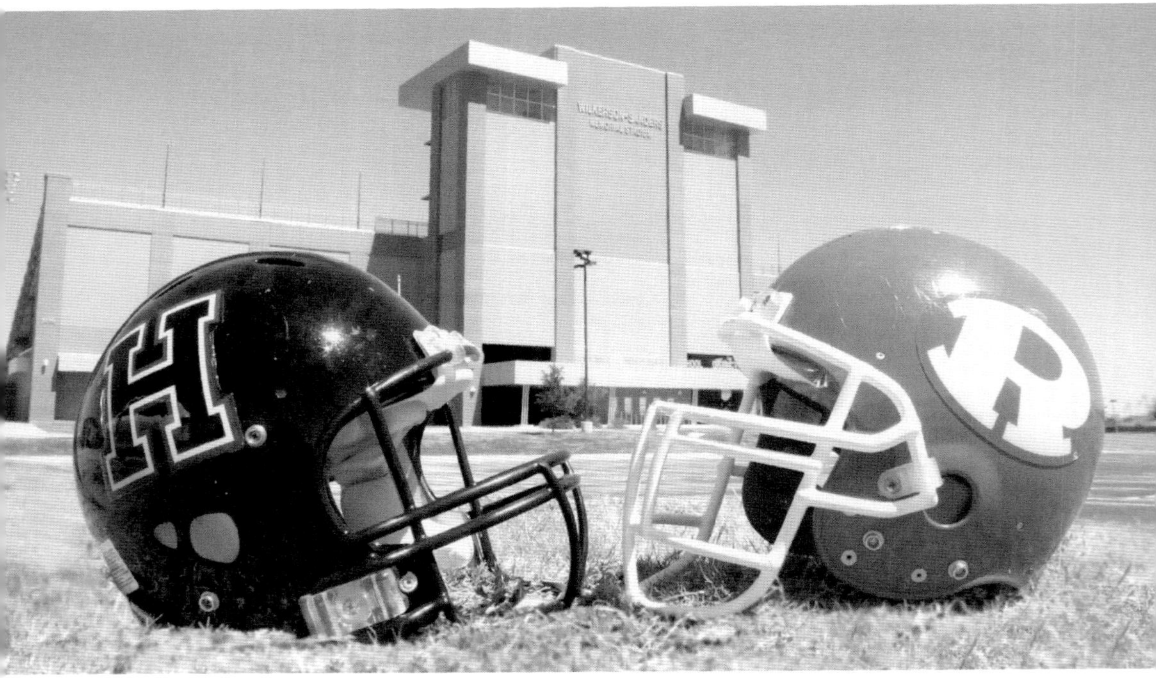

J.A. Wilkerson

J.A. Wilkerson was superintendent of schools for Rockwall ISD but was perhaps best known as the coach of the Yellowjacket football team. During his tenure from 1927 to 1947, he chalked up 145 victories, 49 losses, and 11 ties. He coached teams to the district title seven times, the bi-district title five times, and to two regional championships. Rockwall ISD's Wilkerson-Sanders Memorial Stadium is named in his honor. (Photograph courtesy of RISD.)

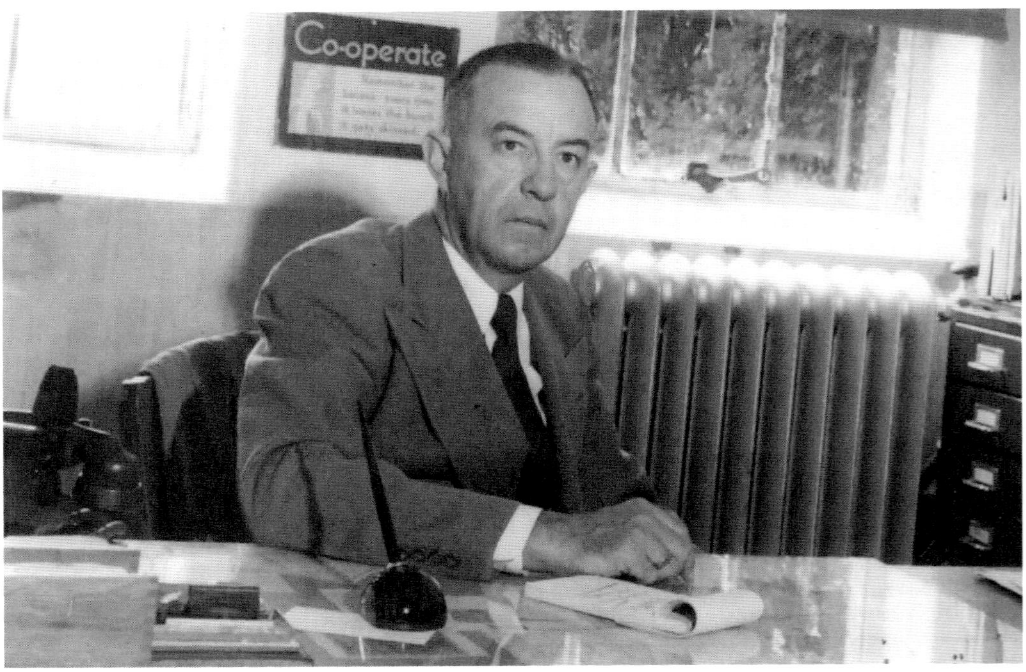

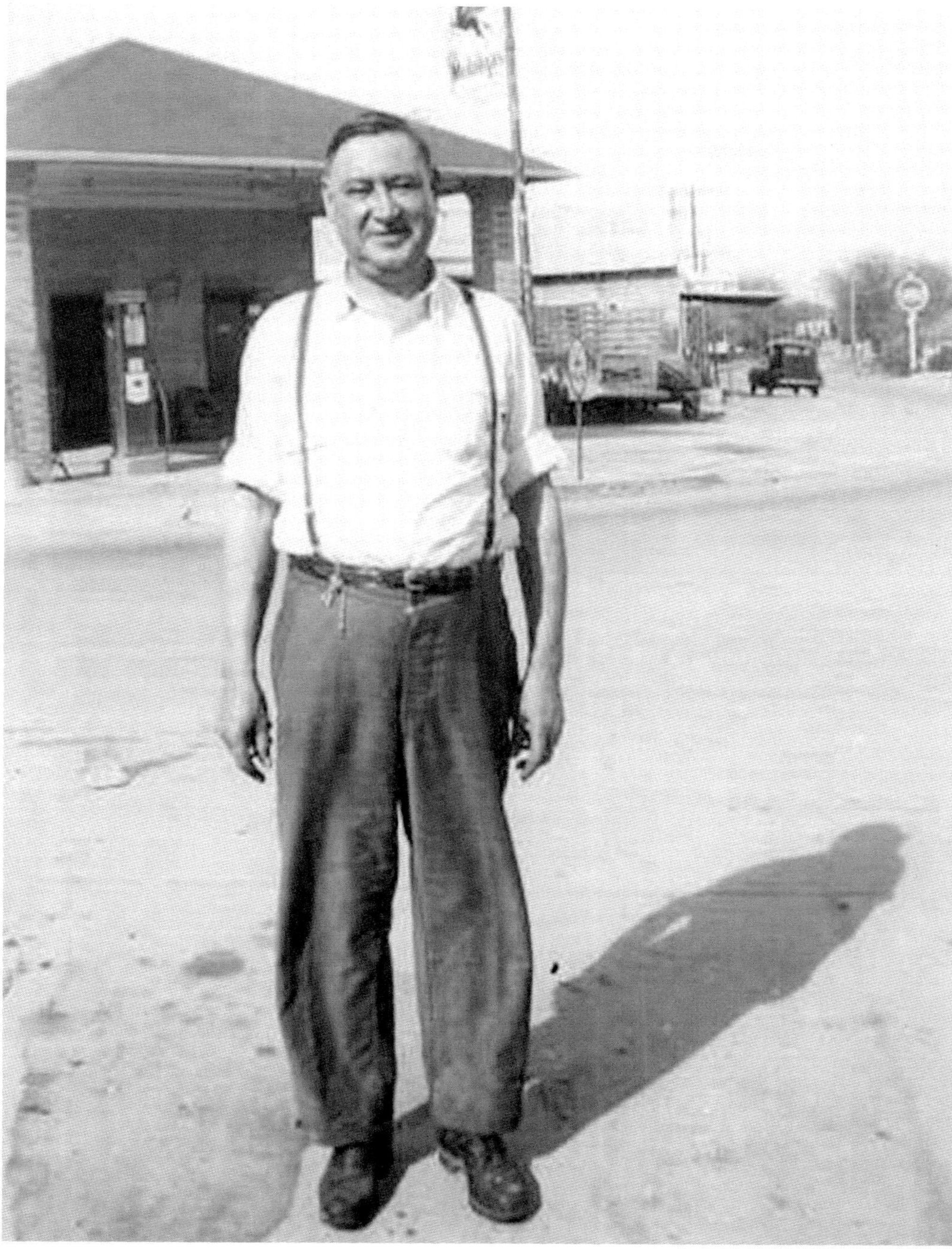

Harvey Sanders

A local businessman, William Harvey Sanders worked as an assistant coach to J.A. Wilkerson for no pay. His love of the game and his ability to help the boys who participated were his only reward. Harvey and his wife owned a sandwich shop on the square, and hungry football players (with or without the cash to pay) were always welcomed with a meal. Rockwall ISD's Wilkerson-Sanders Memorial Stadium is named in his honor. (Photograph courtesy of Rockwall ISD.)

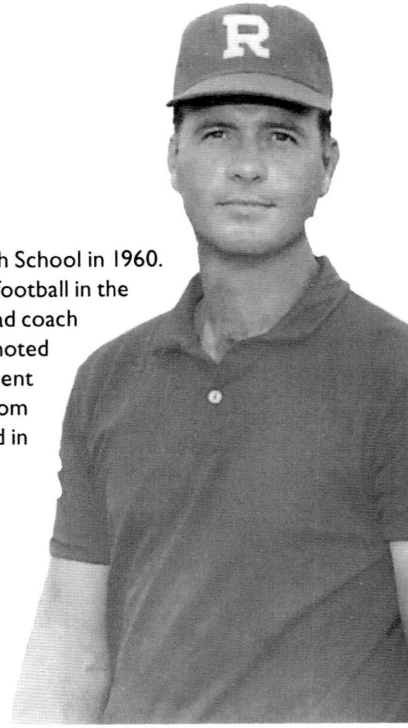

Mickey Florence

A Rockwall native, Mickey Florence graduated from Rockwall High School in 1960. After attending college at East Texas State University, he coached football in the surrounding communities for several years before being named head coach and athletic director for Rockwall ISD in 1970. In 1973, he was promoted to assistant superintendent of schools. In addition to his employment with RISD, Coach Florence also served on the board of trustees from 1994 to 1999. The Mickey Florence Multi-Purpose Facility is named in his honor. (Photograph courtesy of the Florence family.)

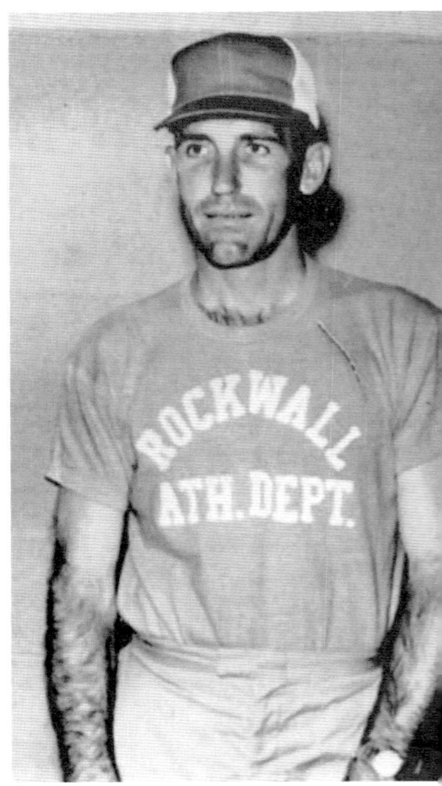

Hobart Wisdom

Wisdom Field, located behind Dobbs Elementary School, is named in honor of coach Hobart Wisdom, who settled in Rockwall after serving in the US Marine Corps and graduating from East Texas State University. Coach Wisdom taught science and driver's education and later served as assistant principal of Rockwall Middle School. He considered being on the coaching staff of the 1963 State Champion Yellowjackets as one of his proudest accomplishments. (Photograph courtesy of RISD.)

CHAPTER FIVE

Business Owners and Professionals

In 1855, the first store was established in Rockwall by John O. Heath and C.L. Jones. It was a general store located two blocks south of the current square. By the time the railroad was built through town in 1886, Rockwall boasted a hardware store, a dry goods business, a blacksmith shop, and a millinery. There were also at least two saloons and several hotels. By 1912, Rockwall's business district had eliminated the "unseemly" elements, and the respectable downtown had two banks, three drugstores, three general merchandise stores, two restaurants, two hardware stores, two harness shops, two furniture stores, two tin shops, three blacksmiths, two wheelwrights, a sawmill, a bakery, a foundry, a machine shop, a newspaper, and a gentlemen's furnishings shop.

Throughout the years, the Rockwall community has been home to hundreds of businesses and business professionals. These include dentists such as Dr. Jessie Castle LaMoreaux (Texas's first formally trained female dentist), journalists such as the Bounds family (who ran the *Rockwall Success* for many decades), veterinarians such as Joe Loftis (who established his practice in 1958), merchants such as D.E. and Paralee Payne (owners of Payne's Appliances, which operated on the square for four decades), and bankers such as Larry Parks (who still offers personalized service to his loyal customers).

Quite honestly, no list could ever encompass the many, many business leaders who have made significant contributions to the Rockwall community. From the early mercantile proprietors who issued credit, to the local farmers waiting for their crops to come in, to recent business owners who champion the community through their steadfast support of the Rockwall Chamber of Commerce and other civic organizations, there is no way to include all those who deserve to be mentioned. Instead, this chapter is designed to include a small sampling of those men and women who have helped shape Rockwall's business culture throughout the years.

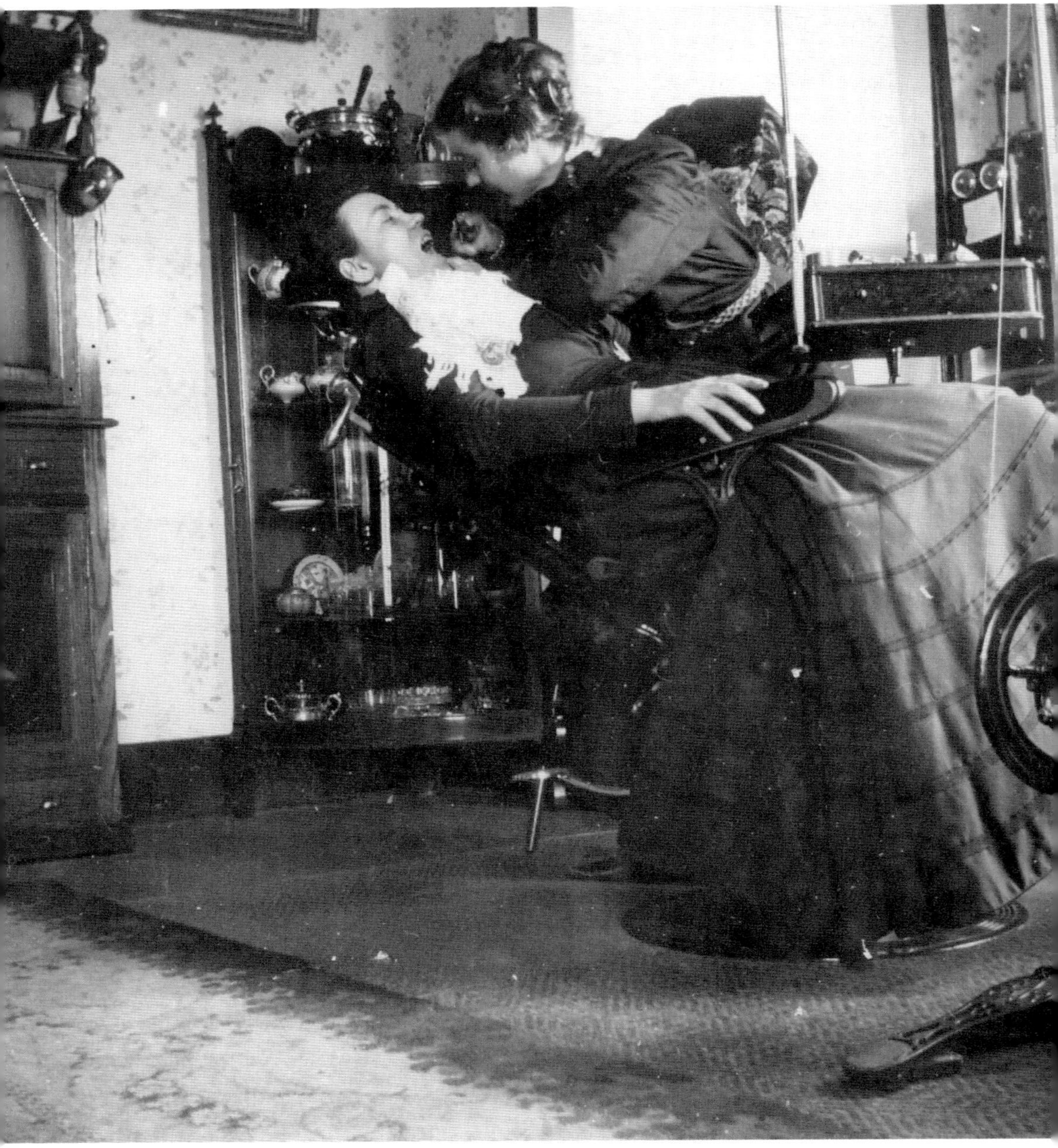

Dr. Jessie Castle LaMoreaux

Dr. LaMoreaux grew up in Michigan and studied dentistry at the University of Michigan, receiving her degree in 1896. After establishing her first dental practice at the Battle Creek Sanitarium in Michigan, she moved to Texas to be closer to her sister, who lived in Rockwall. In 1898, she set up practice in Dallas and became Texas's first formally trained female dentist. In 1901, she relocated her practice and her residence to Rockwall. After many decades of being active in the community, Dr. LaMoreaux passed away in 1954. (Photographs courtesy of the RCHF.)

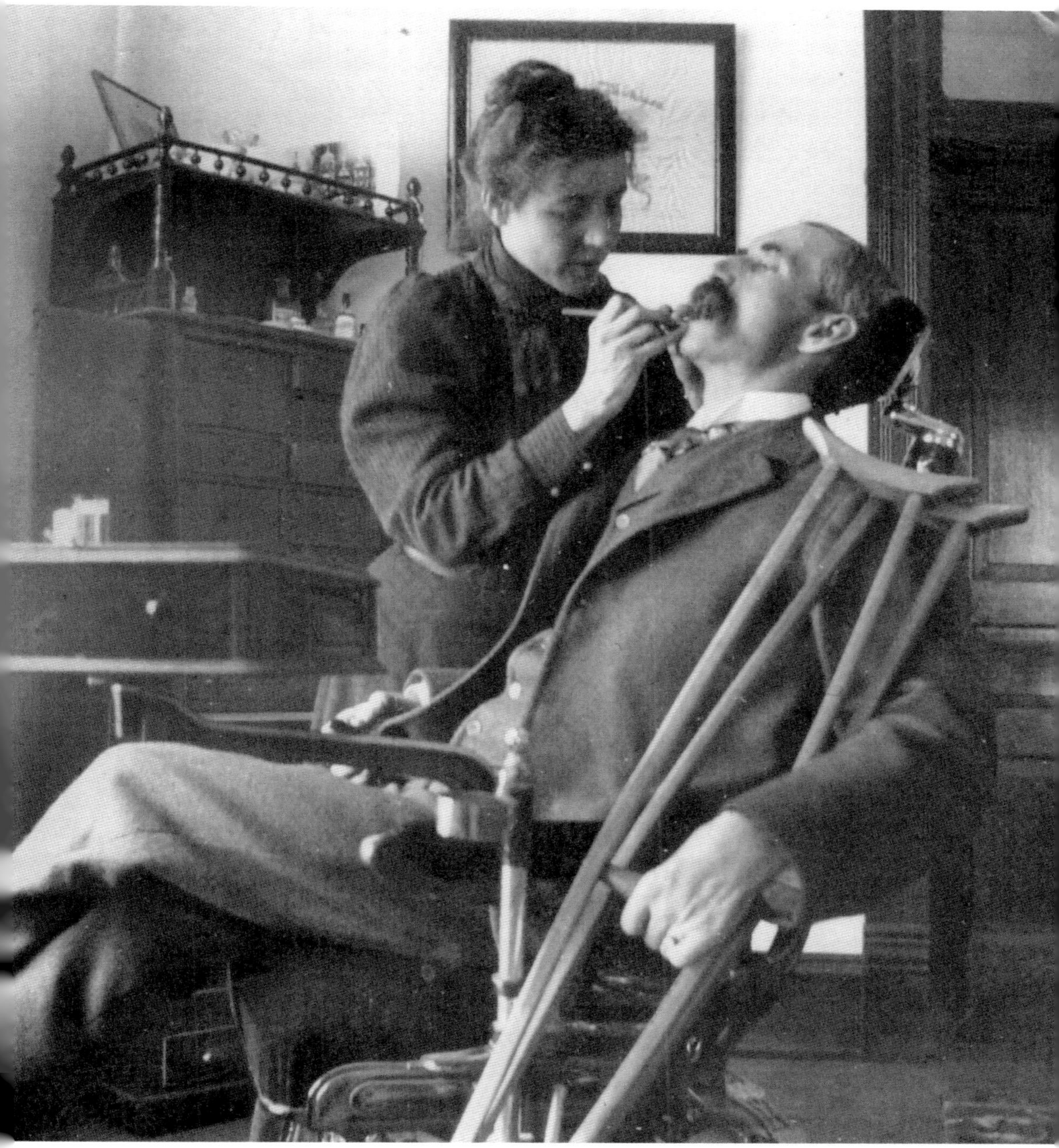

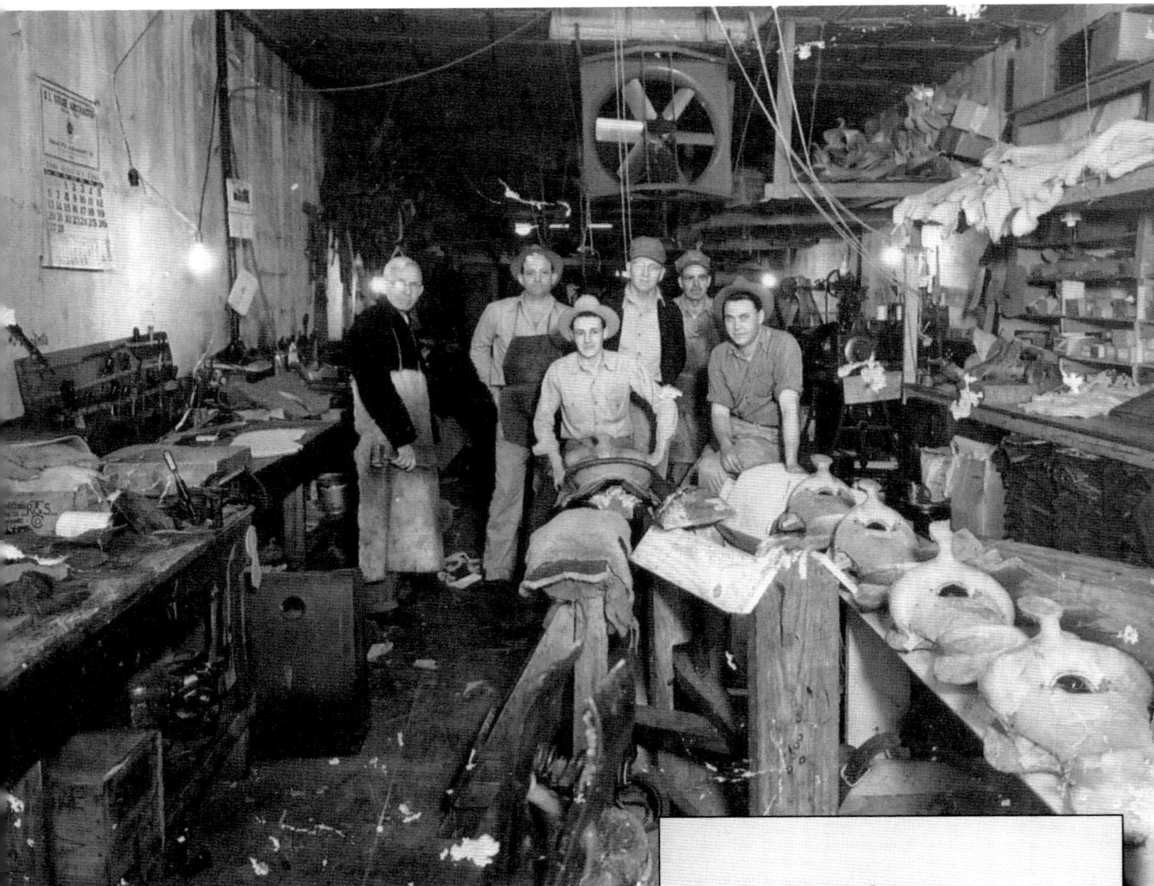

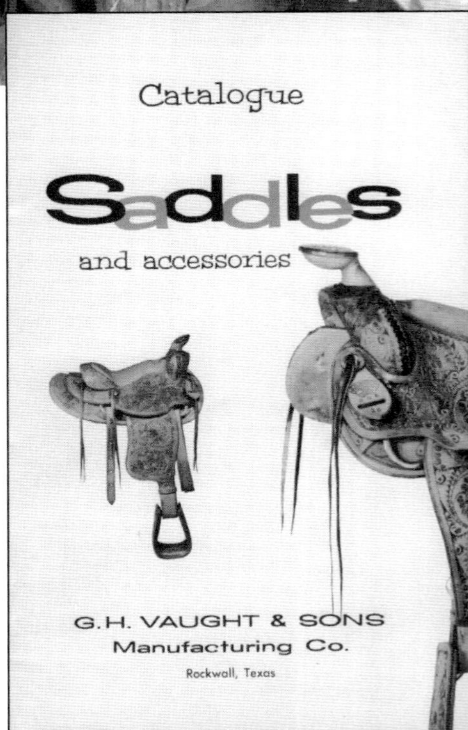

George Vaught
In the 1920s, when he was just 16 years old, G.H. Vaught began his business with just $35 and developed it into a nationally recognized leather goods manufacturing operation and saddle shop. By the 1940s, Vaught saddles and leather accessories were so well known that orders came into the Rockwall-based business from around the country through its mail-order catalogue. Today, Vaught saddles are considered collectible items and can often be found on auction websites. (Above photograph, courtesy of the RCHF; below photograph, author's private collection.)

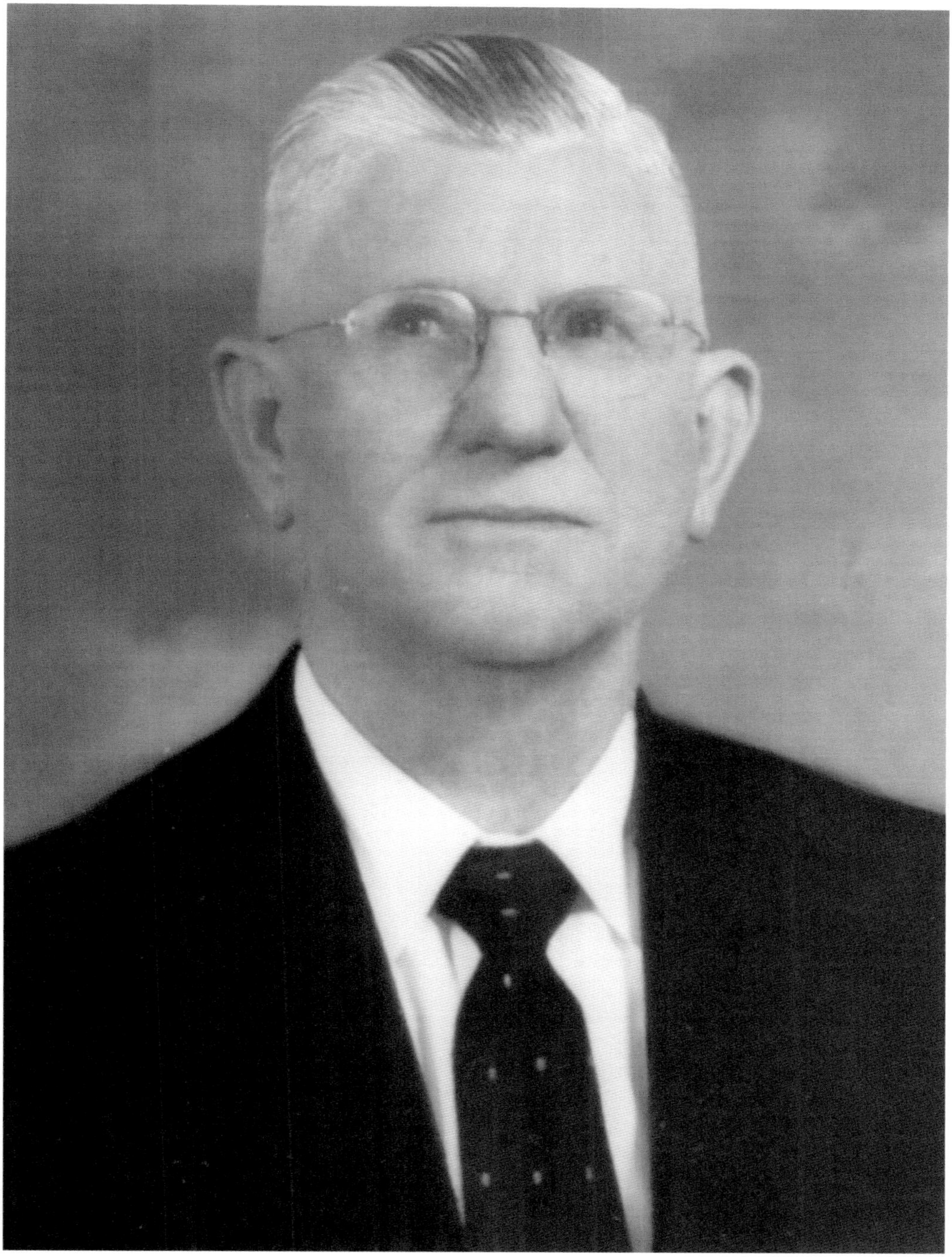

O.L. Steger
A lifelong resident of Rockwall, O.L. Steger Sr. dedicated more than 50 years of civic service to his community. He was a businessman, elected county official, farmer, real estate agent, chamber of commerce leader, mayor of Rockwall, charter member of the Rockwall Rotary Club, church leader, and member of the school board. In addition, he was a local historian who recorded the early days of Rockwall County in his book, *History of Rockwall County 1842–1968*. (Photograph courtesy of Diana Steger Chapman.)

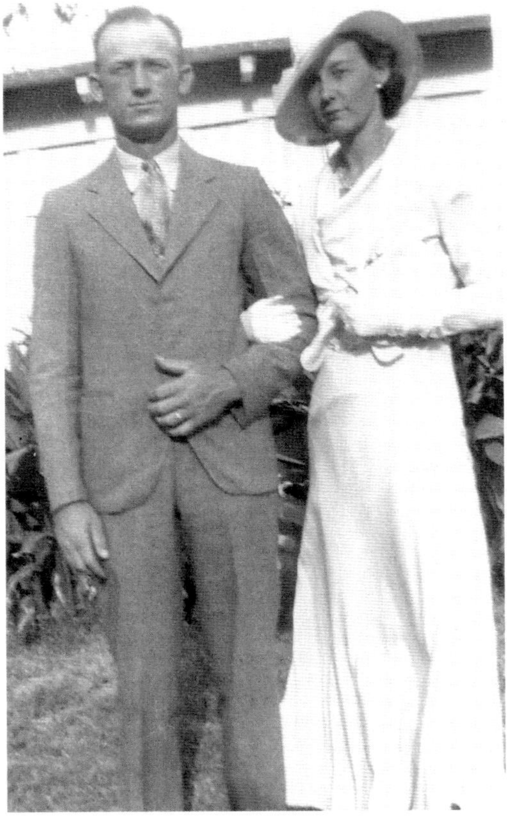

Glenn Cross

Although Glenn Cross was a farmer by trade, in 1936 he became an assistant rural mail carrier for the postal service. After 43 years of service, he retired in 1979. He was married to Orpha Bailey, who made the post office a family business when she took a job as a postal assistant in Royse City for six years. Her father had served as postmaster in Royse City for 15 years. (Photograph courtesy of Lucille Cross Bell.)

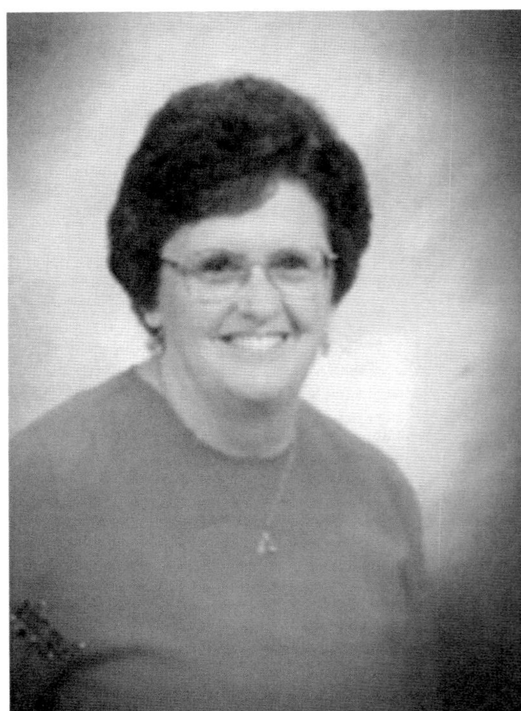

Kathleen Melston

Kathleen "Kathy" Melston was a school librarian for 20 years, mostly in New York State, before she and her husband, Ken, moved to the Rockwall area in 1987. She became director of the Rockwall County Library in 1988, and over the next 20 years she moved the library into the digital age. When Melston became library director, the Rockwall facility was 2,800 square feet. After several moves, the library space had been expanded to 10,000 square feet, which was still inadequate for Rockwall County's growing population. Working with the Friends of the Library and the Library Advisory Board, Kathy was instrumental in getting bond issues on the ballot to both purchase land for and to build a new 52,000-square-foot facility, which opened in 2008. The Quiet Reading Room in the new library is named in Kathy's honor. (Photograph courtesy of Kathy Melston.)

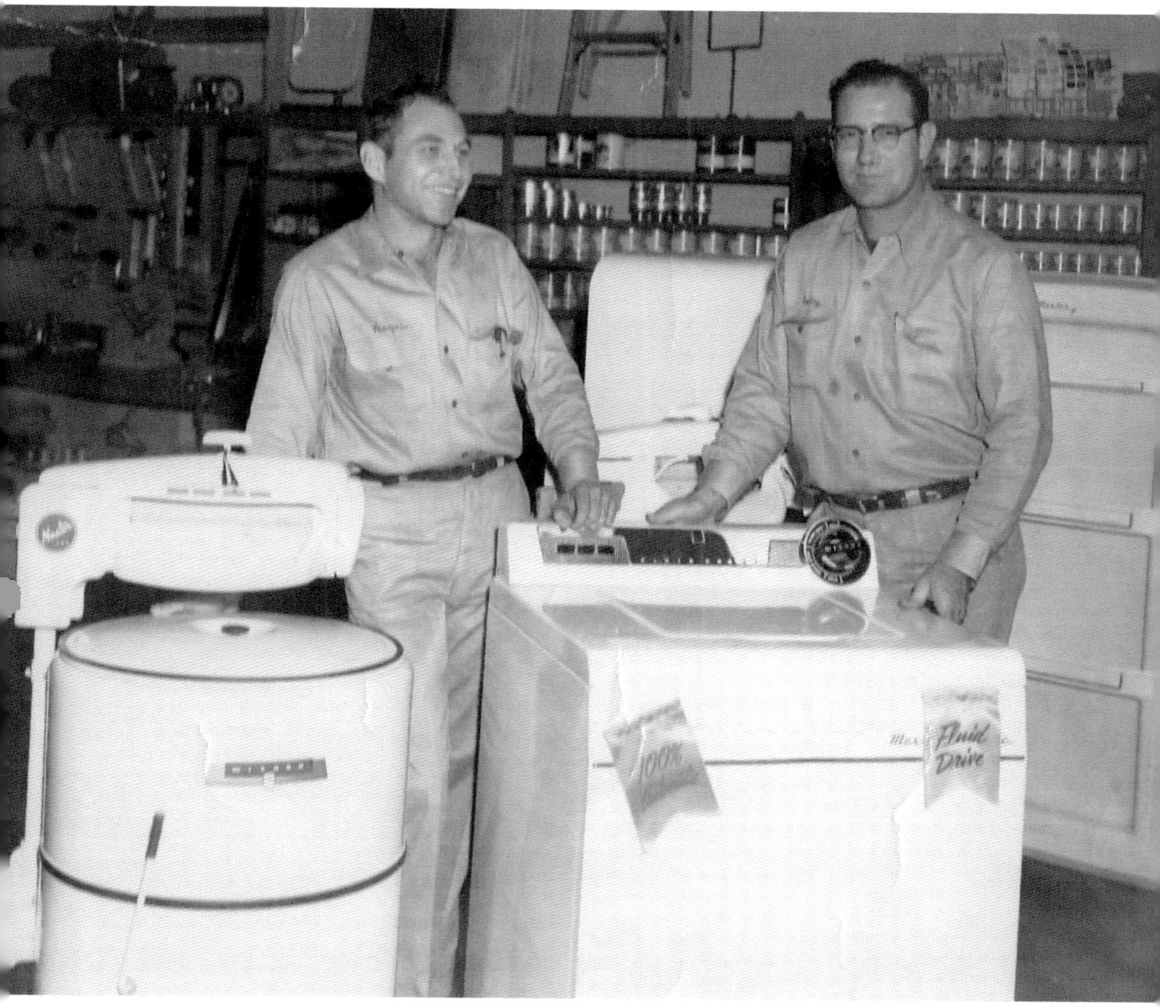

Wayne Rogers

Innis "Wayne" Rogers was born August 16, 1924, in Winters, Texas, to Ira W. and Lucille (Jones) Rogers. He served his country as petty officer first class in the US Navy during World War II. He moved to Rockwall in August 1951 and began his career as a local business owner by purchasing the Western Auto store located on Rusk Street in downtown Rockwall. The small business grew and eventually became Rogers & Rogers Ace Hardware. Wayne suffered a stroke in July 2008, but he continued to be involved in the business that he had nurtured for over six decades until his death in July 2011. In 1952, Wayne joined the Rockwall Volunteer Fire Department. He was fire chief for 12 years and was also voted Fireman of the Year. He served proudly as a volunteer firefighter for over 20 years, until May 1974. Wayne was actively involved in the Rockwall community. He was a member of the Rockwall Firefighters' Support Committee, a Rockwall Rotarian, a Lions Club member, a member of the American Legion, on the Rockwall Planning and Zoning Committee, and a Rockwall City Council member. In addition, he served as mayor pro tem for Rockwall and was an elder in the First Presbyterian Church. Wayne was the recipient of an award, given by the mayor and the Rockwall City Council, expressing appreciation for his dedication to the community and his contribution toward the success of the city of Rockwall. Wayne was married to Wanda (Richardson) Rogers. The couple had one son, Michael Wayne Rogers; and two grandsons, Ari Lara and Ricky Lynn. Ricky preceded Wayne in death. Pictured are Wayne Rogers (left) and Early Darr (right). (Photograph courtesy of the Rogers family.)

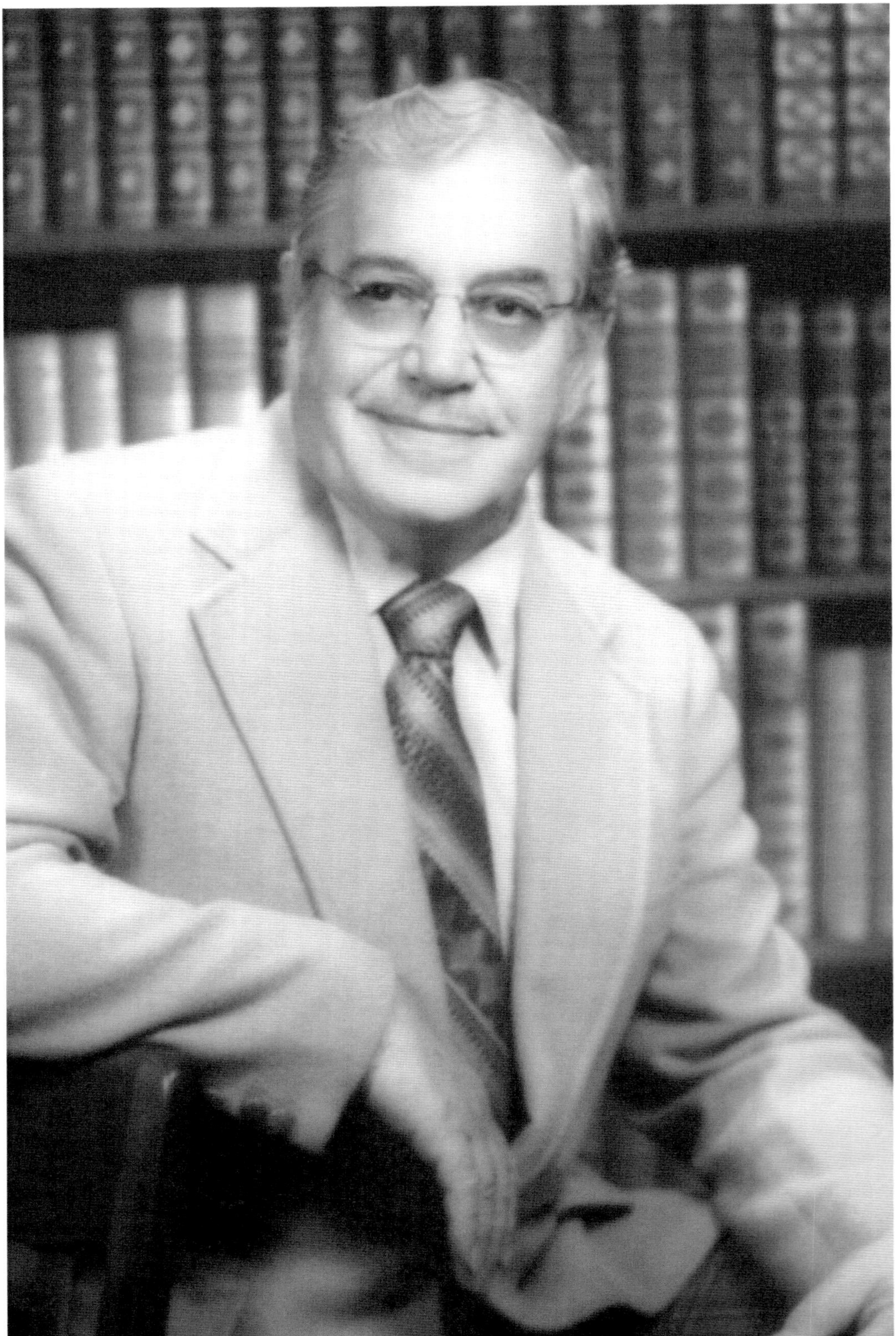

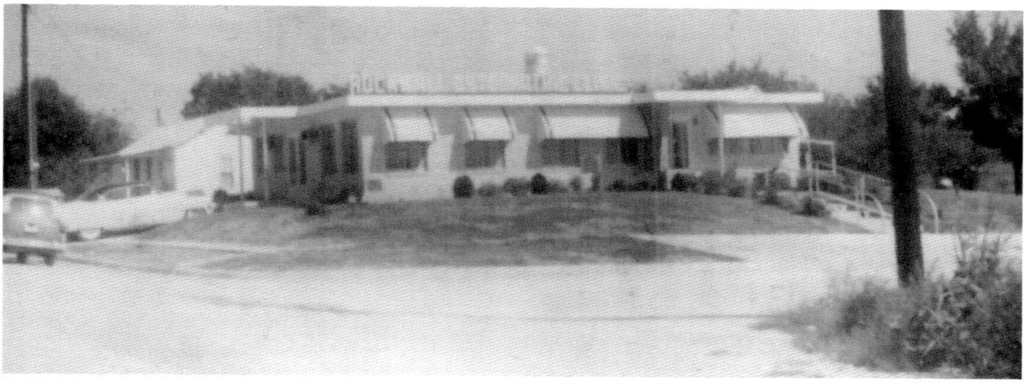

Sherman Sparks

Having moved to Rockwall in the mid-1940s, Sherman Sparks was a physician, a civic leader, the first male president of the Rockwall PTA, civil defense coordinator for Rockwall County, and team physician for the Rockwall Yellowjackets for 30 years. He was also active in politics, holding the first Republican Primary in Rockwall County in 1964, with 11 people voting. A well-known and admired physician, Dr. Sparks provided affordable medical care for the citizens of Rockwall County. The Rockwall Osteopathic Clinic & Laboratory is pictured above. Pictured below, from left to right are Mrs. Billie Sparks, builder Johnnie Parrigan, and Dr. Sparks, ceremoniously placing the clinic's cornerstone in 1952. (Photographs courtesy of Dr. Robert Sparks.)

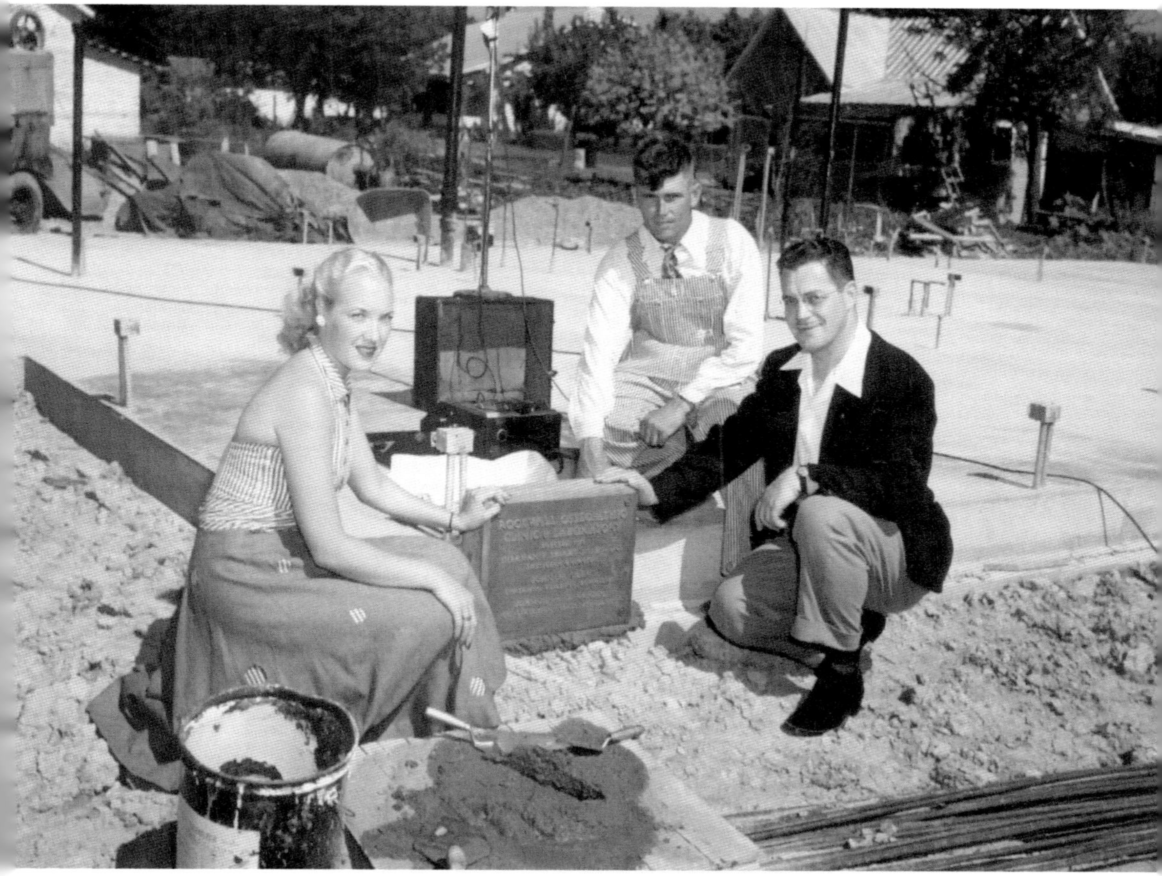

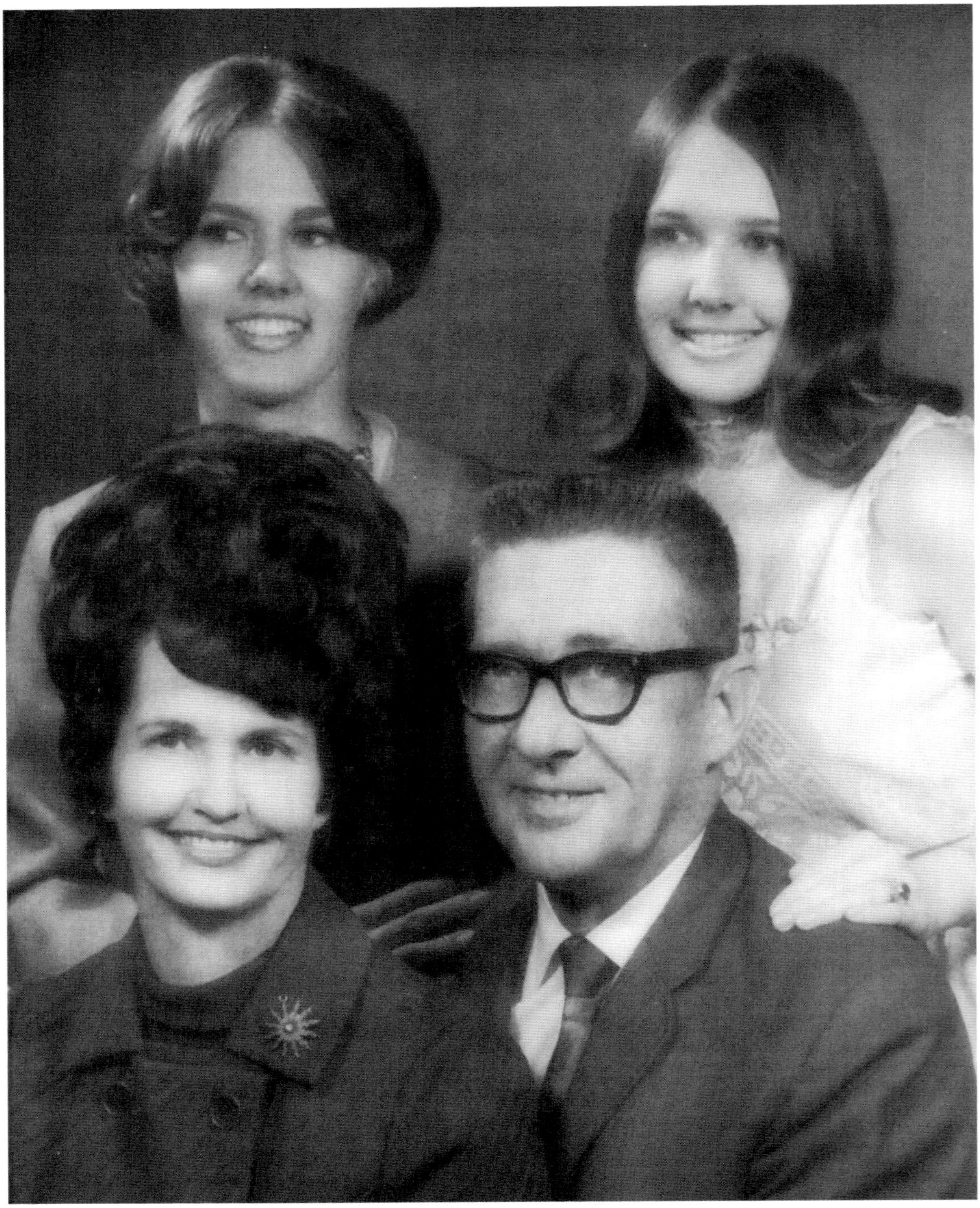

P.J. and Jane Bounds
Founded in 1883, the *Rockwall Success* was a well-established newspaper when the father/son team of P.J. Bounds Sr. and P.J. Bounds Jr. purchased the publication in 1949. After the death of the elder Mr. Bounds in 1955, his wife, Geneva, assumed his role as copublisher until her retirement in 1966. In 1958, daughter-in-law Jane joined her husband and took an active role in the production of the paper. P.J. Bounds Jr. passed away in 1976, and Jane became the publisher, later joined by daughters Jane and Jill, until 1988 when the paper was sold. Both P.J. and Jane were active in the civic affairs of Rockwall County, and Jane holds the distinction of becoming the first woman to become a member of the Rockwall Rotary Club. (Photograph provided courtesy of Jill Bounds Greenwalt.)

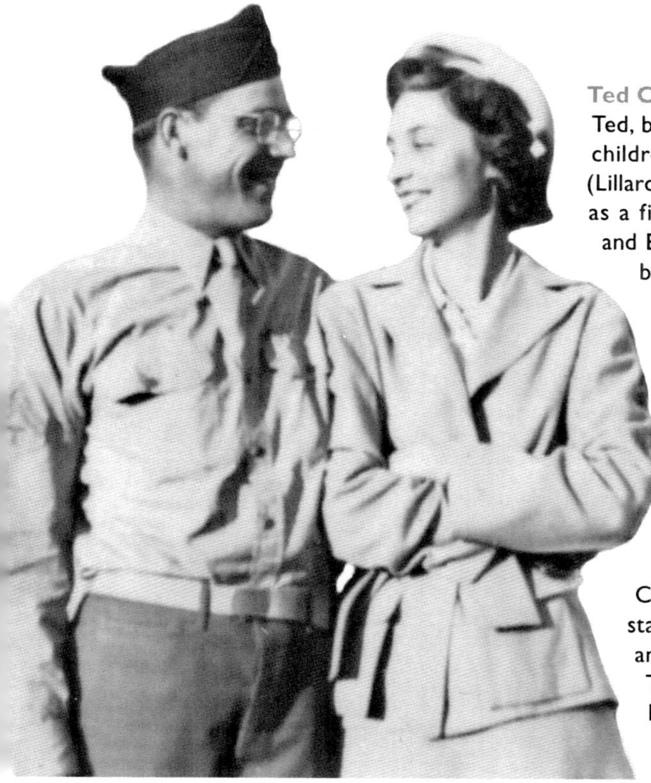

Ted Cain

Ted, born in 1917 in Rockwall, was one of eight children of Jessie Hubert and Sadonia Estelle (Lillard) Cain. During World War II, Ted served as a first sergeant in the US Army in Africa and Europe. In addition to being a flourishing businessman, Ted was an avid member of the First Baptist Church and served many years as a member of the Rockwall Volunteer Fire Department. He was the consummate businessman around town—donating his time to the Rockwall Chamber of Commerce, the Rockwall Rotary Club, the Rockwall Lions Club, and serving two terms on the city council. Ted owned a number of successful businesses, including Ted Cain's Real Estate; Mobil and Texaco service stations, at which he personally pumped gas and changed tires; Cain's Variety Store; and Ted Cain's Used Cars. He was married to Maurine Williamson Cain (also pictured) for 70 years. (Photograph courtesy of the Cain family.)

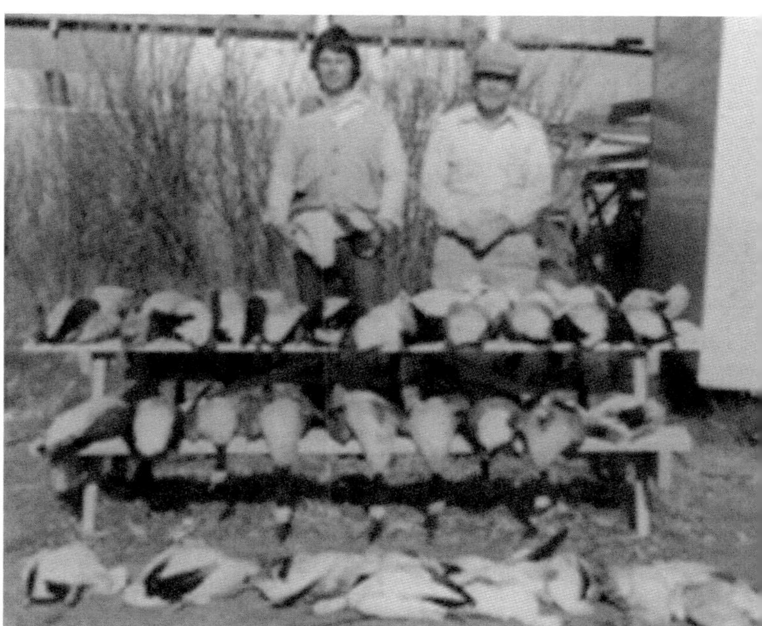

Horace Lee Williams Sr.

After serving in the Air Force during World War II and several subsequent years fulfilling peacetime duties, Horace Lee Williams and his wife, Mary Jean, returned to their native Rockwall and, in 1947, opened the Williams Lumber Company. Williams's longtime friend Frank Lawhorn helped manage the operation, and the men partnered in other ventures as well, including the Lawhorn-Williams Construction Company and the development of the Highwood Addition. Pictured are Horace Lee Williams Jr. (left) and Horace Lee Williams Sr. (Photograph courtesy of Horace Lee Williams Jr.)

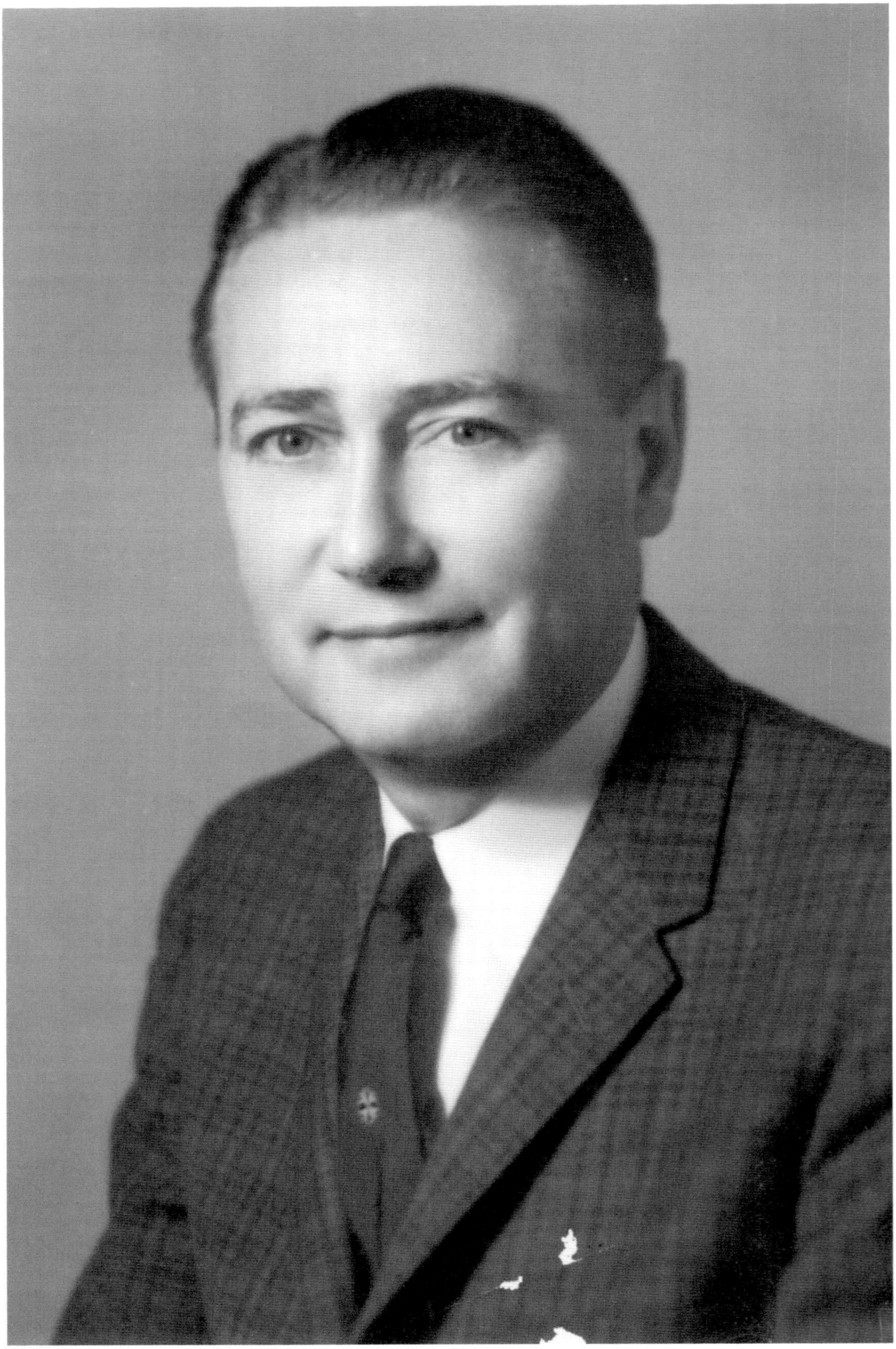

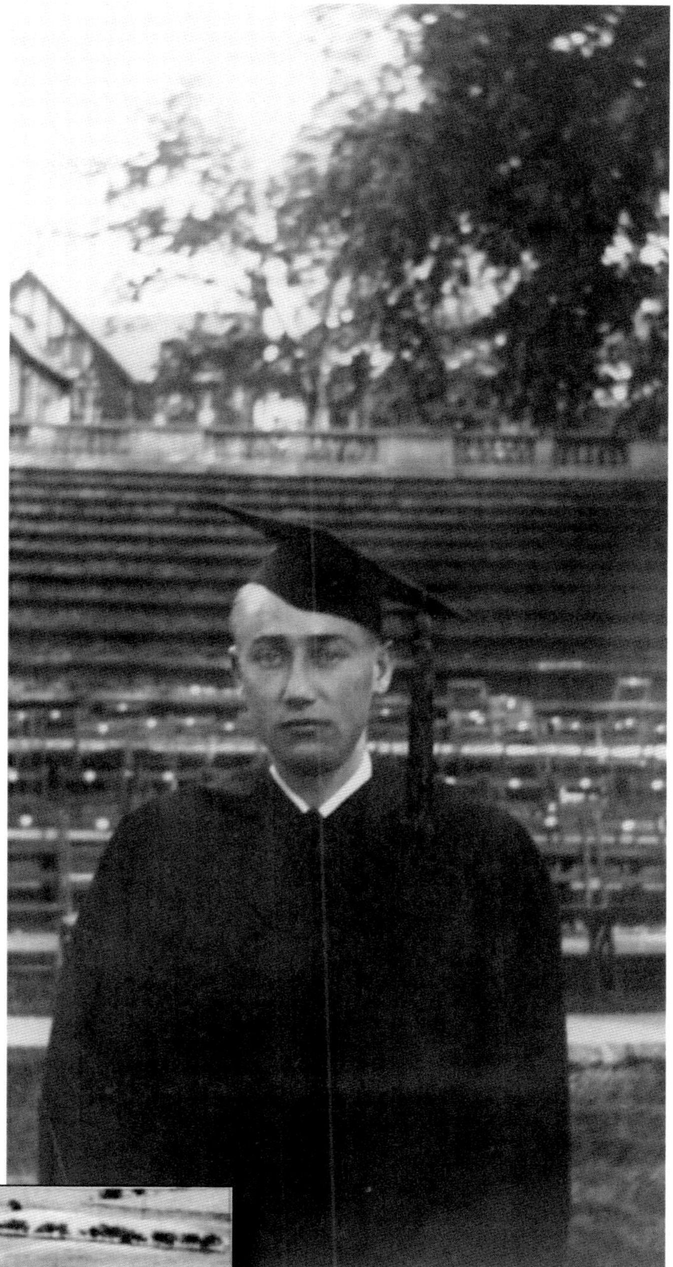

Richard W. Pickens

Born in Ohio, Richard (Dick) Pickens moved his family to Rockwall in 1953 and founded the Texas Aluminum Company, one of the first industrial businesses in the community. He and his wife, Betty, had three daughters, and Mrs. Pickens founded the Girl Scout movement in Rockwall. In honor of Pickens's contribution to the community, Pickens Lake, located in Harry Myers Park near the original site of the Texas Aluminum plant, is named in his honor. Pickens was known for his devotion to the community and to his employees. In a 1966 interview with *East Texas Magazine*, Pickens stated, "No matter where a company operates—no matter how big or small—no matter what its products or services are—the most important ingredient in the formula for success is people—the employee and his family." The Texas Aluminum plant, Rockwall's first major manufacturing company, is pictured below in the 1950s. (Photographs courtesy of Patti Pickens Canup.)

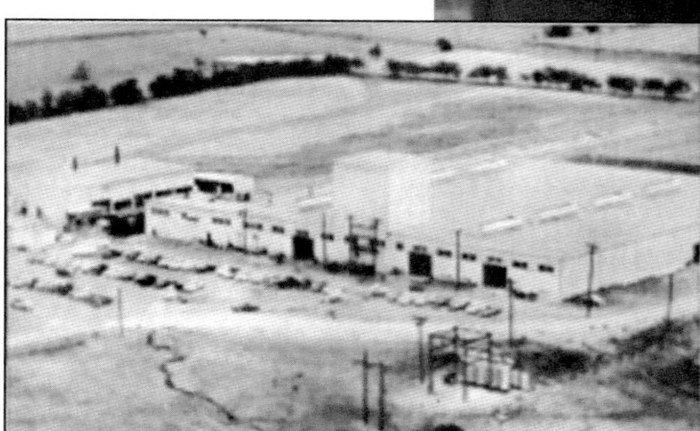

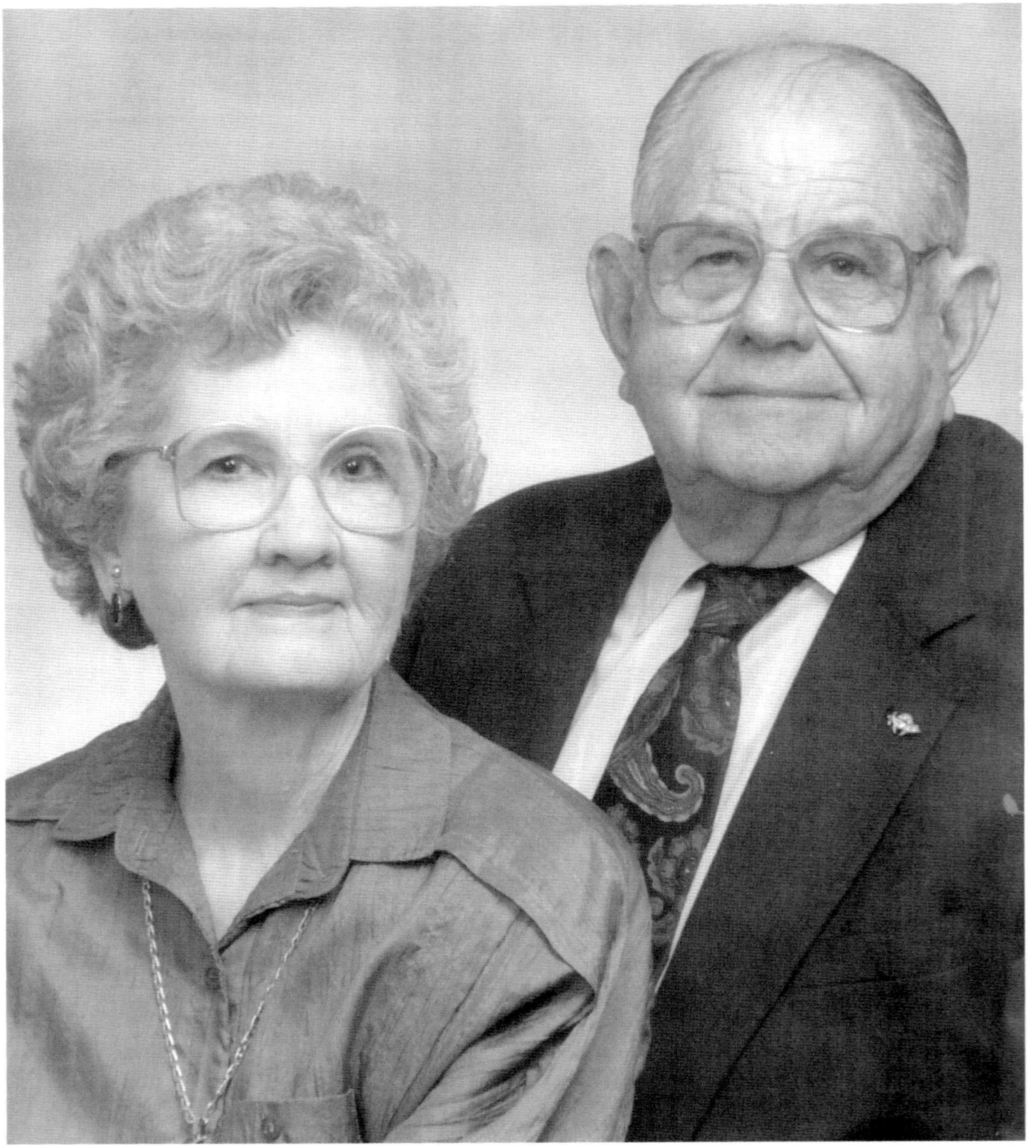

Raymond and Elizabeth Cameron

Raymond Cameron met Elizabeth Rochell while in school at East Texas State Teacher's College, and they were married on September 20, 1942. Raymond served as an instructor in flight engineering schools at several US Army bases during World War II. In addition to being a farmer and a teacher, he and his brother were partners in several real estate developments, including Rockwall's Ridge Road Shopping Center and the Cameron Building. In addition, both Raymond and Elizabeth were active in civic affairs and philanthropic causes. Raymond served on the Rockwall Chamber of Commerce, the Rockwall Independent School Board, the Rockwall Rotary Club Board of Directors, and the Rockwall City Council. Rockwall's Cameron Lake is named in Raymond's honor. Both he and Elizabeth were dedicated to the First United Methodist Church, with Raymond serving as a Sunday school teacher for more than 50 years. The Camerons donated the land for Amanda Rochell Elementary School and gifted thousands of dollars in scholarships to students attending Texas A&M University-Commerce. (Photograph courtesy of Elizabeth Cameron.)

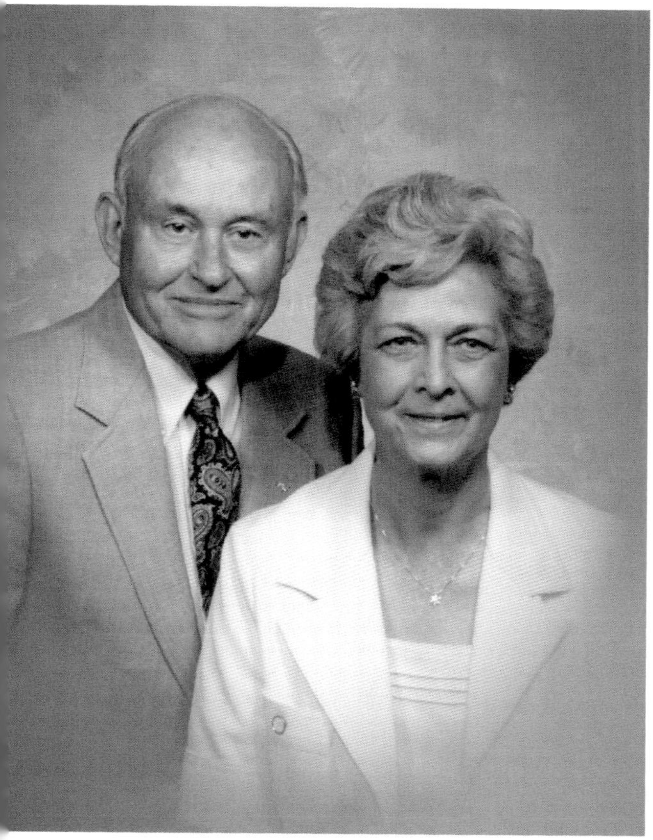

D.E. and Paralee Payne

Denton Elbert Payne (1912–1985) called J.D. after his father, James David, married Mary Paralee McLeod (1913–2006) on February 6, 1932. They had two children, Alfred Eugene and Carol Ann. J.D. served on the Rockwall City Council. Paralee founded the Rockwall Garden Club, taught Sunday school at the First United Methodist Church, and was a member of Eastern Star and of the Business and Professional Women's Club. The Paynes first owned a grocery store in Rockwall in the early 1940s but later opened a furniture and appliance store on the square that sold some of the first televisions in the area. People would gather on the sidewalk to watch the TV in the store's front window on Saturday nights, left on even after the close of business. At one point, the Paynes owned 13 buildings on the square in Rockwall. (Above photograph, courtesy of the Payne family; below photograph, courtesy of the RCHF.)

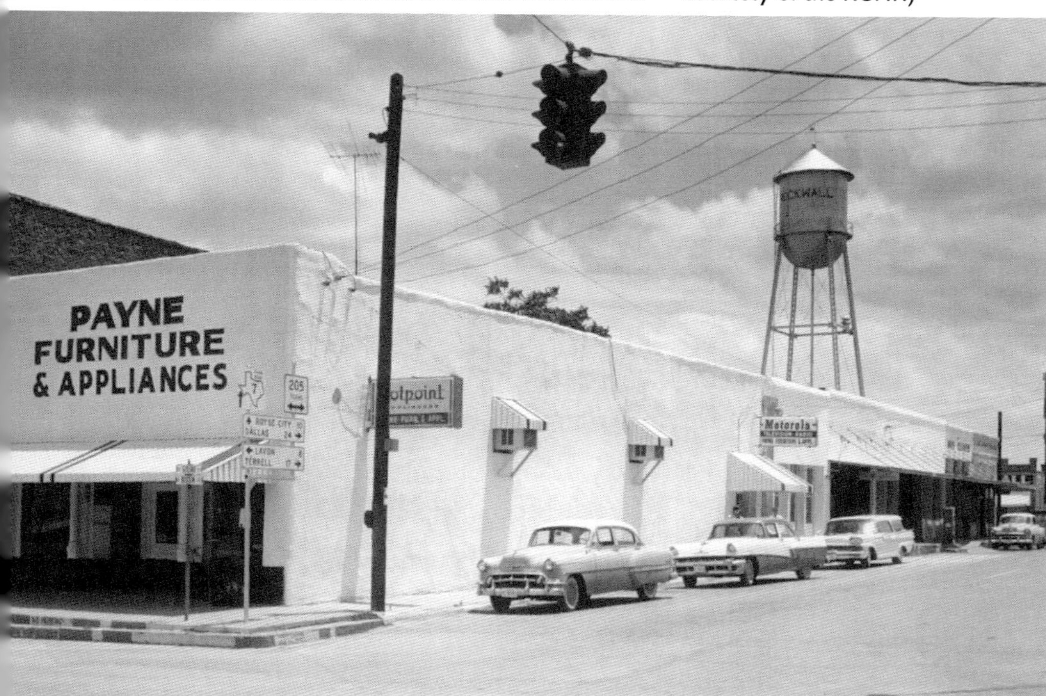

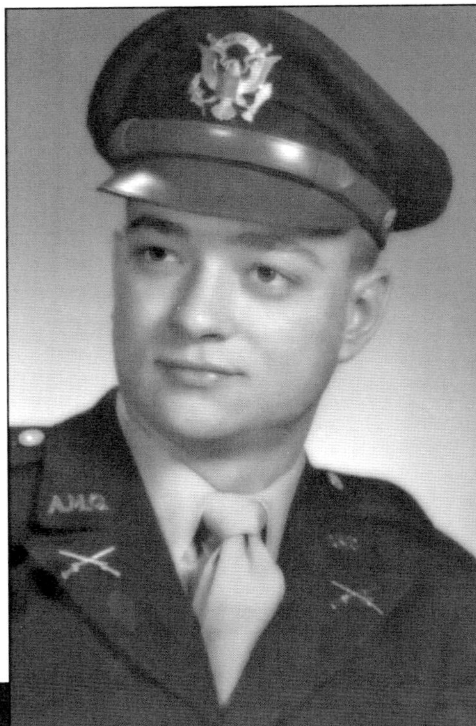

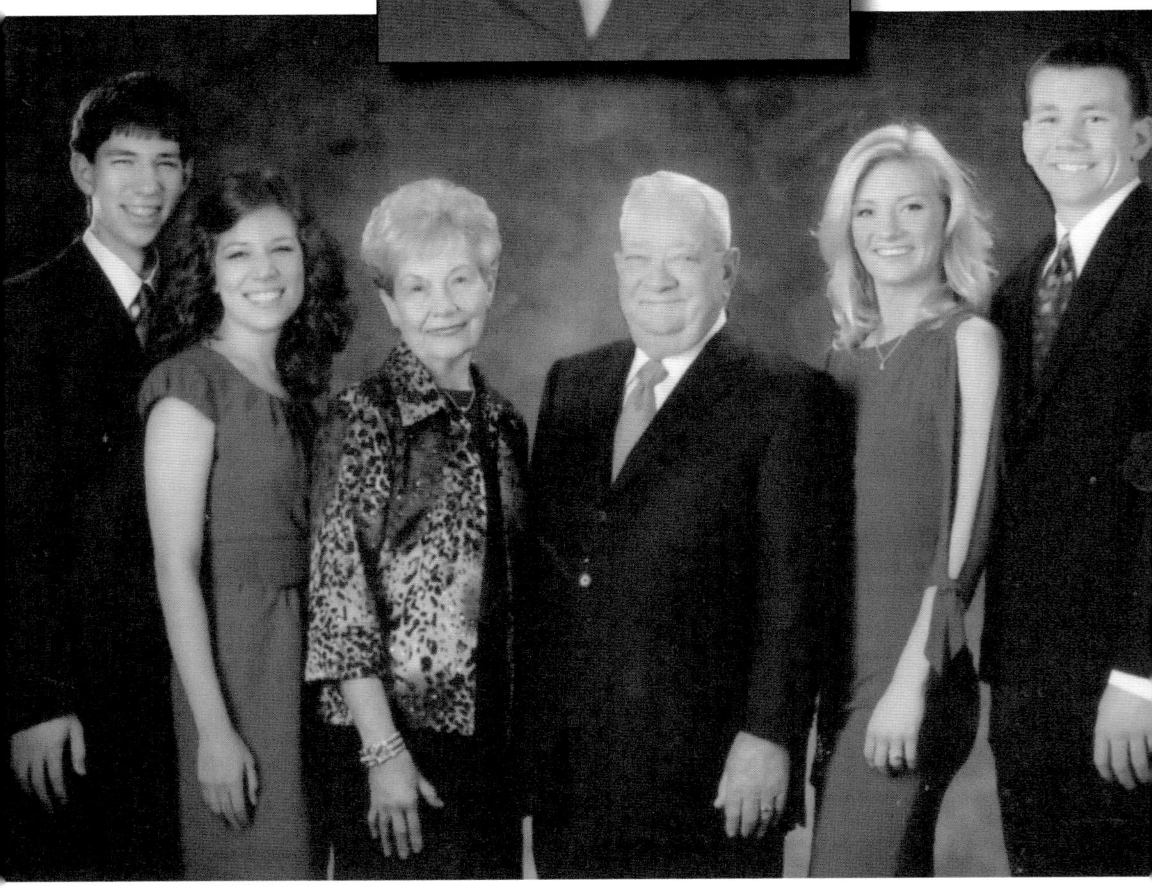

Joe Loftis

Joe Dowell Loftis Sr. was born in Royse City and moved with his family to the Rockwall area when he was in the second grade. He graduated from Rockwall High School in 1952 and earned his doctor of veterinary medicine degree from Texas A&M University in 1958. That same year, he and his wife, Jo Ann Rochell, moved back to Rockwall, where he opened a veterinary practice that is still operating today under the guidance of his son David Loftis. When he first began his practice in 1958, Dr. Joe Loftis said his patients stretched from Crandall to Blue Ridge and from Greenville to Garland. At that time, 90 percent of his business was in large animals. Today, the majority of the patients can be carried into the clinic. (Photographs courtesy of the Loftis family.)

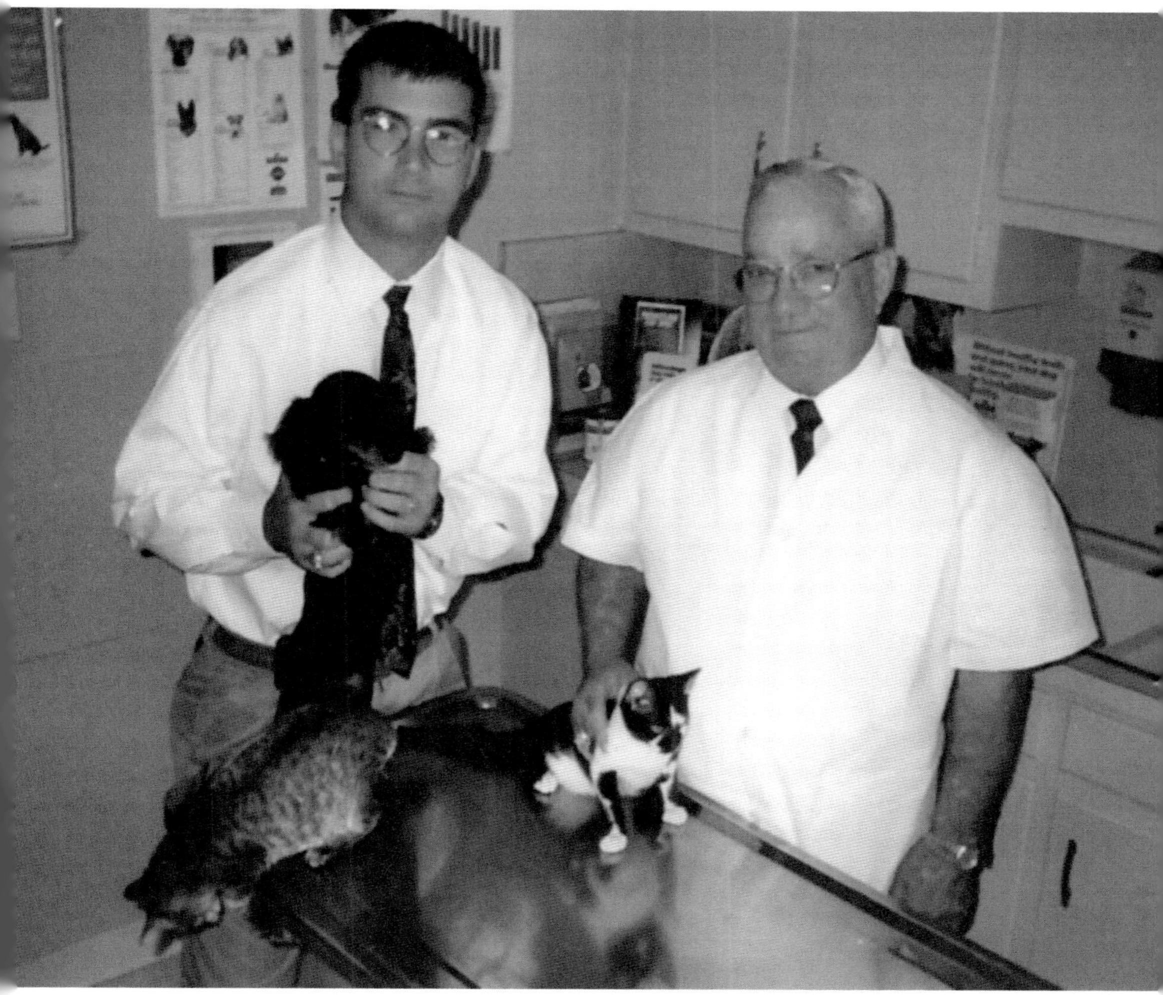

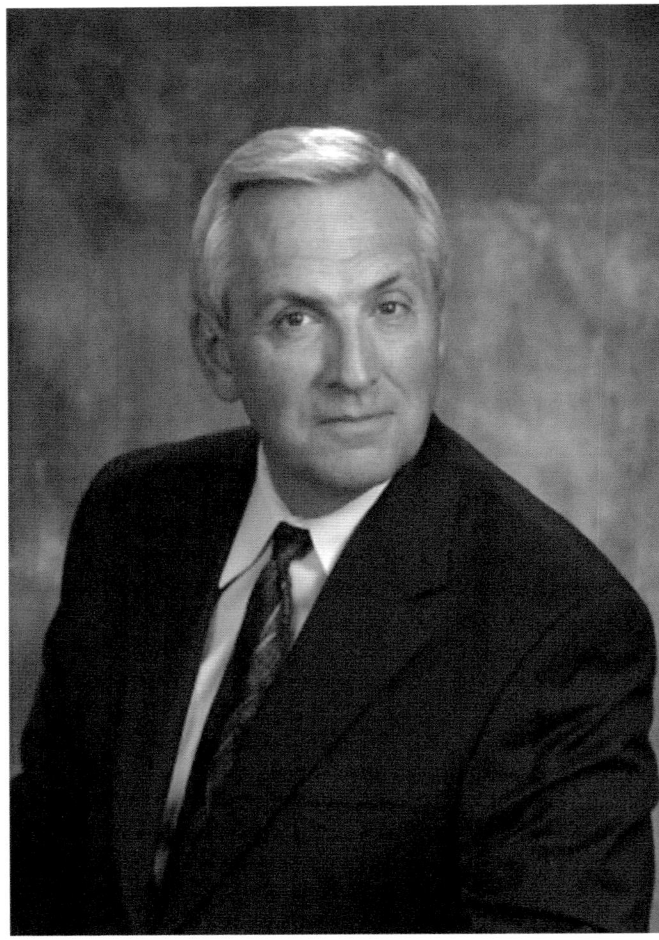

Larry Parks

Larry Parks, born December 7, 1947, in Shamrock, Texas, was raised in Memphis, Texas. He graduated from Memphis High School and attended the University of Texas at Austin on a landman's scholarship but later switched his major to finance, eventually earning a bachelor of business administration degree. Larry then followed his father into the banking industry. He was first employed by the Department of the Treasury as a national bank examiner in the East Texas/Oklahoma area, but he agreed to return to Memphis to the bank where his father was employed for a one-year period in the early 1980s. He started as executive vice president. A year later, when the bank was sold, he was bank president and chief executive officer. Along the way, he also earned a graduate degree in banking from SMU. Larry then began a job search that led him to move to Rockwall on April 15, 1985—or, as he refers to it, "tax-paying day," working for the First State Bank of Rockwall. He became president of the Rockwall office of the American National Bank of Texas in 1990 and was later named later regional president, which title he held until 2008. In 2011, Larry was elected an American National Bank of Texas board member, and he currently serves as the senior vice president of business development in Rockwall. A known UT enthusiast, Larry has endowed a scholarship in the McCombs School of Business at the University of Texas, Austin. Larry is an active participant in community organizations. He is a 30-year member and officer of the Rockwall Area Chamber of Commerce, a 29-year Rockwall Rotarian and club officer, has served 28 years on the board and as an officer of the Rockwall YMCA, devoted 21 years of service as a board member and officer of the North Texas Municipal Water District, spent 16 years on the board of trustees of the Lake Pointe Medical Center, 10 years as a board member and officer of the Consumer Credit Counseling Service of Dallas, and 5 years as a charter board member of the Heath Economic Development Corporation. Larry is also a longstanding member of the First United Methodist Church of Rockwall. To quote Mr. Parks, "The community of Rockwall has always demanded strong educational, cultural, and civic development. It has been a great experience to be a part of that growth." Larry is married, with a daughter, two sons, and two grandchildren. (Above photograph, courtesy of Larry Parks.)

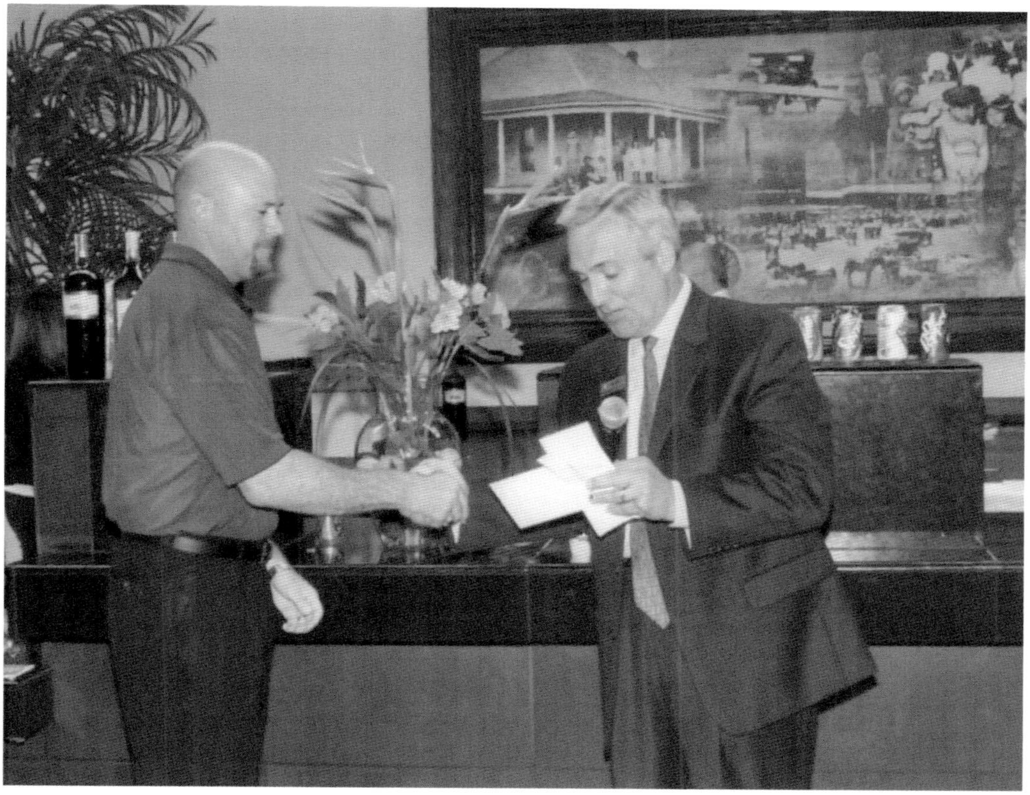

Larry Parks and Randy Hudson are pictured above at a bank-sponsored charity event. (Photograph courtesy of American National Bank of Texas.)

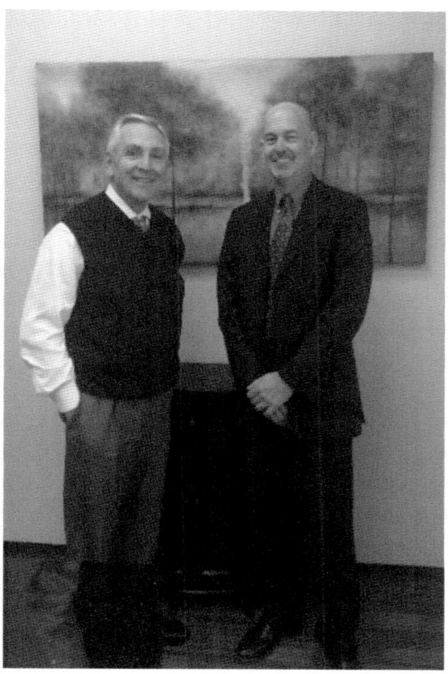

Larry Parks is pictured with Kevin Fowler, who has worked in the Rockwall banking industry for over 15 years and considers Mr. Parks his mentor. (Photograph courtesy of Amanda Fowler.)

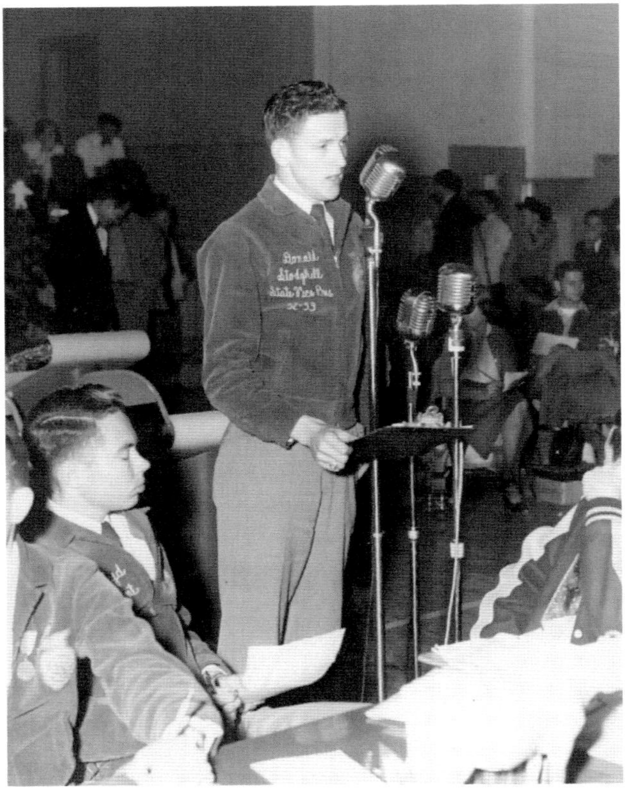

Donald R. Stodghill

A graduate of Rockwall High School, Don Stodghill was a local attorney and civic leader who served as president of the Rockwall Chamber of Commerce, president of the Rockwall Rotary Club, the first president of the Rockwall County Bar Association, and a member of many local clubs and organizations. During high school, he was state vice president of the Future Farmers of America and Rockwall County's only Lone Star Farmer. He received his undergraduate and law degrees from the University of Texas at Austin and worked for Dallas district attorney Henry Wade prior to returning to Rockwall to work in the law practice of Ralph M. Hall. Eventually, he established his own law firm and was well known in the North Texas area for his work in probate and real estate. (Photographs courtesy of the Stodghill family.)

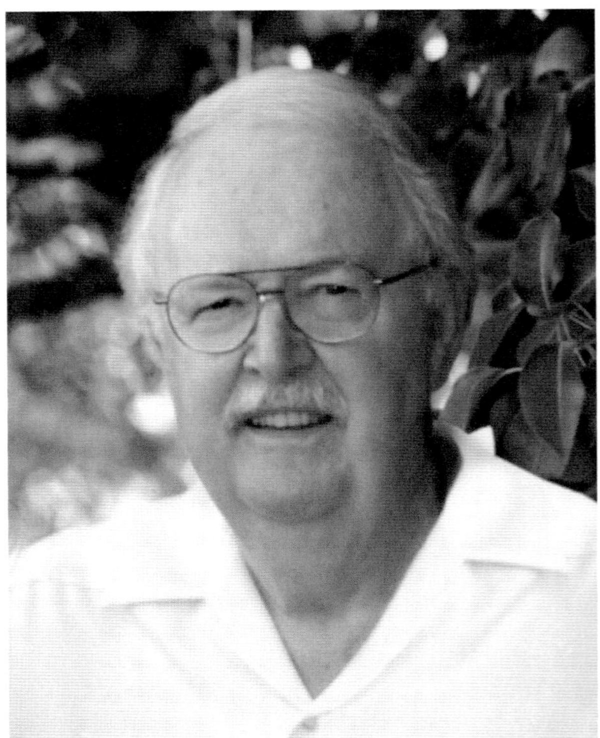

CHAPTER SIX

The Roads We Travel

While Rockwall has many legendary politicians, civic leaders, and businessmen, the backbone of its early economy can be traced to the many farmers who moved to Texas and transformed the blackland near the East Fork of the Trinity River into a thriving and successful farming community. It was not an easy task. Accounts of pioneer settlers describe the soil as so thick that it took eight oxen to pull a plow through it. Early crops included wheat, corn, and cotton, but the closest shipping points were Dallas or Terrell, locations a day's drive away by wagon, so transporting large amounts of crops for shipping proved challenging. This all changed in 1886, when the Missouri-Kansas-Texas railroad was constructed straight through Rockwall County and farmers gained a direct route by which to ship their crops. With this new development, both output and income increased.

By 1900, there were more than 1,000 farms operating in Rockwall County, most of them producing cotton. Eighteen cotton gins operated throughout the county, and Rockwall was representative of the well-known Southern phrase "Cotton is King." For many decades, these farmers provided the basis for the local economy; Rockwall County produced almost 19,000 bales of cotton in 1930—a record high. While their names do not often appear on buildings, these very important legendary locals are remembered through roads named in their honor, often located near their farms—many of which encompassed thousands of acres.

Long-tenured Rockwall residents will most certainly recognize the names Rochell, Bourn, Springer, Cornelius, Crawford, Zollner, Darr, Smirl, and Stodghill—all lifelong farming families who toiled tirelessly to make a decent living from the rich, blackland soil. While county residents travel these roads daily, they may not realize the significant contribution these farmers made to the community the current population of Rockwall now calls home.

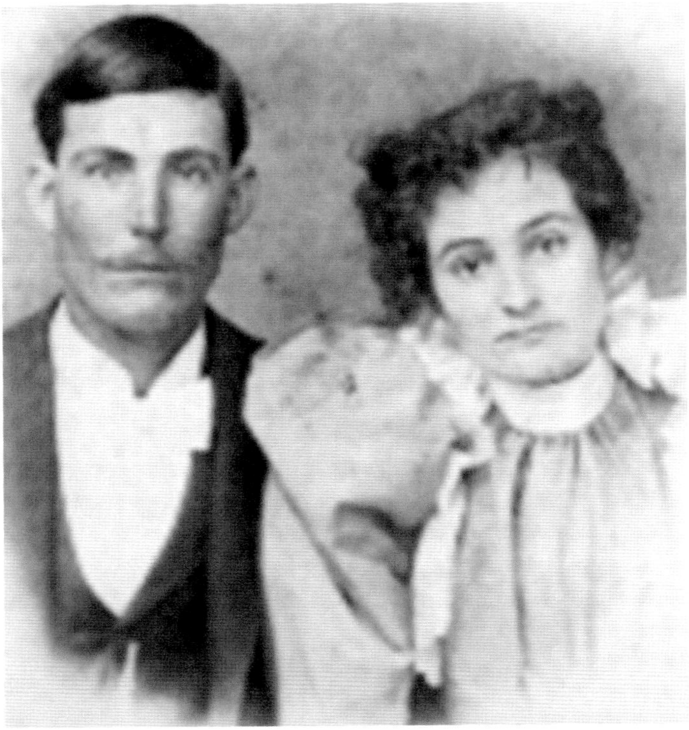

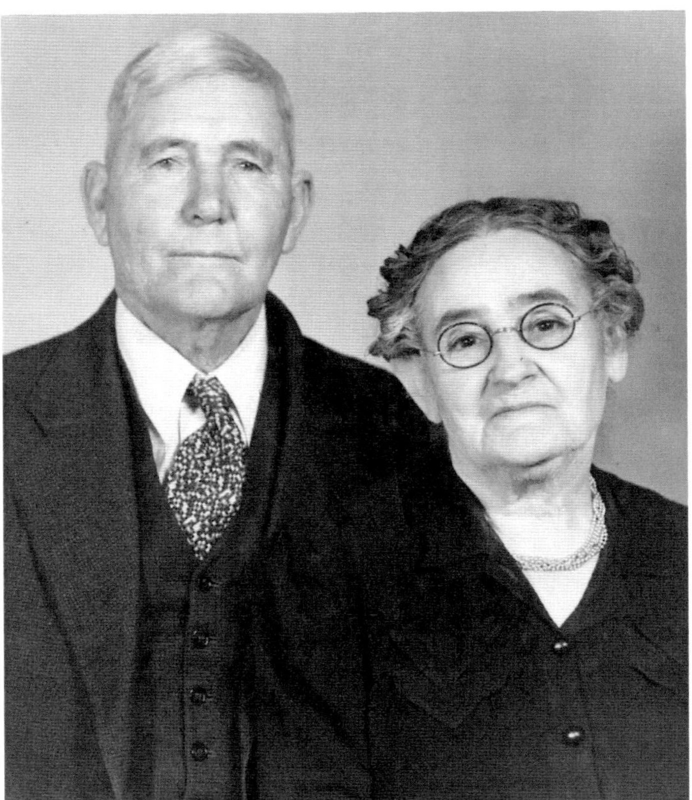

The Bourn Family
Robert Louis Bourn Sr. and his wife, Sarah Lancaster Bourn, traveled from Missouri to Rockwall in a covered wagon in 1856. In 1843, S.A. Rector and his wife, Amanda, had also settled in Rockwall, coming to Texas from Alabama. The two families were united by the marriage of their children, Ruben Louis Bourn Jr. (pictured on the left in both images) and Martha Leona Rector (pictured on the right in both images), who were wed on November 20, 1885, by a Methodist minister in a ceremony that took place in the bride's home. The couple was blessed with seven children. They had six daughters: Marguerite, Marion, Mable, Hattie, Leona, and Winnie, and one son, Ruben Louis Bourn III. The Bourns were a farming family and primarily raised cotton; all the children worked in the fields. Bourn Avenue now winds through land that was once the family farm. (Photographs courtesy of Terry Garrett.)

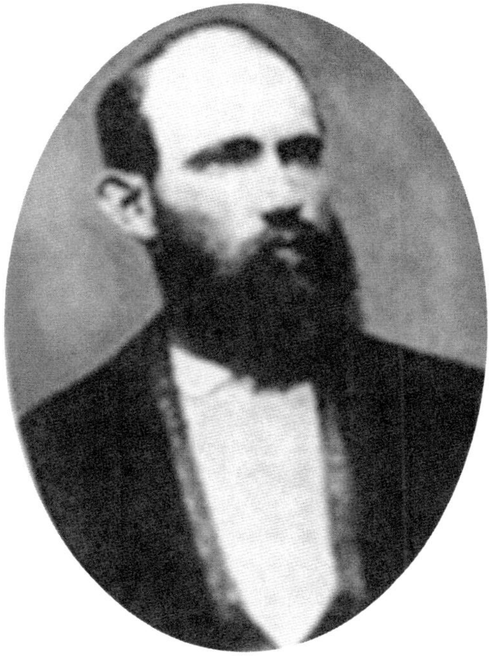

The McLendon Family

Preston Alexander and Anna Louise (Burch) McLendon came from North Carolina to Texas in 1869 and established a farm in the area that would soon bear their family name. By the early 1870s, the area boasted a general store, a cotton gin, and a blacksmith shop. A schoolhouse and church were soon constructed. Although the population remained small throughout the 1900s, the dawn of the 21st century saw a surge of development in the area, and McLendon Road now holds a prominent place in the Rockwall County community. (Photograph from author's private collection.)

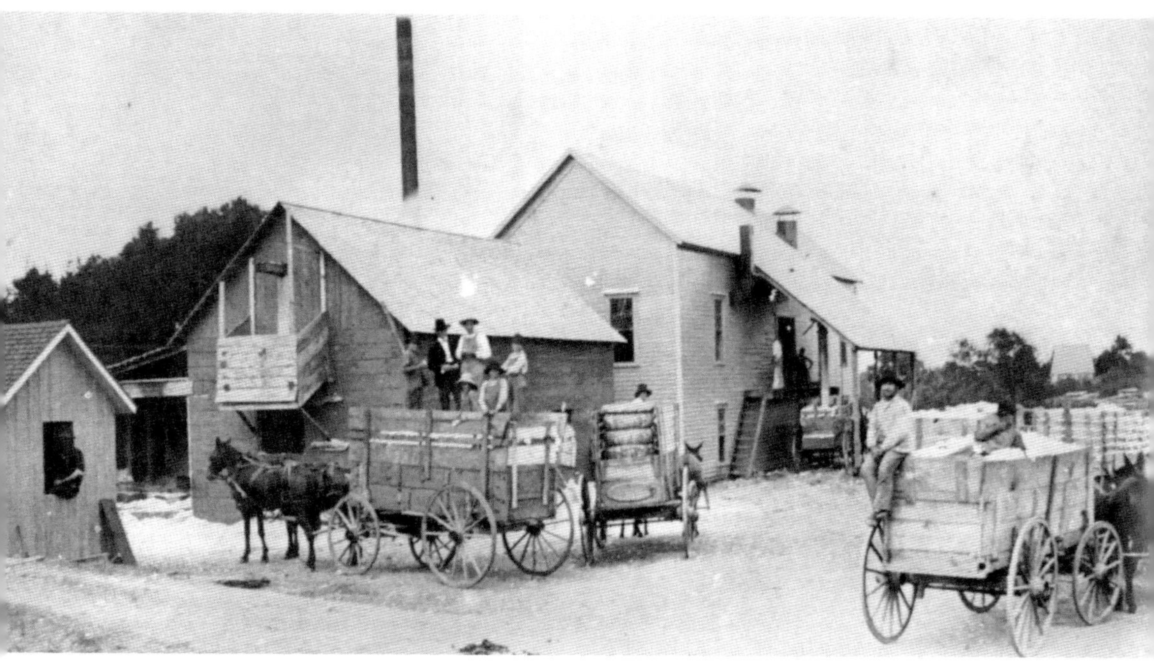

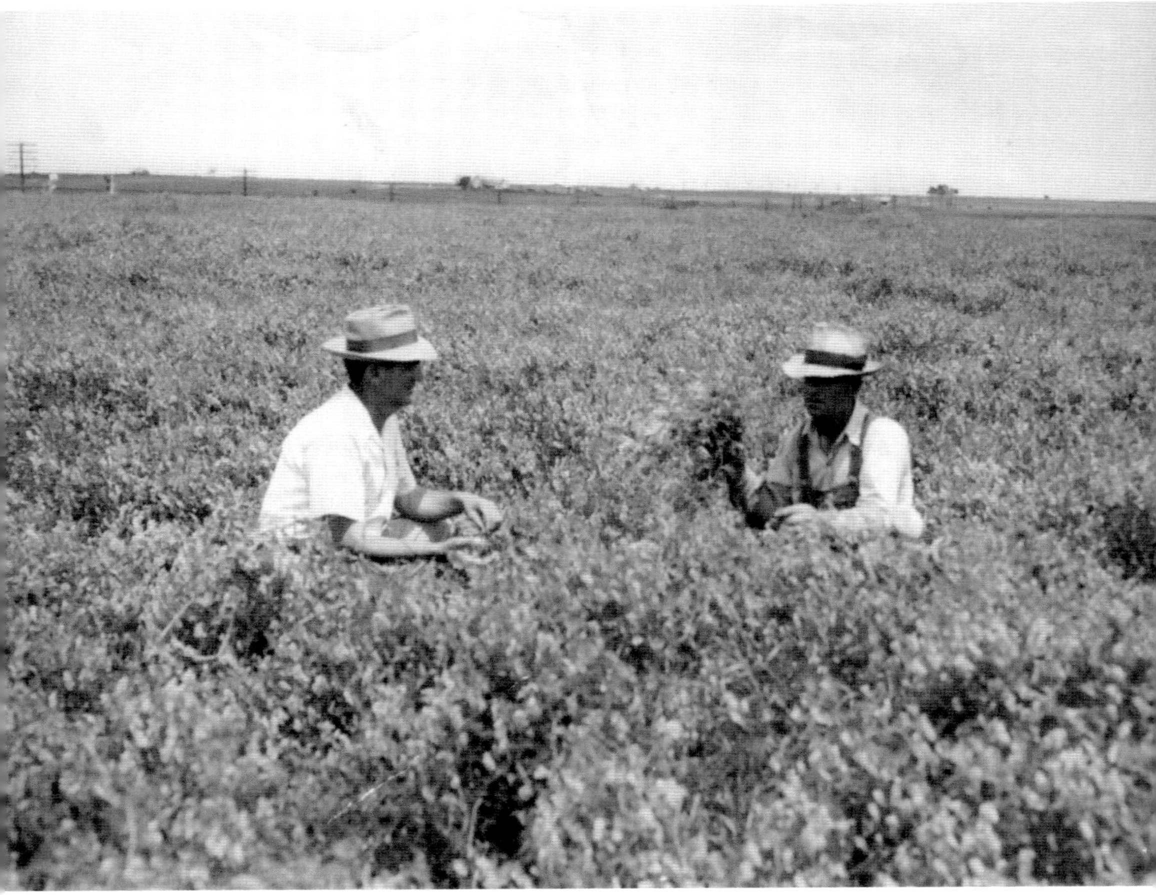

The Springer Family

Robert Springer purchased 80 acres of rich blackland soil east of the city of Rockwall and moved his family to Texas in 1905. The Springer family farm was not just a source of income, but it was also a source of immense pride. Through the years, Mr. Springer expanded his land holdings and implemented the most beneficial farming techniques, including rotating crops and terracing the land. He and his sons helped organize the Soil and Water Conservation District, which assisted farmers with their operations. Springer Road was named in honor of the family's contribution to Rockwall County's agricultural roots. Pictured above are Walter Springer (left) and Herbert Nation. Pictured on the opposite page, above, are Mettie Lou Ellison (left) and Robert Taylor Springer. (Photographs courtesy of the Springer family.)

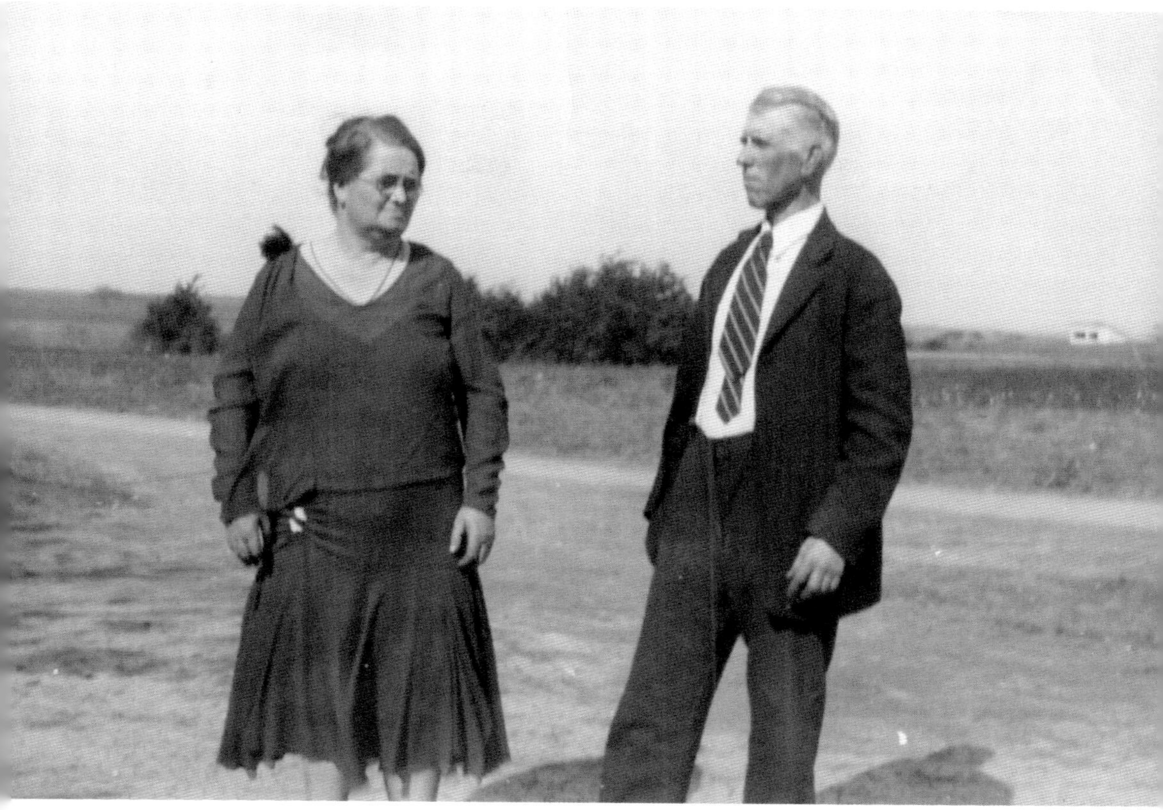

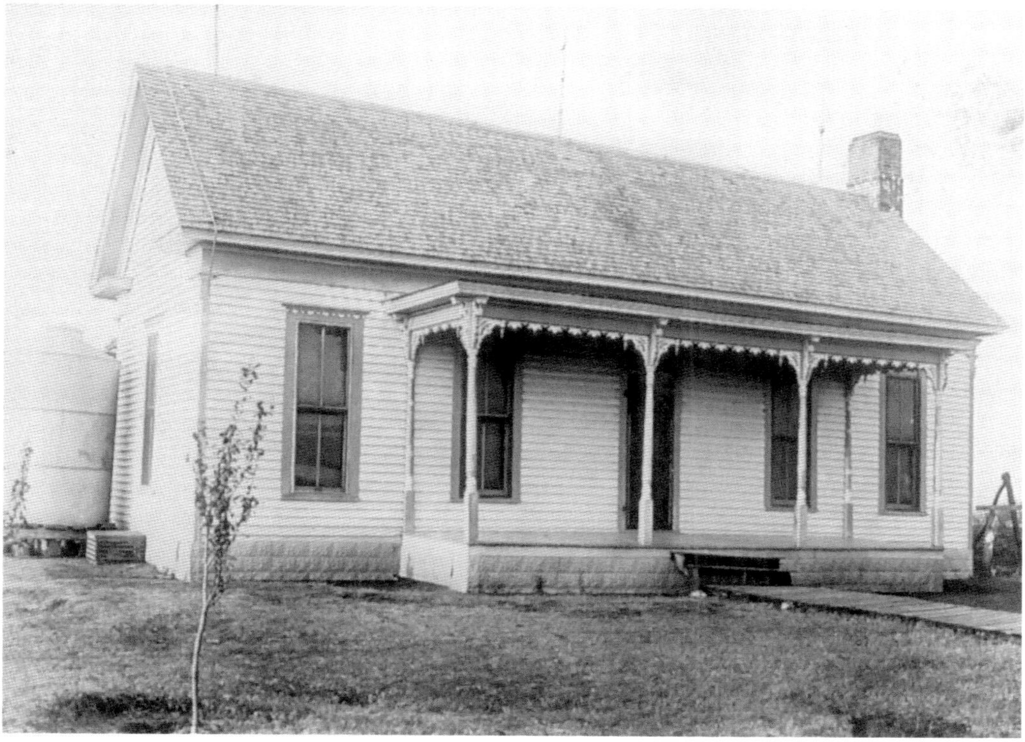

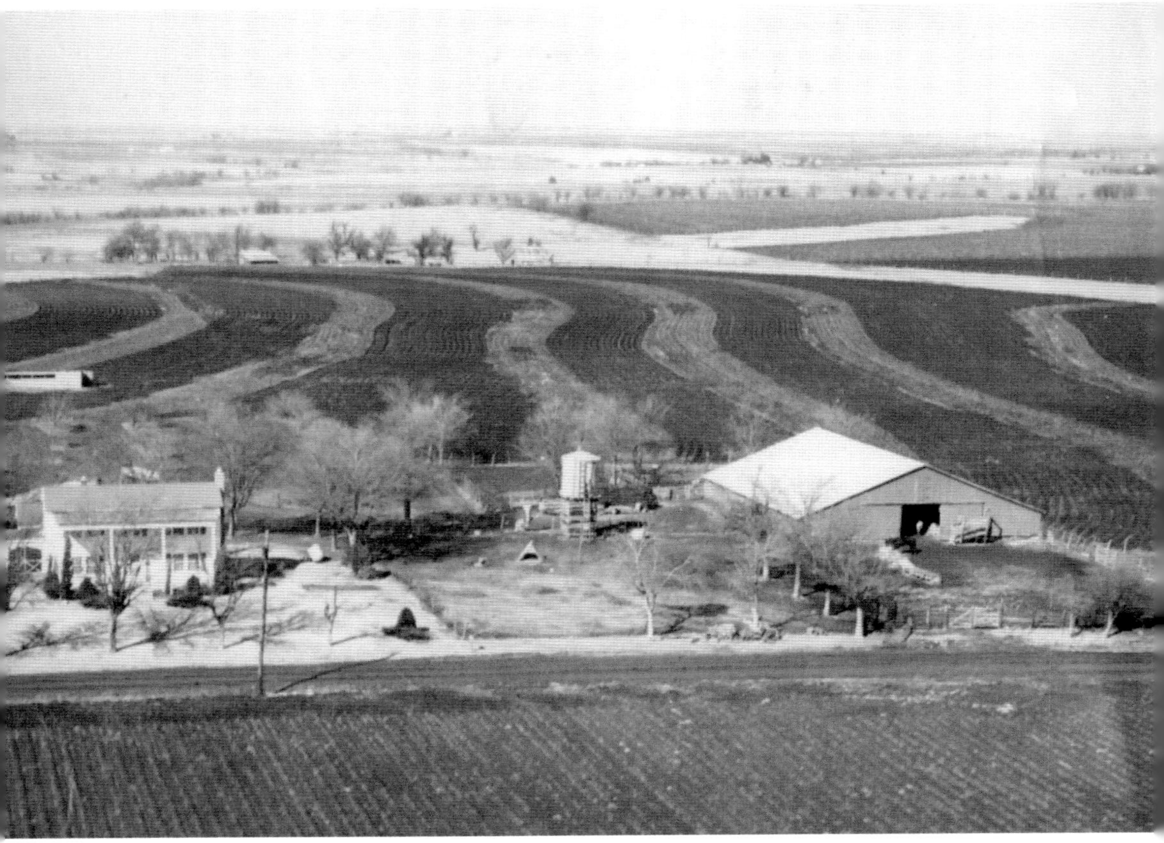

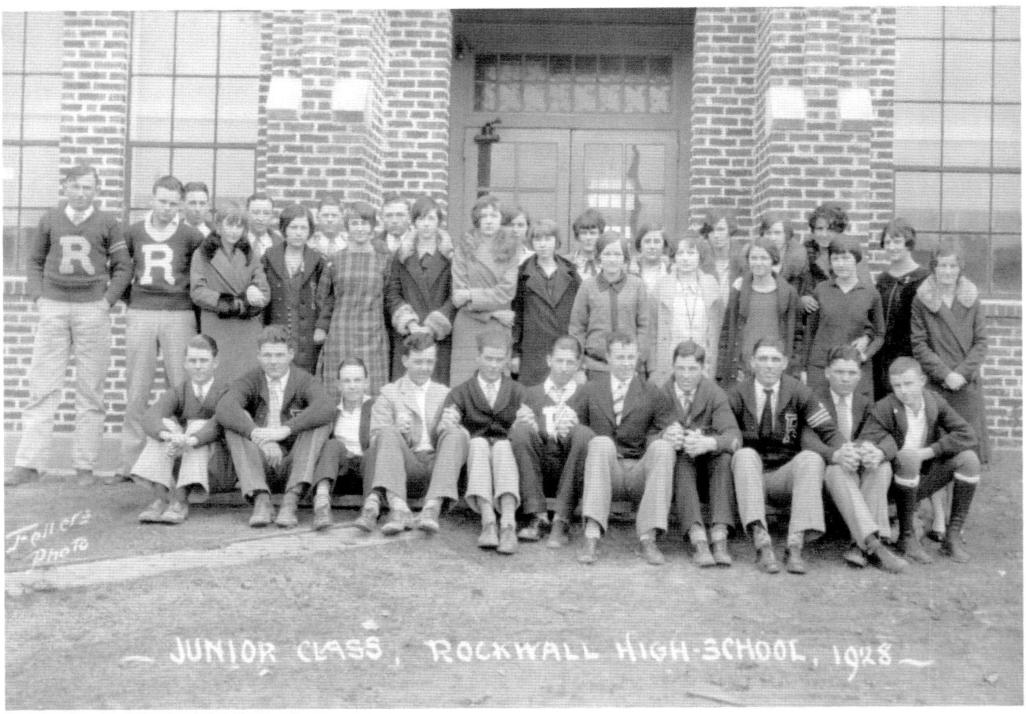
Fellers Photo
JUNIOR CLASS, ROCKWALL HIGH-SCHOOL, 1928

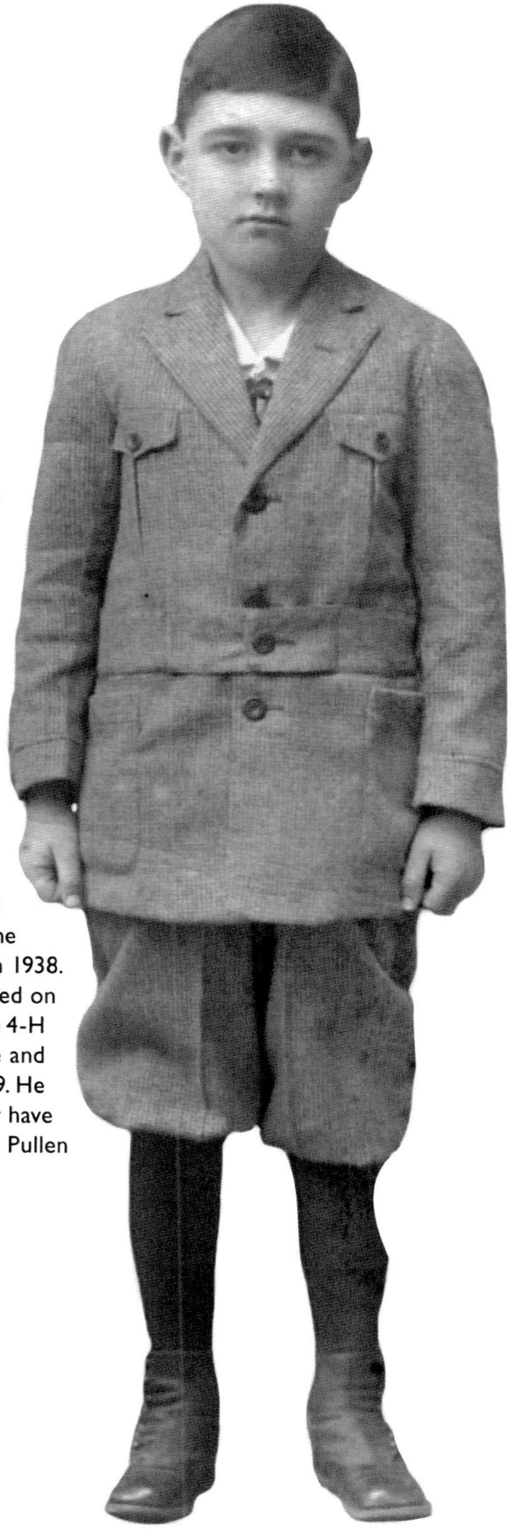

The Pullen Family
Pullen Road is most directly related to Bluford (B.T.) and Lottie Pullen, who moved to the McLendon area in 1981. B.T.'s parents were Martha Elizabeth and James Rayford Pullen, who came to Texas in the early 1900s and began farming on the Griffith League near Chisholm. B.T. married Lottie Bell Tapp in 1908, and they had one son, Jack Pullen, pictured here. The father-and-son team developed a flourishing farming life, both truly loving the hard work and reward brought on by such endeavor. They even made and repaired tools and operated a small blacksmith shop on their property. Jack Pullen was elected Rockwall County sheriff in 1936 and served for eight years. Due to his father's poor health, Jack opted not to seek reelection and instead devoted himself to the growth and development of the family farm. Jack married Dorothy Smith of Fate in 1938. They had one son, Jackie Smith Pullen. Jackie carried on the family farming tradition, as he became involved in 4-H and other agricultural programs through the state and his school. Jackie graduated from Texas A&M in 1969. He married Connie Holt of Vivian, Louisiana, and they have continued to maintain the family farm located on Pullen Road. (Photographs courtesy of the Pullen family.)

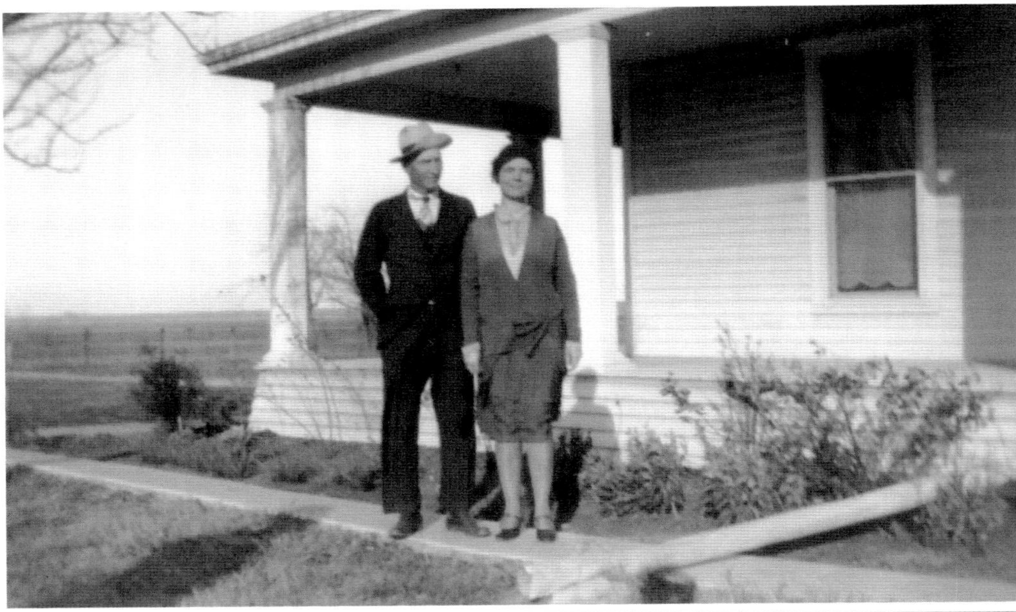

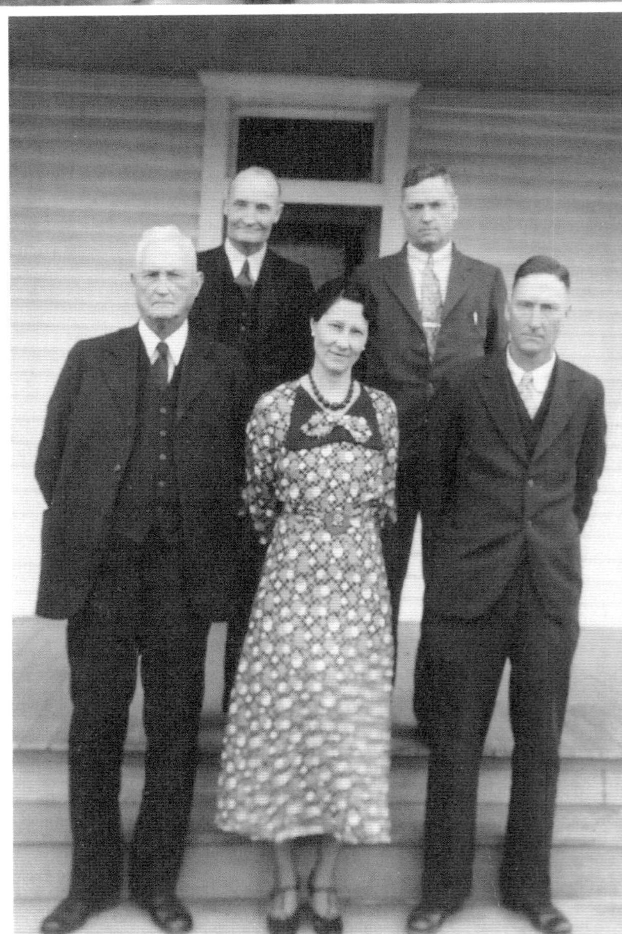

The Rochell Family
Born a poor farm boy in Alabama, Green C. Rochell came to Texas in 1880. Through hard work and determination, he became a successful and prosperous landowner. After the death of his first wife, he married Lanora Josephine Smith. They were the parents of one daughter and two sons. Although they lived in both Fate and Rockwall, the family eventually moved to the community of Nadine. Their home was a white, two-story farmhouse; Mrs. Rochell kept her house immaculately clean and enjoyed gardening. The Rochells occupied this home for many years. Later, their youngest son Henry and his wife, Emma Anderson (pictured above), lived in the home. Henry Rochell continued his family's farming tradition, growing mainly cotton and raising cattle for more than 50 years. Rochell Road, located near the family homestead on State Highway 276, honors this farming family and their contributions to the Rockwall community. (Photographs courtesy of the Rochell family.)

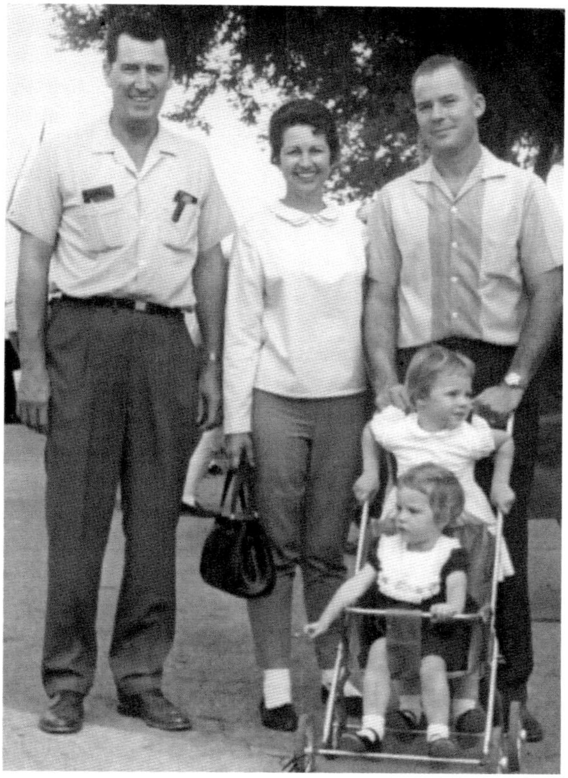

The Clem Family
Calvin and Ellen Clem had two children, John and Fern. Their farm was located northeast of Rockwall. John was a captain in the US Army during World War II, and after he returned home he managed the furniture division of Sanger's Department Store in Dallas. During the mid-1980s, he and Douglas Cullins owned a furniture store in Rockwall. John died in 1978 at the age of 60. Pictured from left to right are John Clem, Ila Cullins, Douglas Cullins, and daughters Danna and Saundra. (Photograph courtesy of the Cullins family.)

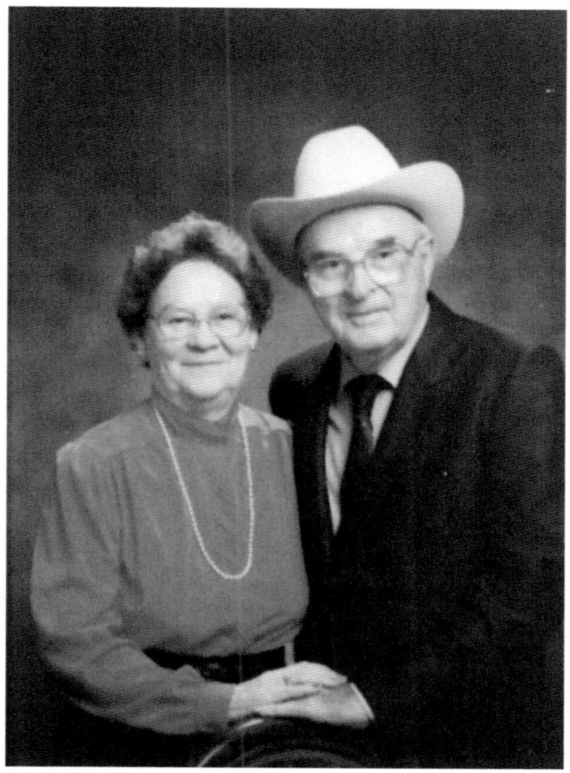

The Cullins Family
Edna and John "J.W." Cullins grew crops and raised cattle on their farm east of Heath. J.W. also served as a policeman in Rockwall and later in Heath. The couple had three sons: Douglas, Richard, and Johnny. Douglas married Ila Phares of Garland; they had daughters Danna, Saundra, and Terri. Richard married JoAnn Frazier of Rowlett; they had daughters Donna and Kym. Johnny married Jane Carney; they had daughters Amy and Kathy. (Photograph courtesy of the Cullins family.

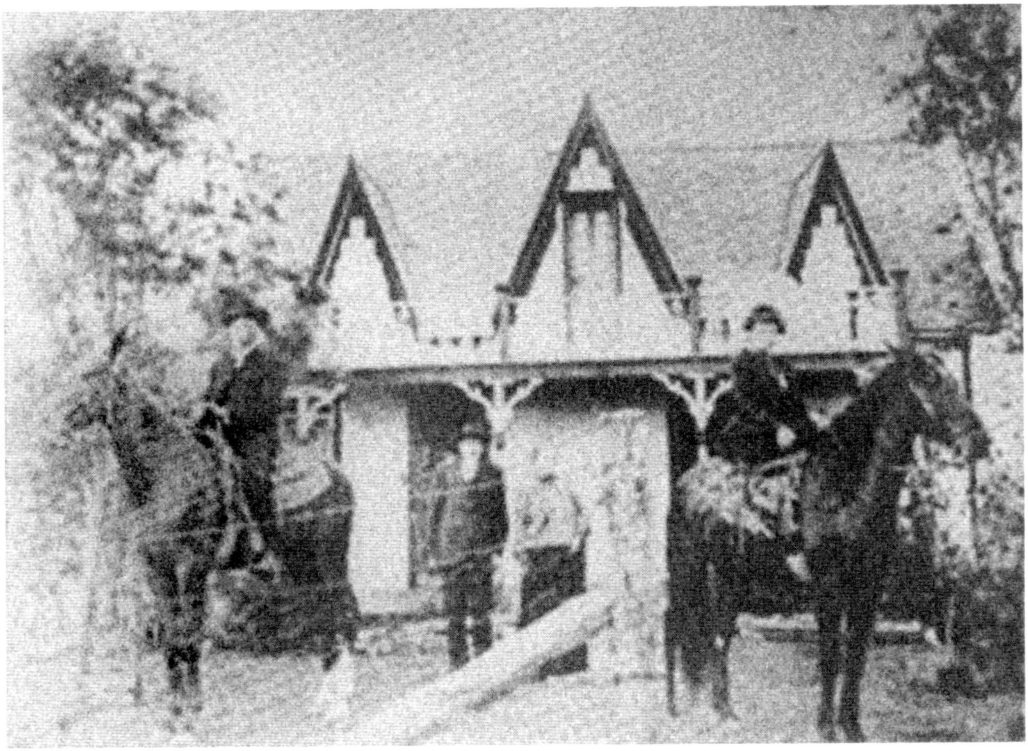

The Cornelius Family

In 1941, Ollie and Bertie Cornelius purchased a Rockwall County farm that had once belonged to his great-grandfather. Bertie concentrated on raising their 10 children and tending the garden, while Ollie farmed an extensive amount of acreage comprised of land he owned as well as land he leased. The road that runs in front of the former Cornelius homestead in northwest Rockwall now bears the name of this pioneer family. (Photograph courtesy of the Cornelius family.)

Mable Sears Dalton

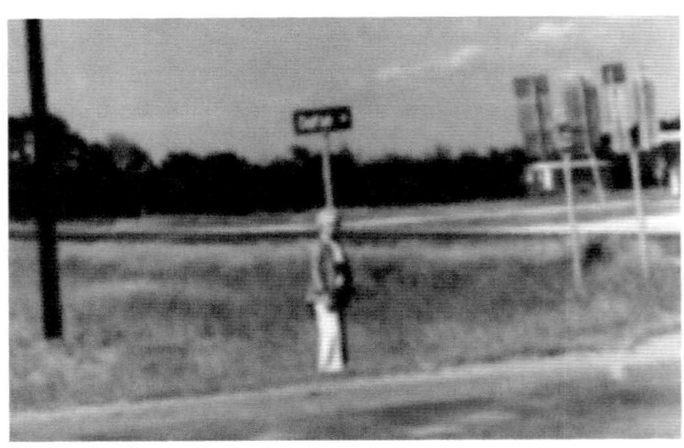

(Zora) Mable Sears Dalton (1908–2006) was born in Royse City but was a lifetime resident of Rockwall. She was a licensed vocational nurse and also held a dental assistant's license. During World War II, Mable manufactured airplanes at Majors Field in Greenville, Texas. She also assisted her husband, "Slim" Dalton, when he was a self-employed contractor for the Highway Department. Mable served as president and secretary of the Business and Professional Women's Organization, was a charter member of the Rockwall County Historical Foundation, a member of Grand Cross of Colors–Order of Rainbow for Girls, and an endowed member of the Order of the Eastern Star. She was also a member of the First United Methodist Church of Rockwall for 86 years. (Photograph courtesy of the Texas Parks and Wildlife Department.)

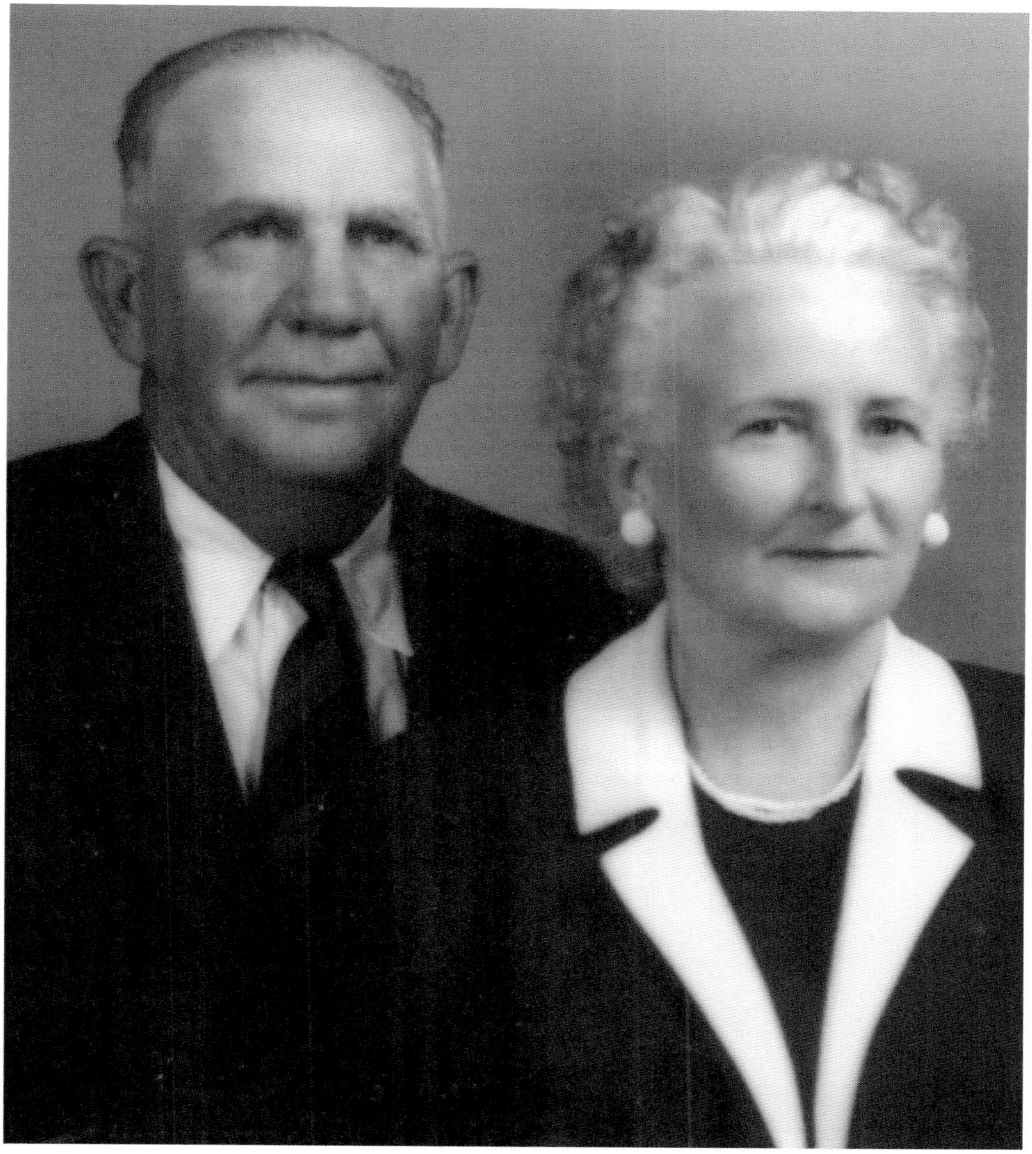

The Garrett Family
Tennessee native Elijah Garrett and his wife, Evalina, came to Texas seeking opportunity—which presented itself in the rich blackland soil and available markets for the cotton and wheat they planned to grow. The family settled on 140 acres just south of Fate and, over the next few decades, worked the farm that Elijah eventually transferred to his son William "Bill" Elijah, 1 of 10 Garrett children. After returning home from the war in France, Bill married Lockie Wooldridge in October 1919, and in 1925 Bill, Lockie, and their young daughter, Runelle, moved to the family farm in Fate and began building a life in the community. Daughter Billie Marian came along two years later, born in the back room of their little house. Like so many families in that time and place, their lives were centered around farm and family; work began before dawn six days a week, and Sundays were reserved for church and visiting. Their traditional values and strong character were typical of their generation, and they helped build a vibrant community. Along with raising crops and livestock, they also raised two career public school teachers. Lockie passed away in 1969, and Bill died in 1977. (Photograph courtesy of Billie Stevenson.)

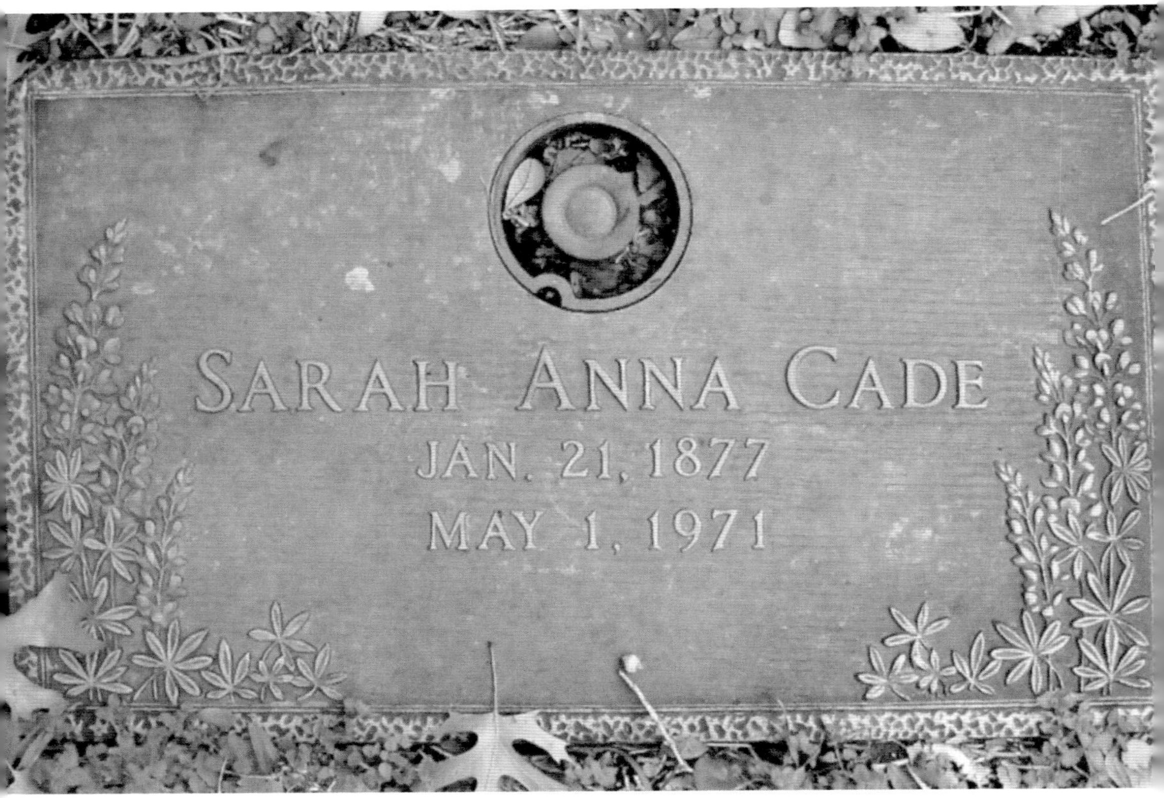

Sarah Anna Cade
George Edward Cade was born May 25, 1846, in Mississippi, the youngest of four children. He had two sisters, Sallie and Lizzie, and one brother. During the Civil War, George Edward was in the drum corps while his older friends were joining the army—some enlisting in the Confederate troops and some in the Union ranks—and George didn't want to fight any of his friends. He was 16 years old, and he wanted to farm the land and be a good citizen. George decided to journey to Texas with his sister Sallie and her husband, Melvin Douglas Penry. The trio arrived in Poetry, Texas, not far from Forney, on Christmas Eve, 1863; George Edward had 15¢ in his pocket. He stayed with his sister's family for several months, until they were settled in their new home, and then George traveled north through Kaufman County until he reached the Stephen Horn Gardenhire home north of Rockwall. He took a job as a day laborer and proved himself dependable and agreeable. On December 31, 1868, George married Mr. and Mrs. Gardenhire's daughter, Mary Alice, in the family home. George and Mary Alice had eight children: James Henry, Stephen Horn, Lee, Sarah Anna, Nora, Stella, Ada, and Robert Benjamin. George Edward Cade died January 19, 1909, and Mary Alice passed away November 26, 1935.

Sarah Anna Cade continued to live at the home place into her nineties. On the morning of May 13, 1968, the house, which was built in 1887, was struck and destroyed by a tornado. At approximately 4:30 a.m., Anna Cade was sleeping on the back porch when the force of the tornado blew her to the north fence of the property. She was pinned there by wire and lumber for 14 hours during the storm, finally discovered early that evening, about 6:30 p.m., by her nephew Foy Cade McCurry. He summoned help, and she was rushed to Baylor Hospital in Dallas, where she remained for 14 weeks. She contracted pneumonia, underwent thoracentesis (a procedure in which fluid is removed from the lungs by use of a needle inserted into the chest wall), and was confined to intensive care. Anna was then moved to a rest home, where she convalesced for an additional two months. After that, she went to live at the home of her niece, Mrs. Edward Savage, of Denton. Anna Cade passed away on May 1, 1971, at the age of 94. (Photograph courtesy of Restland Memorial Park, Dallas.)

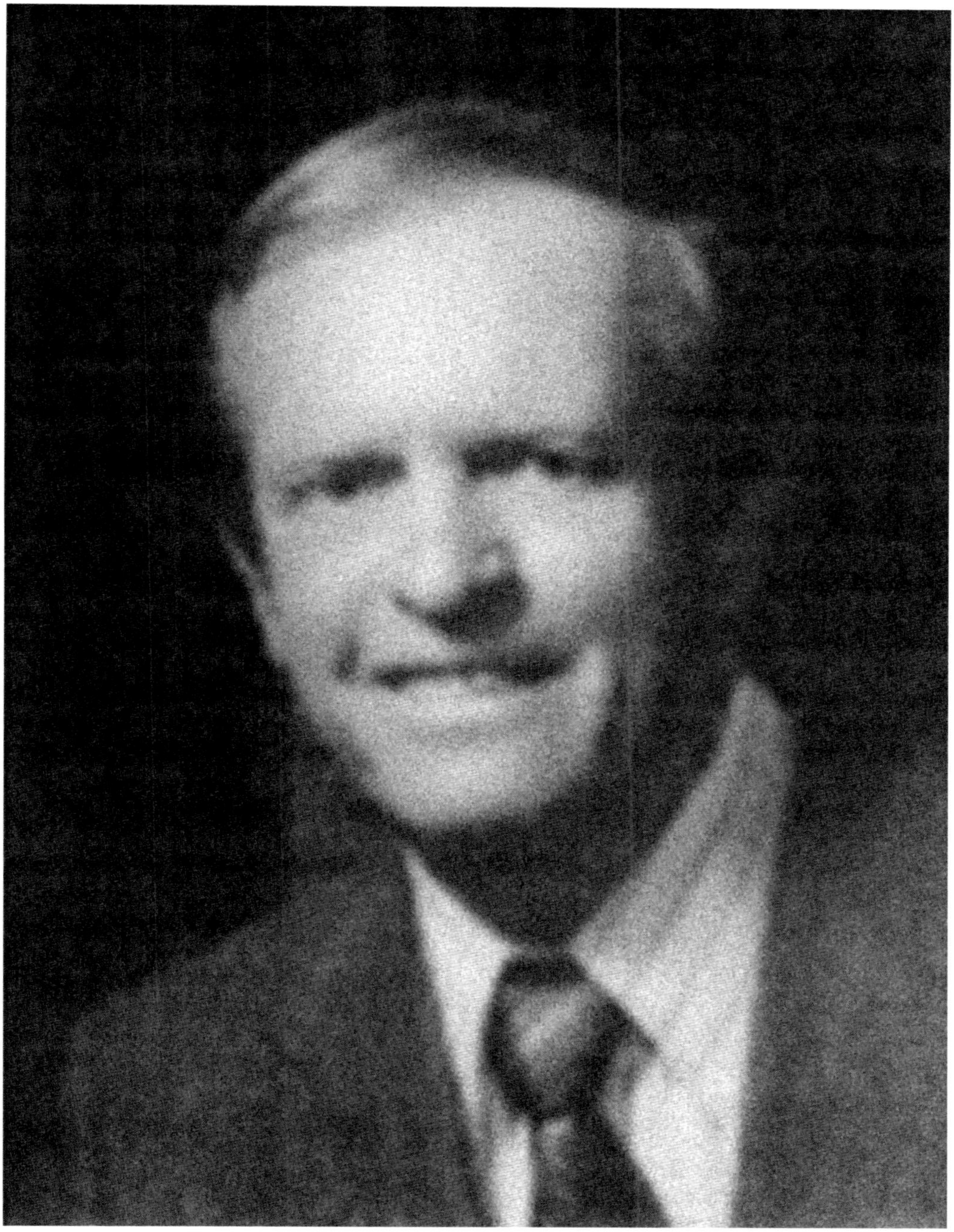

William Earl "Bill" Crawford
Descending from a pioneer farming family, Bill Crawford became the mayor of Fate in 1957. Prior to holding office, he was a successful farmer and rancher. He managed the Blackland Gin for 20 years, implementing new equipment and modernization techniques. W.E. Crawford Avenue is named in his honor. Working closely with his team and the city council, under Bill's guidance the Rockwall County community acquired modern water and sewage facilities. He served 26 years as mayor, always instilling in his constituents a sense of pride in their heritage. (Photograph courtesy of the Cullins family.)

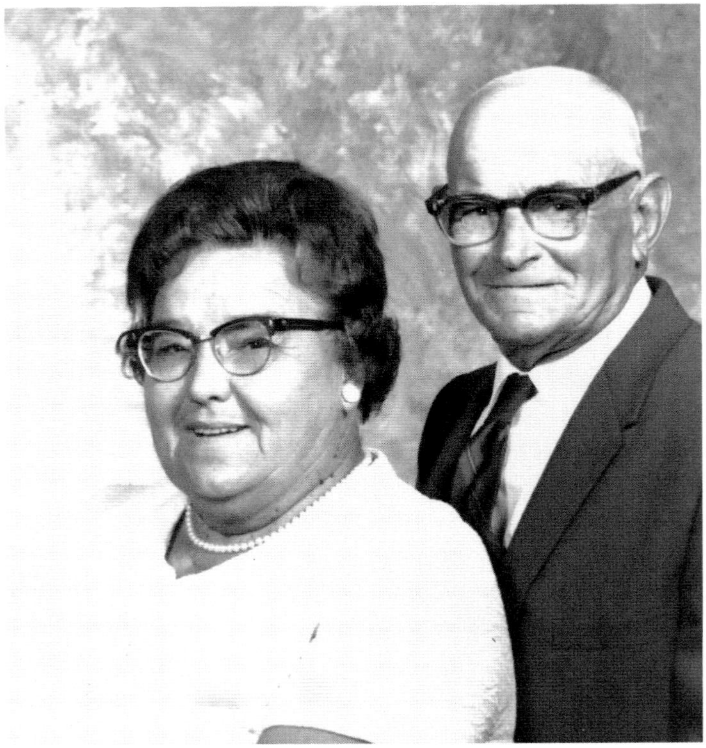

Rosa Lee (Darr) Seabolt and Will Seabolt (Photograph courtesy of Rosemary Klutts.)

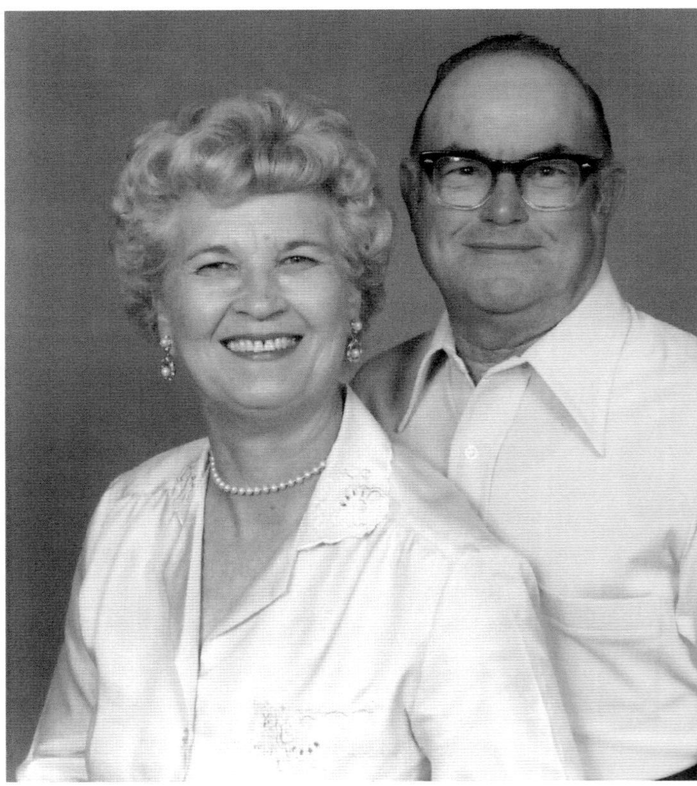

Jean and Bill Seabolt (Photograph courtesy of Rosemary Klutts.)

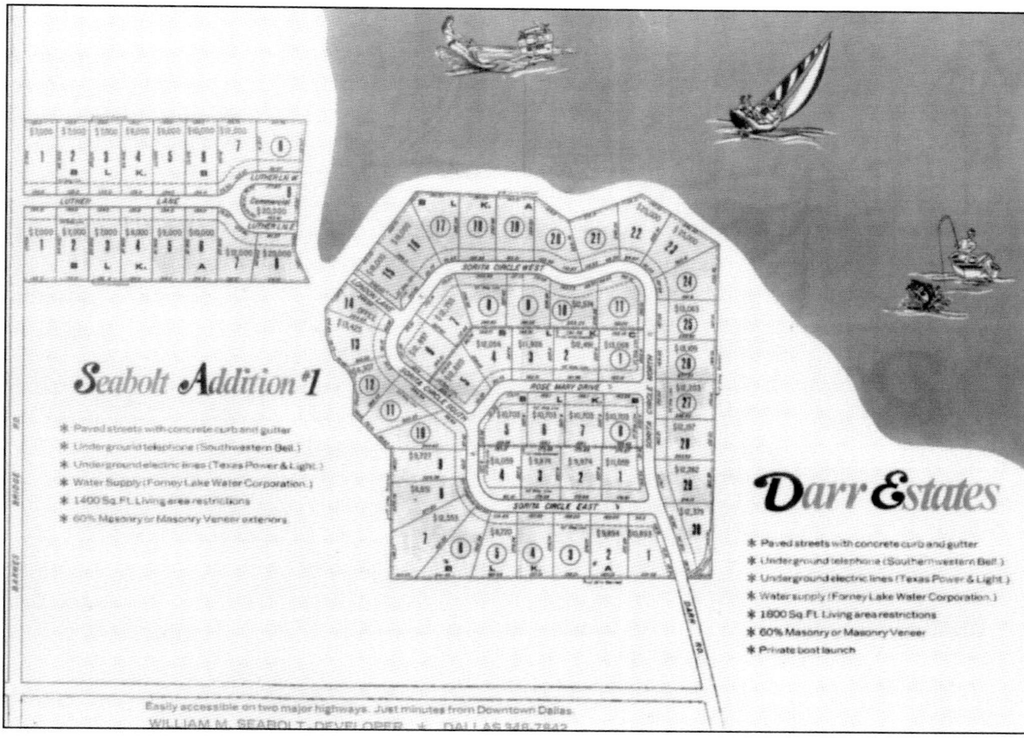

The Darr Family

Felix L. Darr was born June 10, 1857, in Rockwall County and married Mary Jane Adams on February 6, 1898. (Mary Jane was born in Georgia on January 2, 1878.) They made their home on what is now known as Darr Road. To this union, two daughters were born: Emma, who died in infancy; and Rosa Lee (Darr) Seabolt, born on April 1, 1900. William Thomas Seabolt and Rosa Lee wed in 1916 and began their married life on Darr Road, which was nothing but a dirt lane at the time. To this union, three sons, Willie Lee, William "Bill" Maon, and Michael Gene, and two daughters, Rosemary (Klutts) and Sorita Lou (Frasier), were born. The family farmed the land in cotton and corn and raised cattle, pigs, and turkeys. When Lake Ray Hubbard was created, Bill Seabolt convinced his parents, Will and Rosa Lee, that it would be a good idea to develop the property they owned around the new lake into home sites. The development of the 49.96-acre Darr Estates in Heath, Texas, began in 1967 under the title of Rosalee Development Co., Inc., owned jointly by W.T. Seabolt and Rosa Lee Seabolt. The platting of Darr Estates was engineered by Harold Evans and approved by Alvis Nash, mayor of Heath, on October 9, 1967. Two of the streets in Darr Estates are named Rosemary Drive and Sorita Circle, after the Seabolt sisters. The first lot in Darr Estates was sold to Jack Woodard on April 15, 1969. Will and Rosa Lee Seabolt lived to see Darr Estates completed and to witness two of their children build homes on the property. Quite frequently, during the construction phase of Darr Estates, Will could be observed leaving his home in Heath and heading to the site on his red Farmall tractor, as he was not allowed to drive Rosa Lee's car. As for Rosa Lee, she enjoyed driving her big red car around the development with a hoe in her hand, tidying up around the trees and street curbs. After the completion of Darr Estates, Will and Rosa Lee's son Bill Seabolt developed the 18 acres of the Seabolt Addition on Terry Lane (formerly known as Barnes Bridge Road) in Heath, Texas. Luther Lane in the Seabolt Addition is named after Bill and Jean Seabolt's son Luther. (Map courtesy of Rosemary Klutts.)

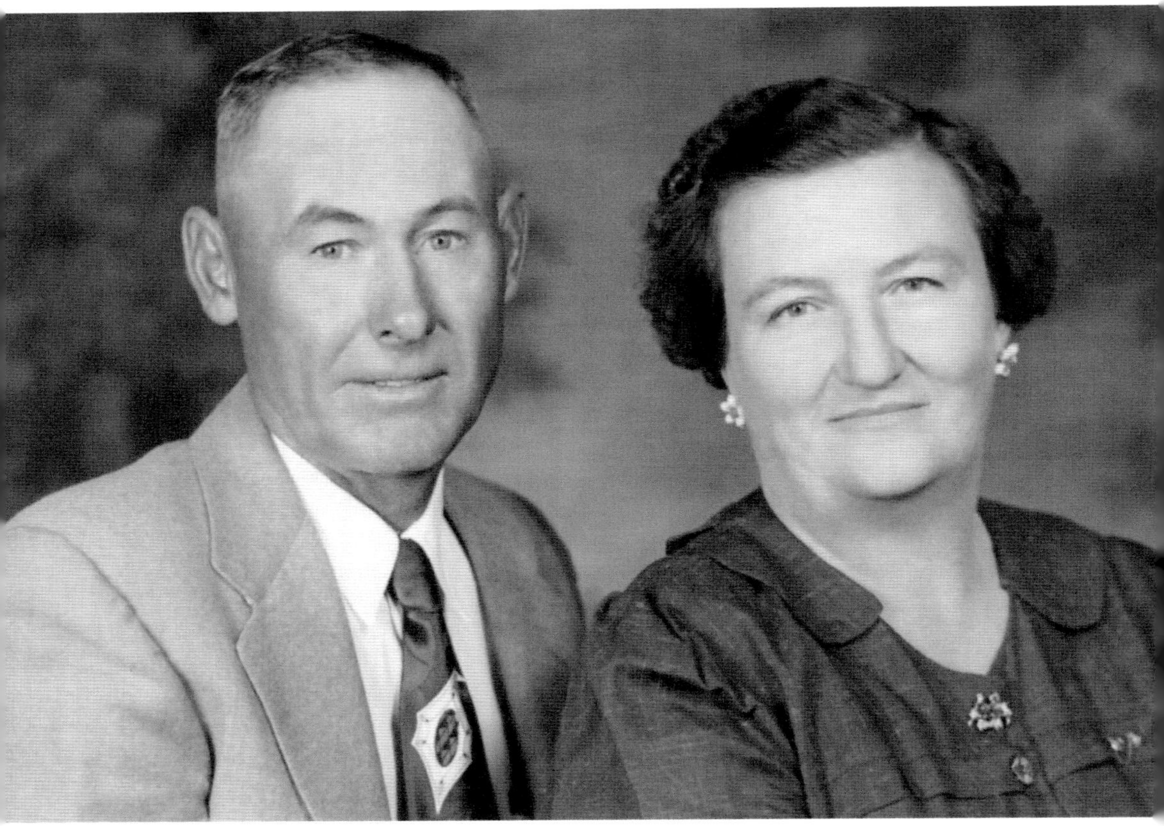

The Smirl Family

The Smirl family lived on a one-way concrete slab road that is now Laurence Drive in Heath. Clarence Smirl was a farmer who worked the land with his father-in-law, Milton Evans, for several years. He and Gladys Evans Smirl had six children: Neta, Theresa, Clarice, Huey, Claudetta, and Carolyn. In 1942, he decided to buy a farm along what is now known as Smirl Drive. The farmland was grown over and in bad condition, and Clarence asked his children if they would work and help pay for it. They worked hard to cut down trees and remove stumps from the rich bottomland. Clarence took his children to the cotton fields when they were just six years old and let them pick cotton into onion sacks. As they grew older, they were given four-foot sacks of their own. Clarence was also an avid hunter and fisherman. He caught abundant amounts of fish for his family to eat and hunted mink in the winter months. He would skin the mink and dry them on boards and then sell the skins for income. Smirl Drive was a dirt road in 1942. The children had to walk a half mile to catch the bus in order to attend school at Heath, and they always started the fall school term late because they could not attend classes until the family's cotton was harvested and they were no longer needed as pickers. It became a two-lane paved road in 1952. All six children grew up in Heath, were married in Heath, and for most of their lives have lived in Heath, within two miles of one another. Four of the children have homes that front Smirl Drive and are built on part of the land that Clarence farmed; the other two built homes on what is now Laurence Drive. The best part of the farmland Clarence owned was covered by Lake Ray Hubbard in 1968. Another part of the farm was sold to a developer who built homes in the Cove Ridge subdivision. The sale of the land to the state for the lake and the development of Cove Ridge supported Clarence and his family as he decreased active farming. Years after Clarence passed away, Gladys continued to raise cattle on what remained of the farm. As time passed, she sold more land to support herself financially until her death. Later, two more subdivisions were built on this land and developed as Cedar Glen Estates and Woodbridge Creek Estate. Pictured here are Clarence and Gladys Smirl. (Photograph courtesy of the Smirl family.)

Pictured from left to right are patriarch Clarence Smirl, matriarch Gladys Smirl, baby Jeffrey Jones, Neta Smirl Jones, Wayne Jones, Theresa Smirl Lindsey, baby Denise Lindsey, Dennis Lindsey, Carolyn Smirl, Huey Smirl, Claudetta Smirl, Clarice Smirl Isbell, and Joe Frank Isbell. (Photograph courtesy of the Smirl family.)

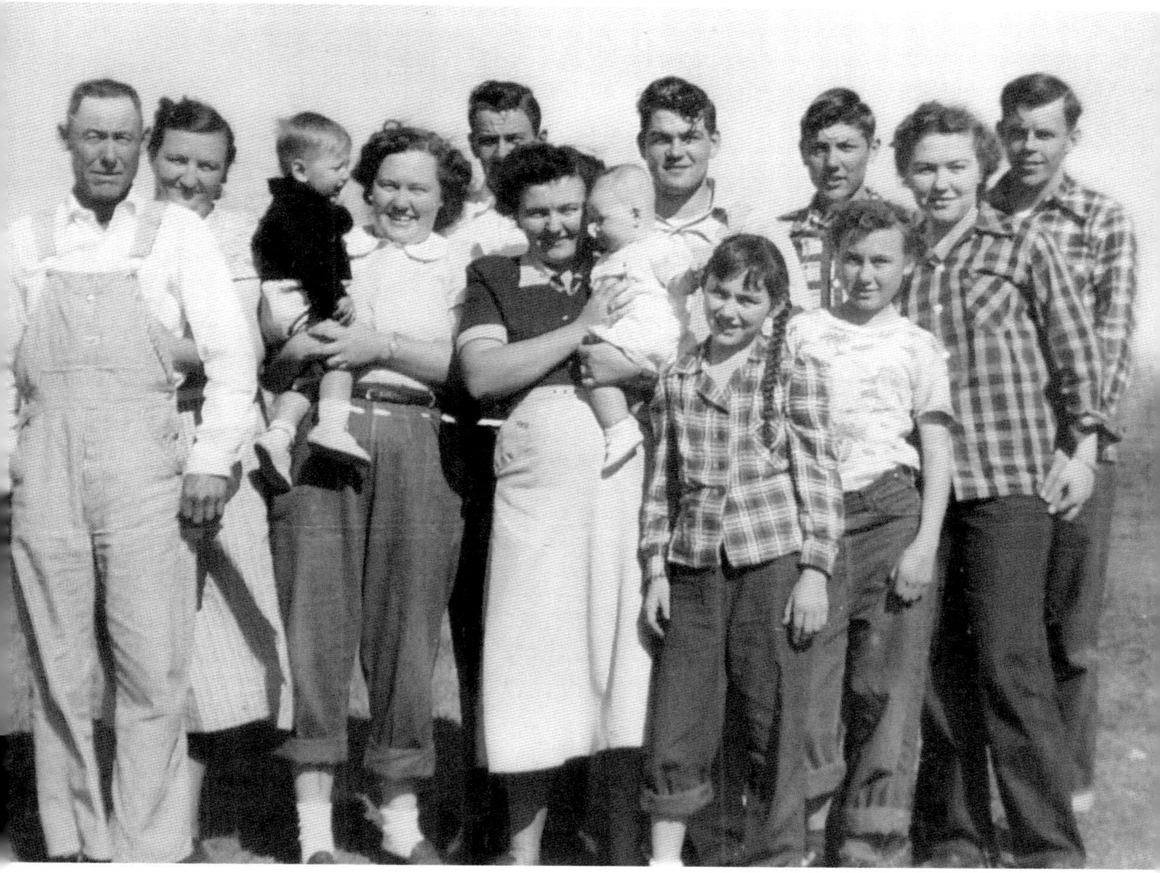

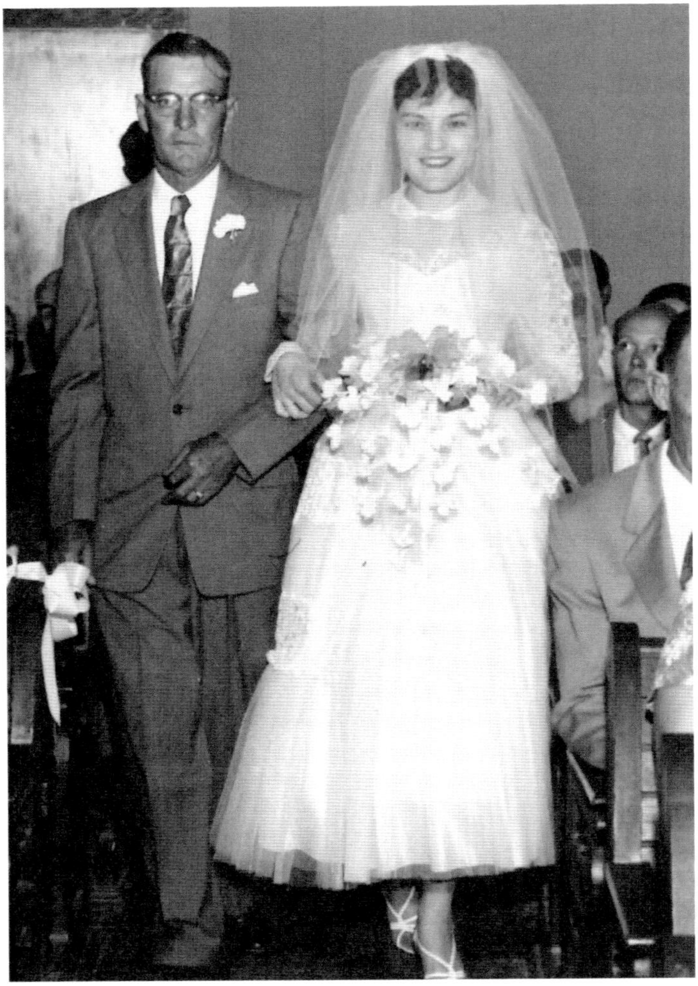

The Terry Family

The Terrys were one of the earliest families to settle in Heath; their farm was located near the Barnes Bridge section of the Trinity River. Many large pecan trees grew on their land. Elijah "Lige" Washington Terry (1879–1957) came from Tennessee and settled in Texas with his wife, Alaska Masonhammer (1882–1908), and their three young children, Elmer, Faye, and Mable. After Alaska's death from pneumonia, Lige married Ina Nancy Robertson Lemmons, who had one son, Alton, from her previous marriage. Together, the couple raised an additional eight children: twins Waymond and Raymond, Austin, Lorene, Mildred, Clyde, Mary Jo, and James Leon. Another child, Preston, died in infancy.

Waymond Terry married Louella Lincoln after his first wife passed away. They had three daughters: Barbara, Betty, and Charlotte. Louella died giving birth to Charlotte, so Raymond (Waymond's twin), knowing that his brother would have his hands full raising two growing girls on his own, adopted Charlotte at birth, and he and his wife raised Charlotte as their own child. Later, Waymond married Aileen Evans, and they had children Ronnie and Kennedy. In later years, both Waymond and his youngest son, Mark, resided in Fate.

Raymond Terry, often called "Cotton," was born in Archer City, Texas, on March 17, 1910. He married Leona Elvada (1908–1972), and they moved their young family to Heath in Rockwall County. They had two children of their own, Charles Ray and Joy Faye, as well as Charlotte. Cotton was a farmer and was Rockwall County commissioner for 22 years. He and Leona were active, faithful parishioners of the Heath Baptist Church; he became a deacon in 1940 and served in that capacity until his death in 1978. Their home was located across the street from the church, and Leona served as custodian of the church for many years; she and Raymond also took care of the Heath cemetery. After Leona died, Raymond married Virginia Canup, and they moved to Rockwall in 1975.

The grandchildren of Lige Terry fondly remember the fun-filled days at the farm in Heath. Sometimes, there would be as many as 10 grandchildren visiting at once, playing in the cane patch and the cottonseed bin and having picnics down by the river. Granddaddy Lige would say, "It takes me all day Monday to get this place back in shape after you kids have been here," but deep inside he loved those visits so much.

Pictured above is Raymond walking Charlotte down the aisle of the First Baptist Church of Heath on her wedding day. (Photograph courtesy of the Terry family.)

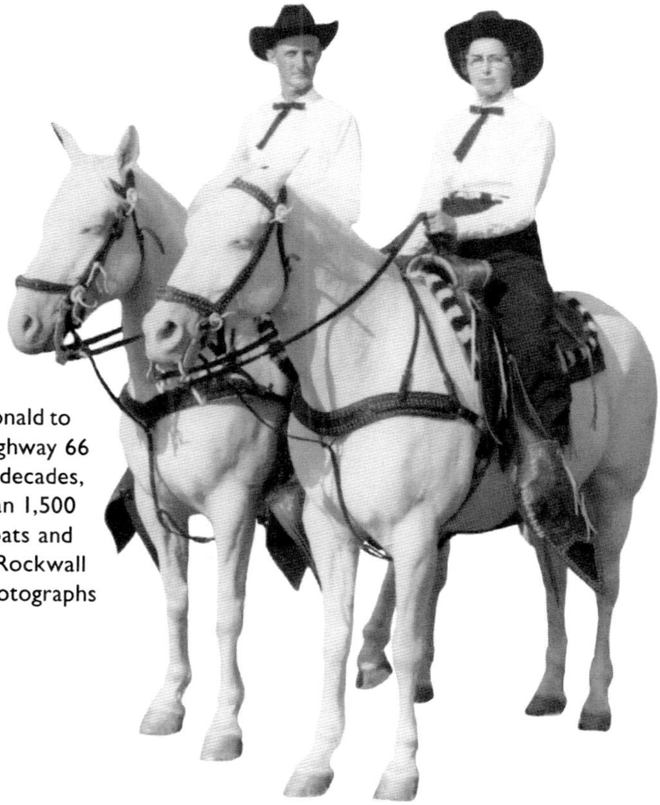

The Stodghill Family
Woodrow Stodghill married Willie Myers in 1932, and they soon took up farming in Rockwall County. In the 1940s, they moved with their son Donald to the corner of present-day State Highway 66 and FM 3549. Through the next five decades, the Stodghill family farmed more than 1,500 acres of land, growing cotton and oats and raising cattle. In 2010, the City of Rockwall named FM 3549 Stodghill Road. (Photographs from author's private collection.)

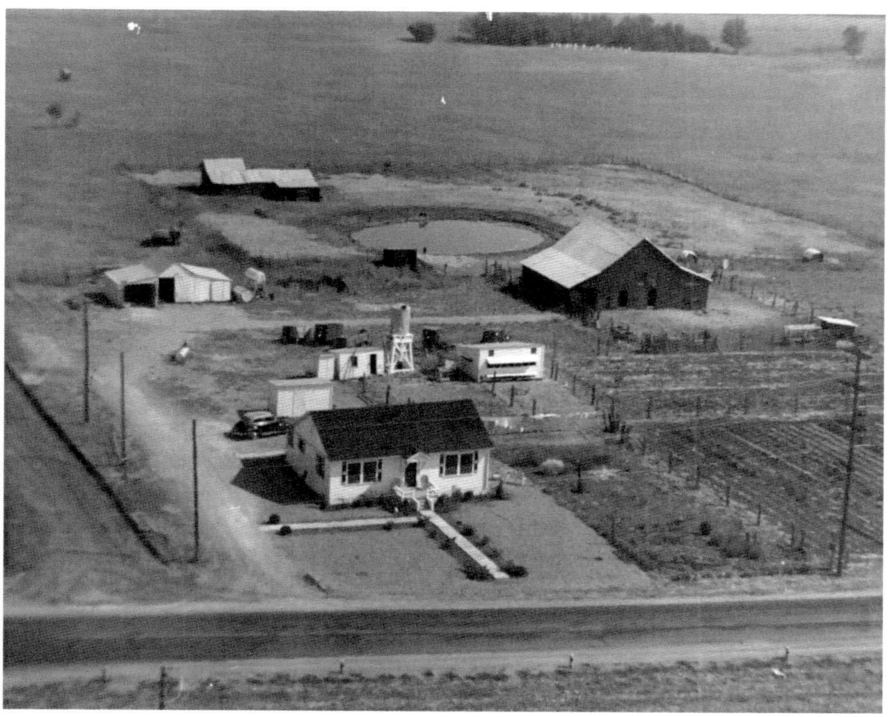

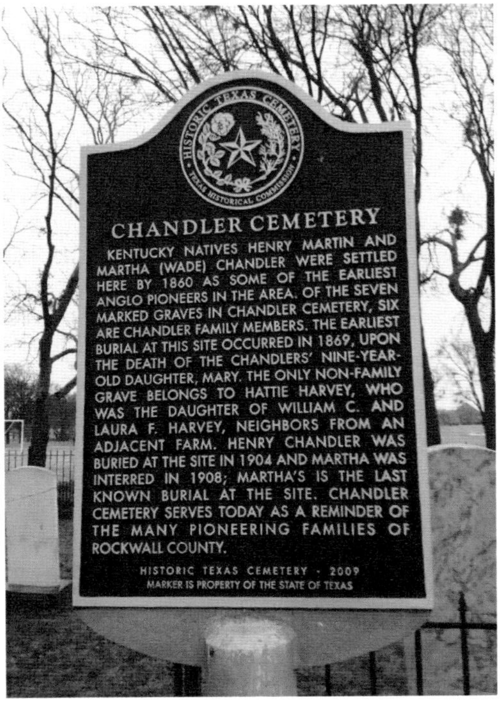

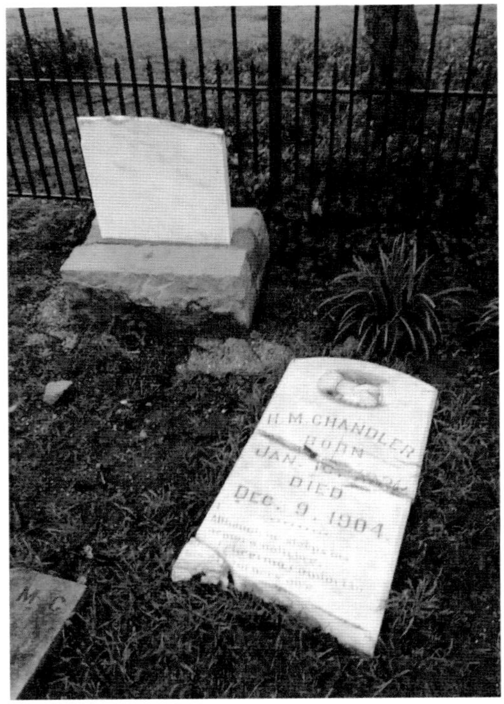

The Chandler Family

In 1859, after serving as a cavalryman in a Kentucky regiment of the Confederate army, Henry M. Chandler took his wife, Martha Ann, and their two young sons and headed for Texas, eventually making his way to frontier Rockwall. In 1866, Henry purchased 200 acres of blackland soil suitable for farming and 40 acres of bottom timberland on the Trinity River. Henry proved to be a good farmer, raising cotton, corn, oats, and wheat. In 1884, he acquired 86 additional acres contiguous to his existing property.

Henry and Martha Ann had four children: Hardin, Jesse (who was killed in a hunting accident), Rosa, and Mary (who died when she was nine years old). Henry is remembered as a stern, strong-willed businessman who had absolutely no use for banks. He kept his money—in gold—at home, and he loaned money to neighbors by parceling it out from a hidden sack. In fact, it is rumored that, shortly after settling in Rockwall, Henry and his oldest son, Hardin, journeyed back to their Kentucky farm and retrieved a "wagonload" of money buried there; reportedly, they were away for three months.

In his later years, Chandler was described as "wearing his white beard long over his chest." He sold parcels of land "for love, affection, and $1" to his son Hardin and his daughter Rosa. Henry died December 9, 1904, at the age of 83, of influenza, and his wife, Martha Ann, passed away four years later. The cemetery where they are buried was created on the land Henry gave his daughter Rosa; the Chandlers' daughter Mary and son Jesse are buried there, as well.

Henry's distrust of banks did not affect his son Hardin. Hardin also became a prominent landholder, and he was president of the Farmers National Bank in Rockwall for two decades preceding his death in 1926.

Although it is unknown exactly when it was built, in the 1940s and for several decades thereafter a large, white, two-story house sat atop the hill near the cemetery on the Chandler property. The section of the road in front of this house was known locally as "the double corner," because it turned first in one sharp, 90-degree angle and then, a short distance down the road, into another 90-degree turn.

In honor of this Texas patriarch, the entry to Chandler's Landing is named Henry M. Chandler Drive, and the community beyond is Chandler's Landing. (Photographs courtesy of Sue Ann Yasger.)

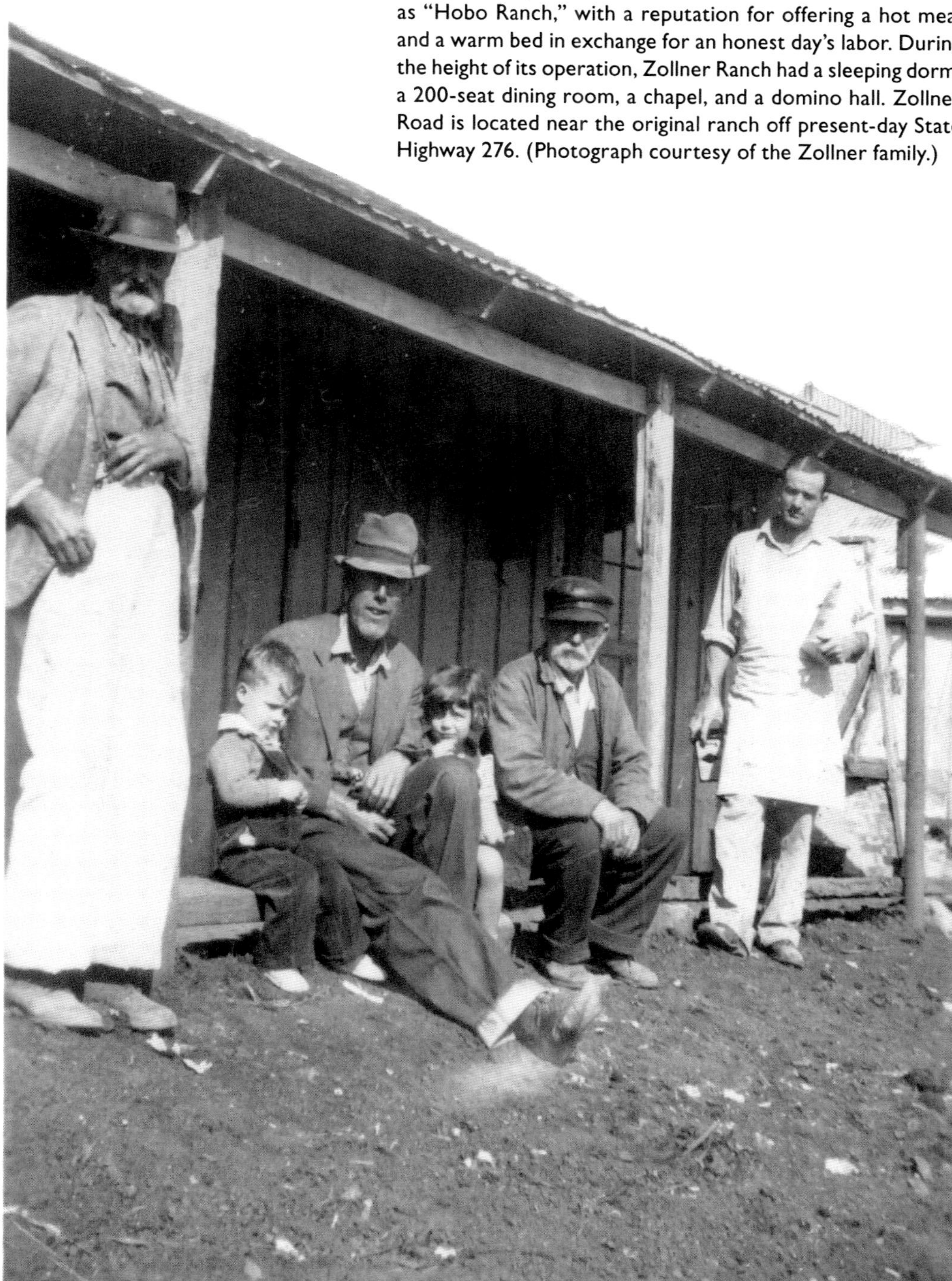

The Zollner Family

The Zollner Ranch was established in Rockwall County in 1876 and soon became a well-known farming and ranching operation. The Zollners welcomed transient men looking for an opportunity for work, and soon the ranch became known as "Hobo Ranch," with a reputation for offering a hot meal and a warm bed in exchange for an honest day's labor. During the height of its operation, Zollner Ranch had a sleeping dorm, a 200-seat dining room, a chapel, and a domino hall. Zollner Road is located near the original ranch off present-day State Highway 276. (Photograph courtesy of the Zollner family.)

John King

John King was born on August 25, 1940, in Kenedy, Texas. His father was J.T. King, the famous Texas Tech head football coach, and John earned a bachelor of business administration degree in industrial management from Texas Tech University in 1964. After college, John became a pilot in the US Air Force and served his country in Vietnam and by flying reconnaissance missions during the Cold War. He accumulated more than 6,000 flying hours during his military career. He received numerous decorations and awards, including the Air Force Commendation Medal with 2 Oak Leaf Clusters, the Meritorious Service Medal with 4 Oak Leaf Clusters, and the Air Medal with 23 Oak Leaf Clusters. He was also awarded the Silver Star, the third-highest military decoration for valor awarded to members of the US armed forces, given for gallantry in action against an enemy of the United States. Air Force pilots flying fighter aircraft are often considered eligible to receive the Silver Star upon becoming an "Ace," which entails the pilot intentionally and successfully risking his life multiple times under combat conditions and emerging victorious. The Vietnam War was the last conflict to produce US fighter Aces, most of whom were also awarded the Distinguished Flying Cross, as was John King. During the Vietnam War, high-ranking officers often received this medal for directing combat operations from aircraft. In July 1989, Lieutenant Colonel King assumed command of Detachment 2, 2762nd Logistics Squadron at E Systems in Greenville, a position he held until his retirement in March 1993. John was a vibrant member of the Rockwall community and served as a member of the city council for seven years. He was also on the Planning and Zoning Committee, was a board member of the Rockwall Economic Development Corporation, and was president of the Rockwall Breakfast Rotary Club. In March 2007, the Texas House of Representatives recognized John King with a proclamation presented by State Representative Laubenberg for service to country and community. John was married, with a son, a daughter, and two grandchildren. He died in December 2006. (Photograph courtesy of the King family.)

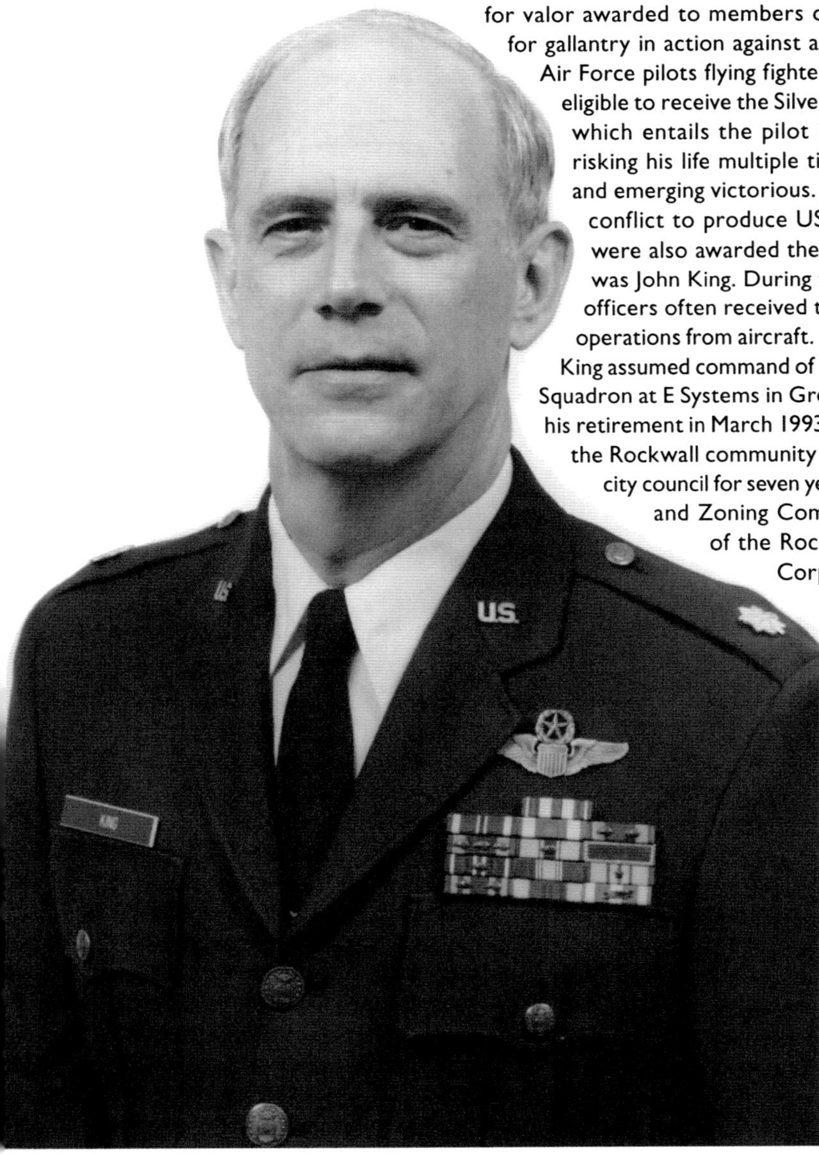

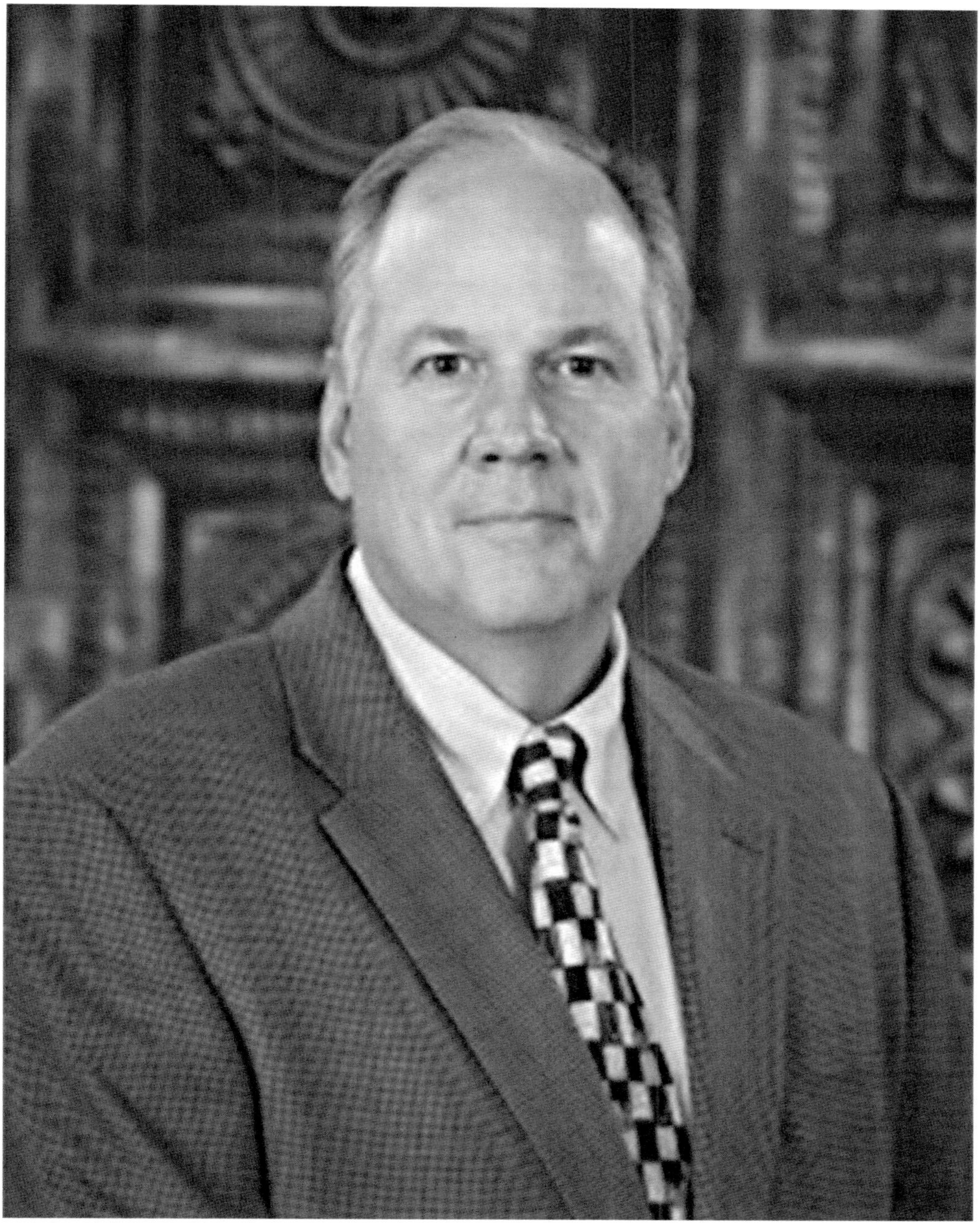

Chris Cuny

Chris Cuny is the president of FC Cuny Corporation, a civil engineering and architectural design firm based in Heath. He is a graduate of Rockwall High School and obtained a bachelor of science degree in civil engineering from Texas A&M University in 1983. Besides his professional accomplishments, Cuny has dedicated much of his time to public service. He was a member of the city council of Heath from 1990 to 1994 and served as the mayor of the city of Heath from 1994 to 2004. He is currently an elected member of the Rockwall ISD Board of Trustees. He has also been a member of the Rockwall Chamber of Commerce, a past member of the noon Rotary Club, and chairman of the American Cancer Society's Relay for Life. Chris Cuny Parkway is named in his honor. (Photograph courtesy of the Cuny family.)

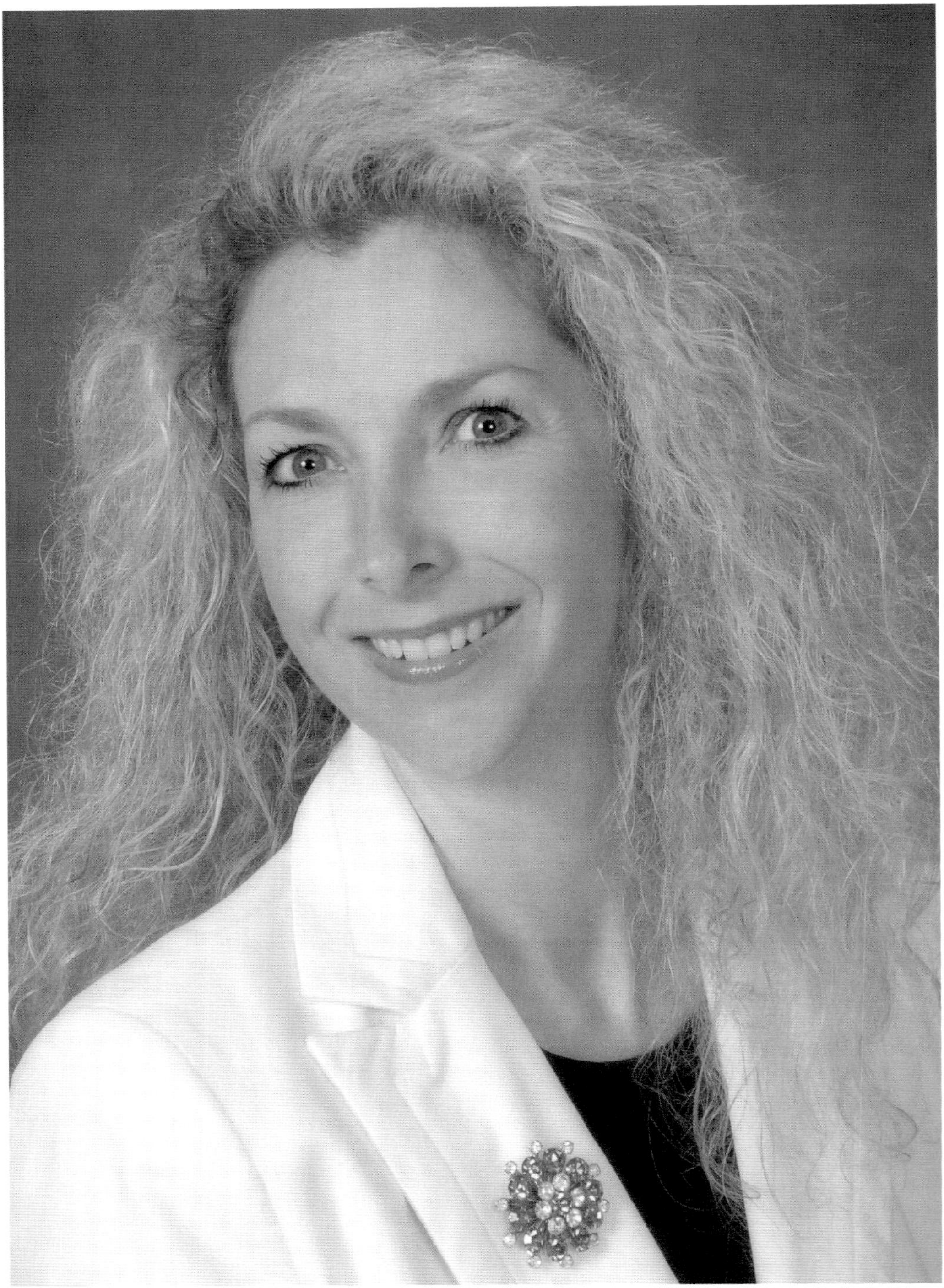

Sheri Stodghill Fowler Parks

Sheri was born on May 31, 1967, to Patsy (Hall) Stodghill of Heath and Donald R. Stodghill of Rockwall. She attended the University of Texas at Austin, where she earned degrees in radio-television-film and journalism. After college, Sheri worked as an assistant editor and copywriter for *Texas Monthly* magazine. She was also a freelance writer for numerous publications, including the *Dallas Morning News*. Sheri married Kevin Fowler in 1990, and the couple had two children, Jake and Grace. The family moved to Rockwall in 2000, settling on land Sheri's grandparents had farmed and upon which her father had been raised. She was the sixth generation of her family to call Rockwall County home, and she was proud to raise her children as the fourth generation living on family land. Sheri loved living in Rockwall and was extremely interested in the stories of pioneer families that settled in the area. Her passion led her to author four books: *Rockwall* (Images of America), *Rockwall* (Then & Now), *Royse City*, and this volume, *Legendary Locals of Rockwall*. In 2006, Sheri was hired as chief information officer for the Rockwall Independent School District. She served in the superintendent's cabinet for more than eight years and elevated RISD's Teacher of the Year program to one of the best in the state. Sheri was also committed to civic service in Rockwall. Some of the organizations that benefitted from her efforts include the Rockwall County Friends of the Library, the Rockwall County Alliance for the Arts, the Rockwall Independent School District Education Foundation, and the Rockwall County Historical Foundation. Sheri was also a devoted mother, interested and involved in all her children's activities. She was a den mother when her son was in Boy Scouts (Jake attained the level of Eagle Scout), and she enthusiastically participated with daughter Grace in National Charity League service for six years. In 2007, Sheri met the man she called "the love of my life," Stacy Parks. Following a four-year engagement, the couple was married on November 29, 2014. Sheri passed away from cancer on January 22, 2015. (Photograph courtesy of RISD.)

ABOUT THE ROCKWALL COUNTY HISTORICAL FOUNDATION

Records of the Rockwall County Historical Foundation state, "Rockwall County Historical Foundation was organized January 16, 1978, with 21 people attending the first meeting at the Chamber of Commerce building. The desire to preserve the heritage of Rockwall County was the main focus of these people as they adopted by-laws and elected officers and directors. Charter members numbered sixty-two."

The RCHF maintains a museum housed in the Manson-LaMoreaux-Hartman House, which is considered to be the oldest home in Rockwall County, with its original structure dating to the mid-1850s. The museum is located in Harry Myers Park at 901 East Washington Street in Rockwall. For museum hours or more information about the Rockwall County Historical Foundation, please call (972) 722-1507.

In addition to maintaining historical artifacts and written and oral histories, the RCHF has developed an extensive photograph archive. Numerous families have contributed to this project, and many of the photographs contained in this volume were generously provided by the Foundation. (Photograph below courtesy of the RCHF.)

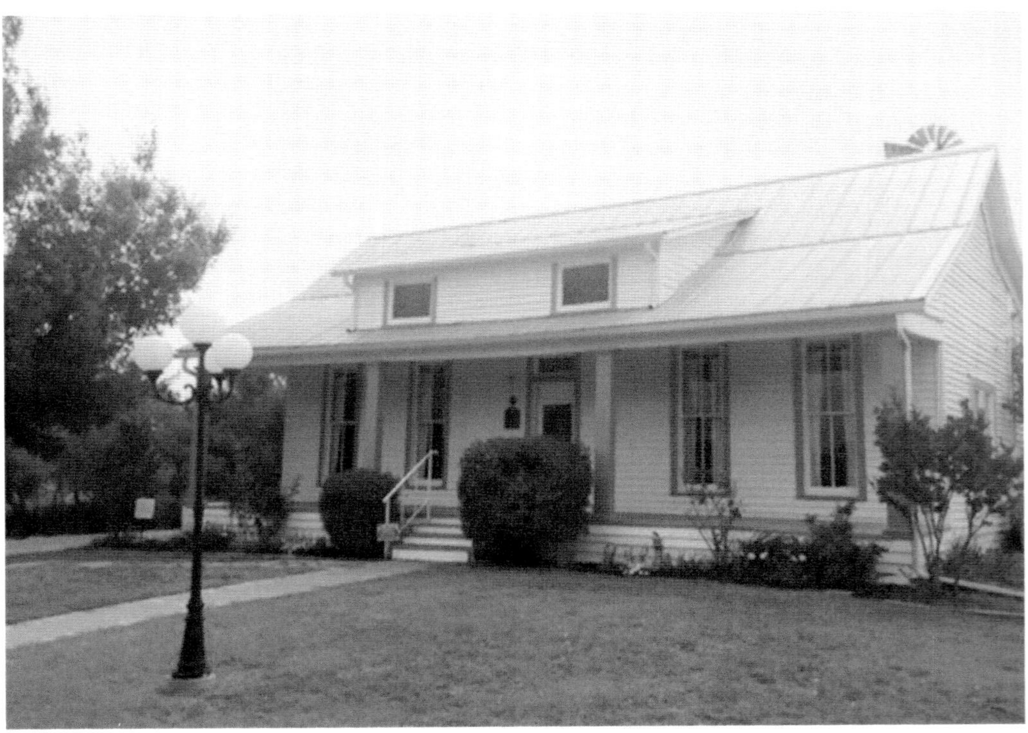

INDEX